NAMIBIA
DISCOVERED

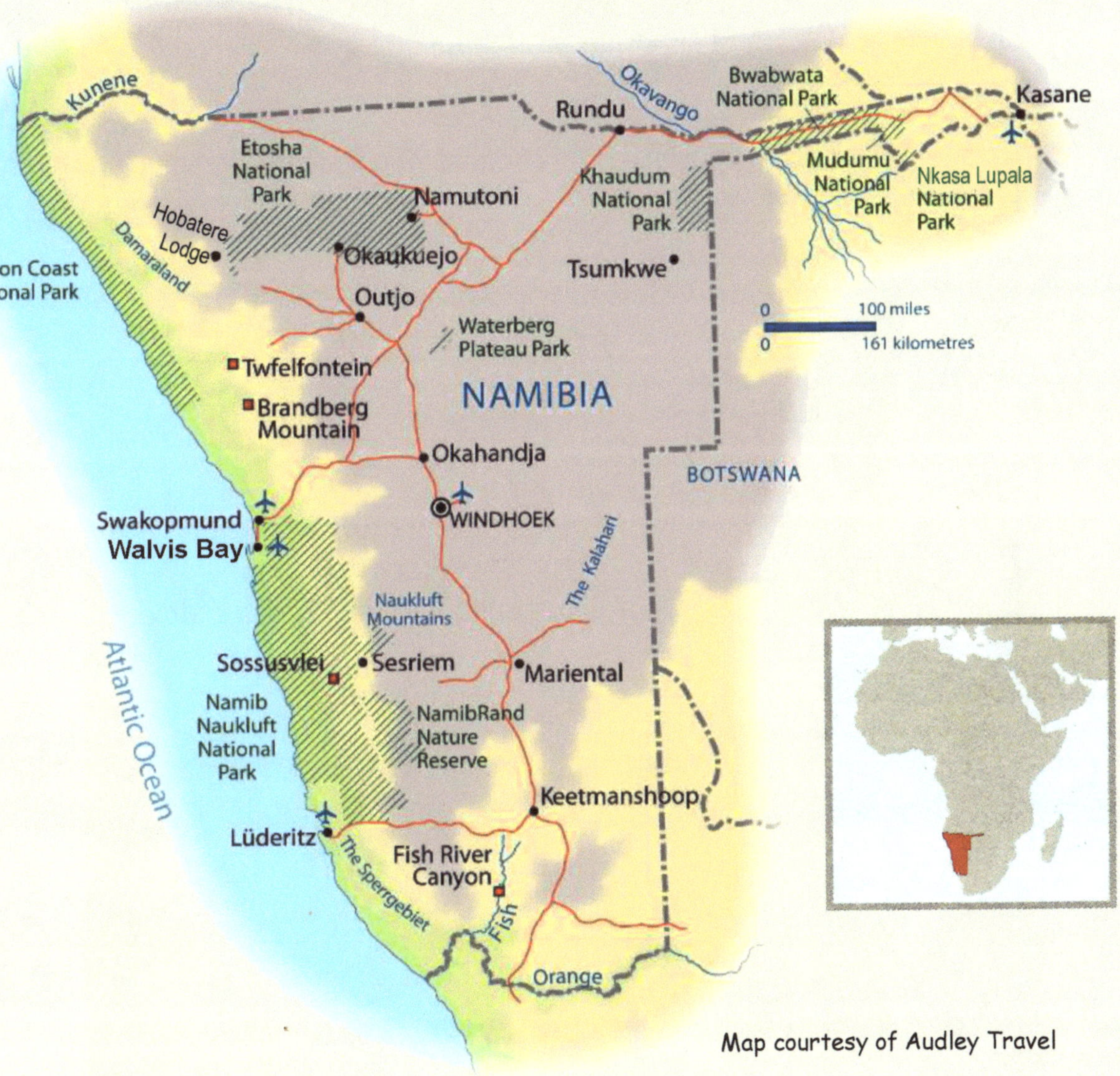

Map courtesy of Audley Travel

A souvenir journal by Joe McDaniel

ISBN 978-1-943650-28-6

Published by BookCrafters,
Parker, Colorado, USA
http://bookcrafters.net
bookcrafterscolorado@gmail.com

This book may be ordered from online bookstores

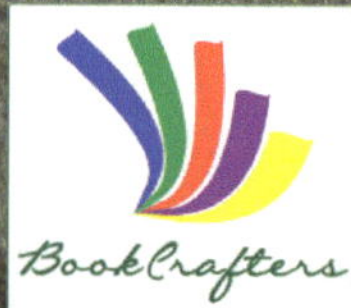

Photographs ©2016 Joe McDaniel

Namibia has been described as..."*a country of vast potential and promise. Rich in natural resources and spectacular beauty, it has also inherited from its colonial and African roots a solid and modern infrastructure and a diversity of cultures and national origins: Herero, San, Khoikhoi, Owambo, Afrikaner, German, Asian and others. Its attractions are unparalleled in Africa..."*

This book records a self-drive 15-day tour beginning with arrival in Windhoek on 28 March and ending with departure on 12 April, 2016. The tour included Sossusvlei and Deadvlei in the Namib-Naukluft Park, Swakopmund and Walvis Bay on the coast, Camp Kipwe and Twyfelfontein in Damaraland, six days in Etosha National Park and two nights at Okonjima Plains Camp.

For maps of *Etosha National Park*, see pages 122 & 123.
Namibia Facts are on page 124.

*Southern Africa - Lonely Planet Publications, 2nd edition

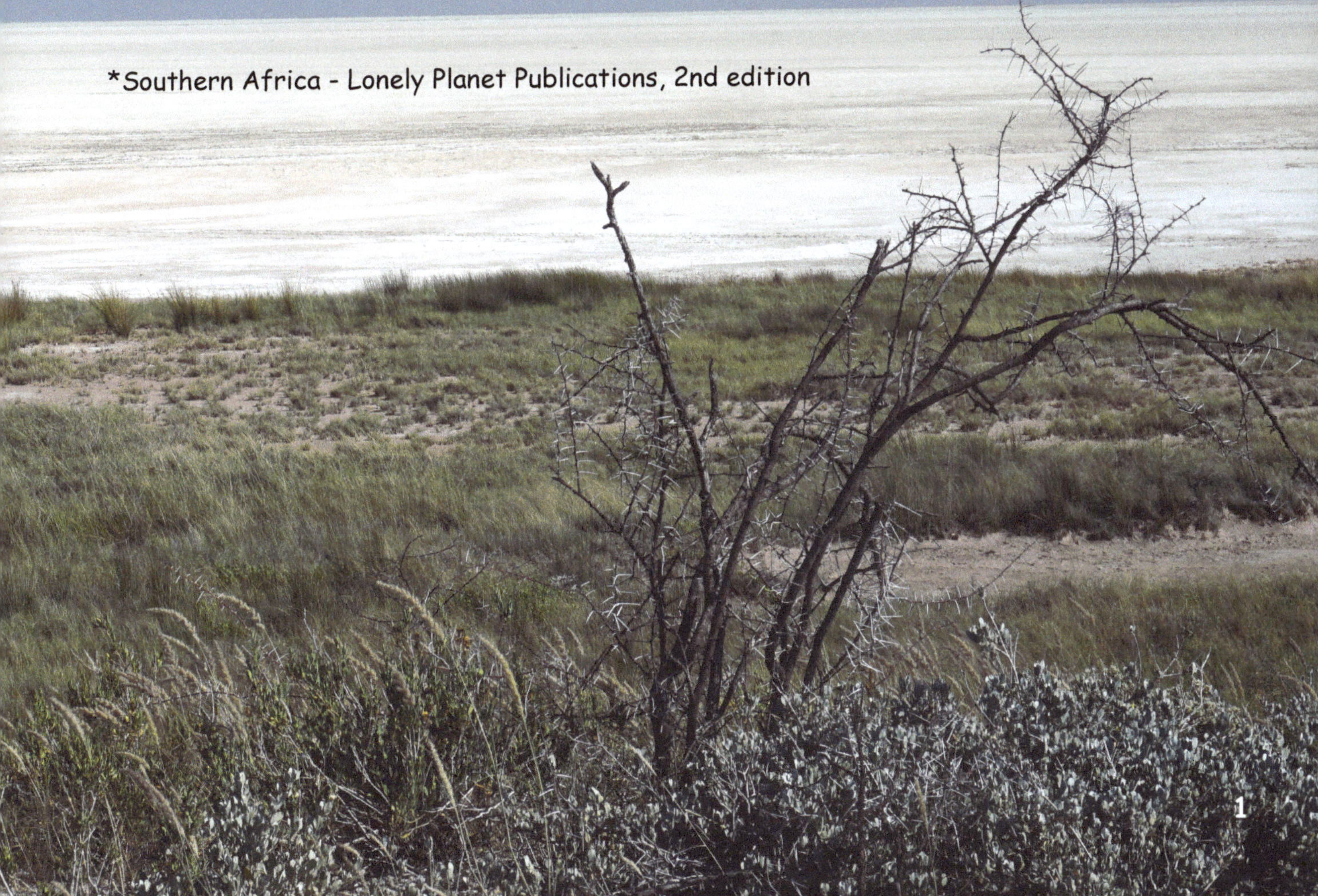

1

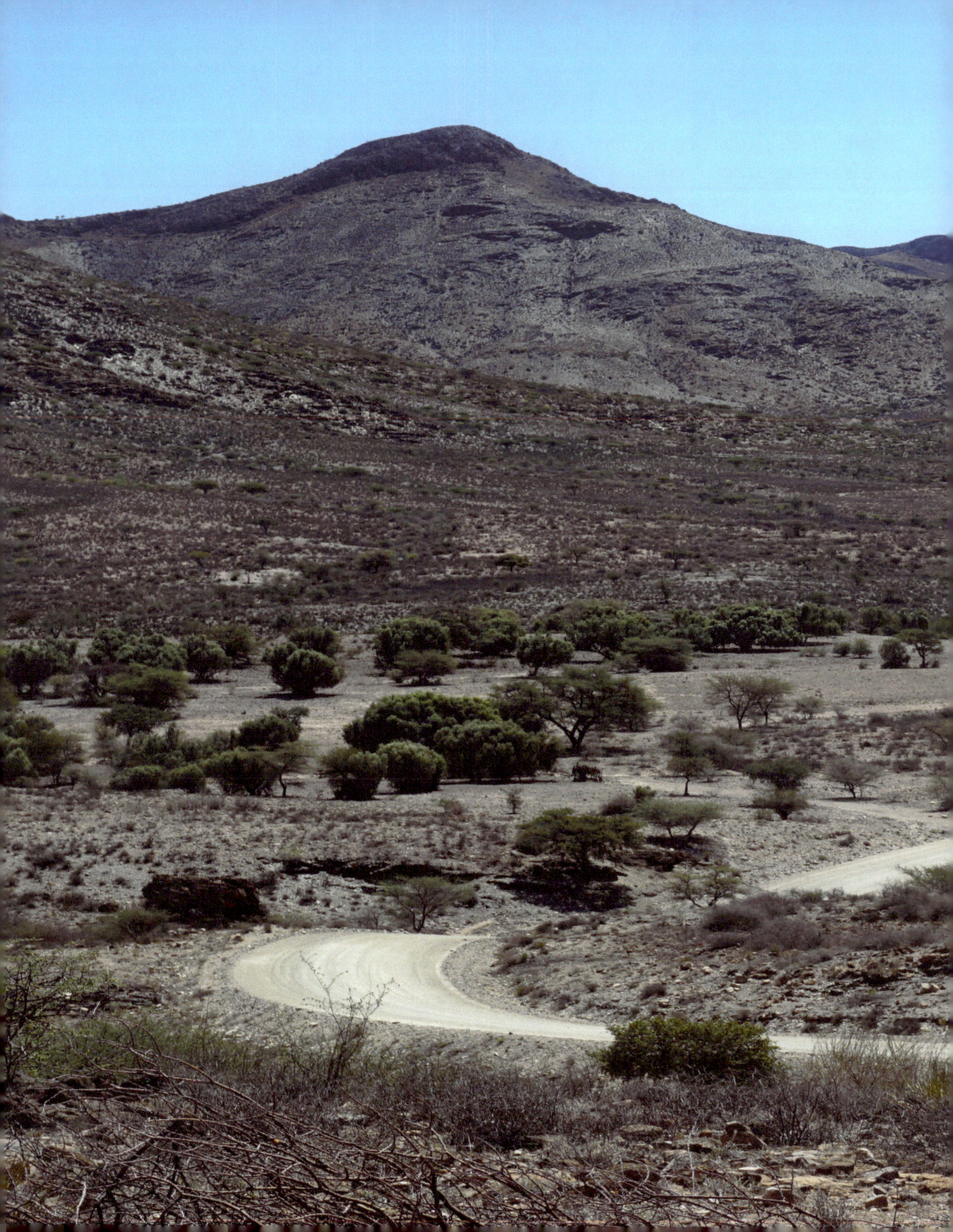

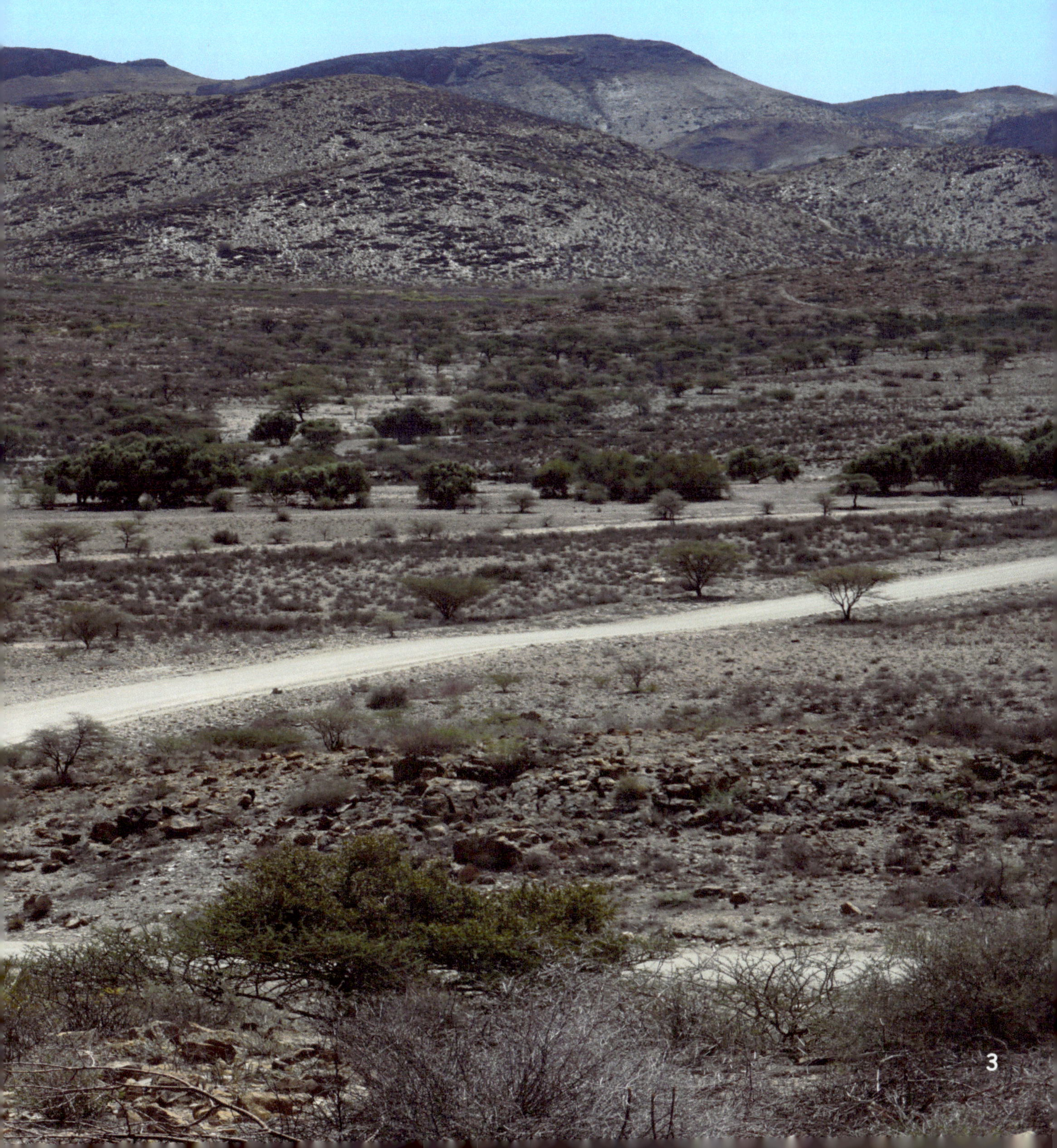

Scenic road (C24) from Highway B1 to Solitaire en route to Sesriem and Sossusvlei.

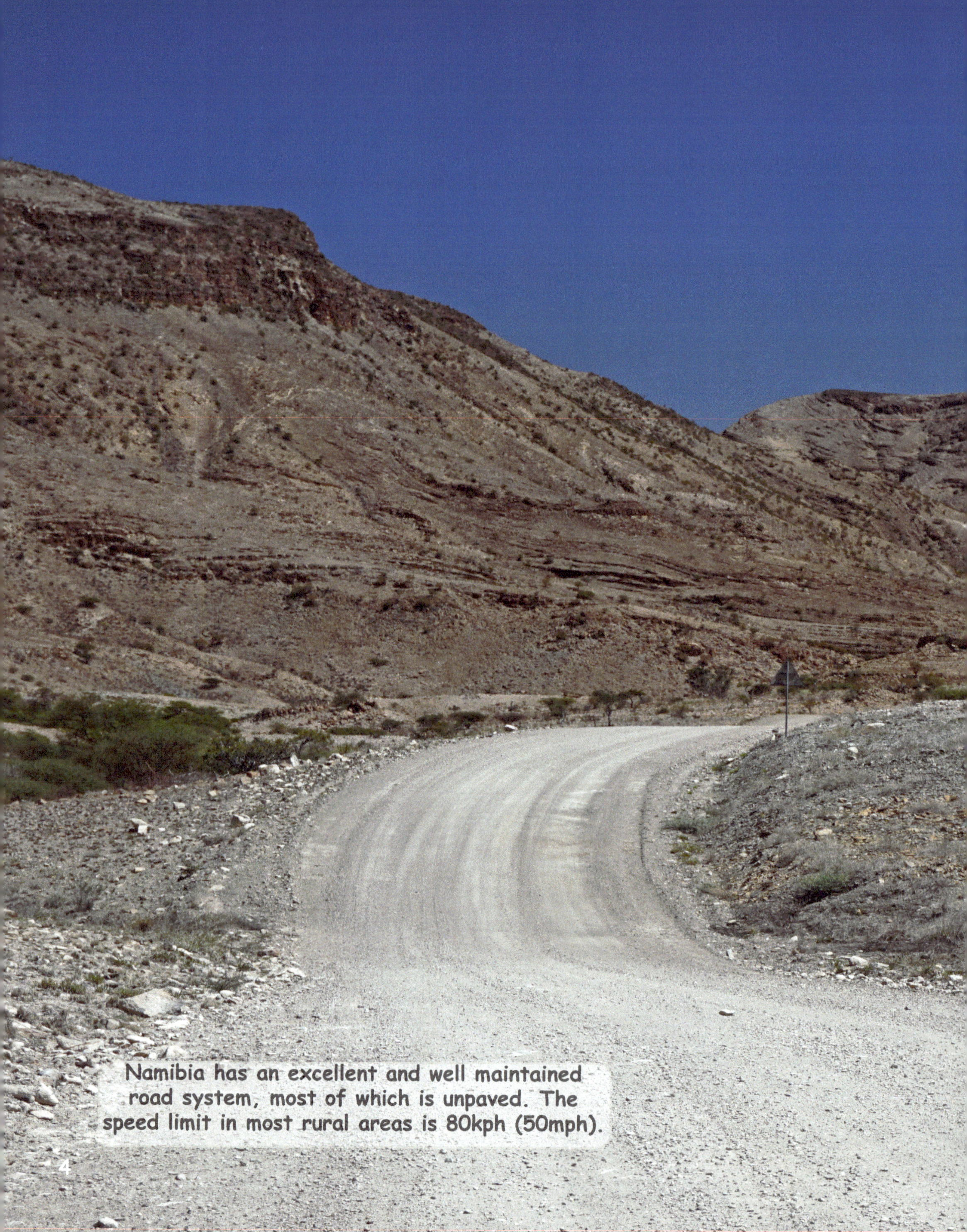
Namibia has an excellent and well maintained
road system, most of which is unpaved. The
speed limit in most rural areas is 80kph (50mph).

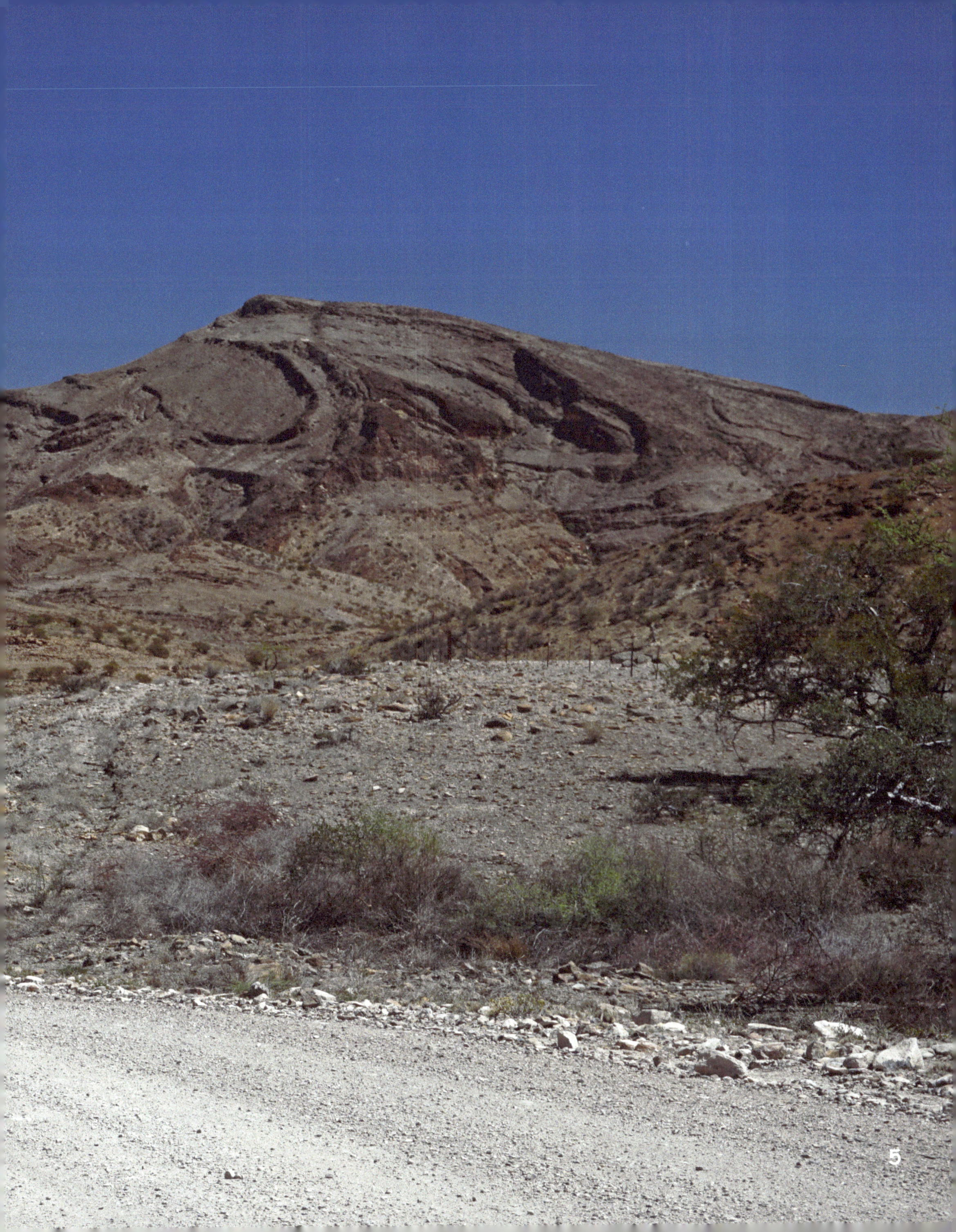

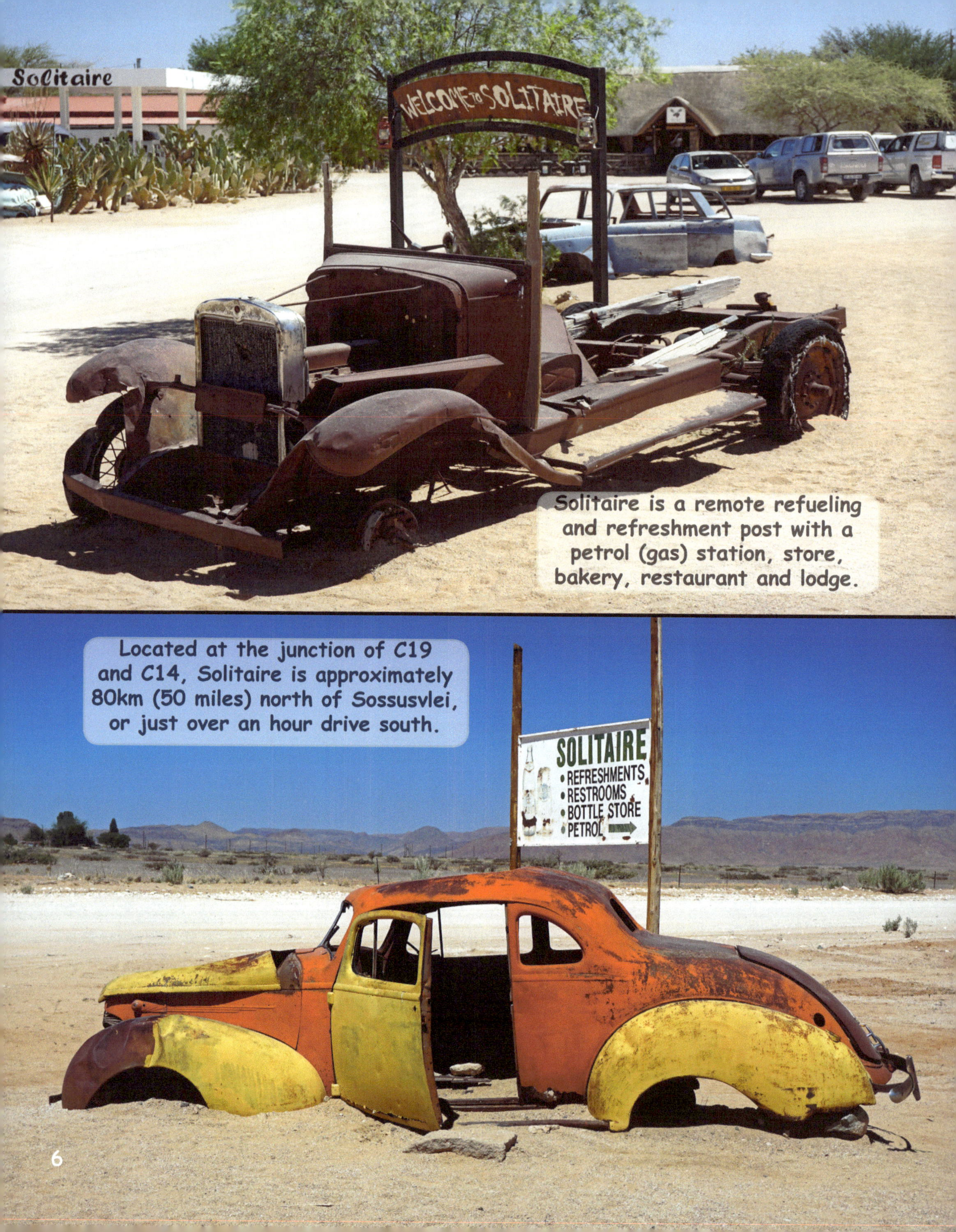

Solitaire is a remote refueling and refreshment post with a petrol (gas) station, store, bakery, restaurant and lodge.

Located at the junction of C19 and C14, Solitaire is approximately 80km (50 miles) north of Sossusvlei, or just over an hour drive south.

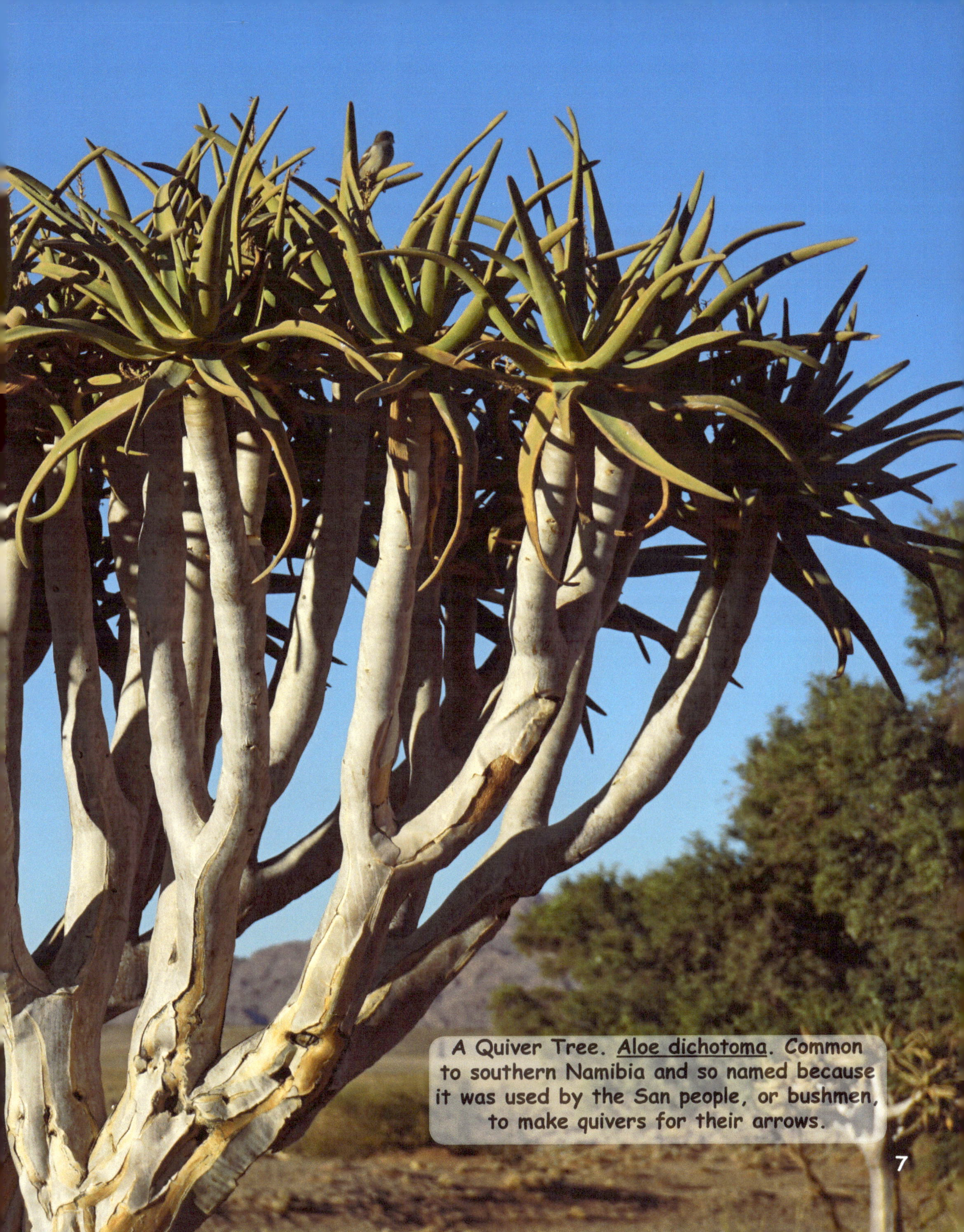

A Quiver Tree. _Aloe dichotoma_. Common to southern Namibia and so named because it was used by the San people, or bushmen, to make quivers for their arrows.

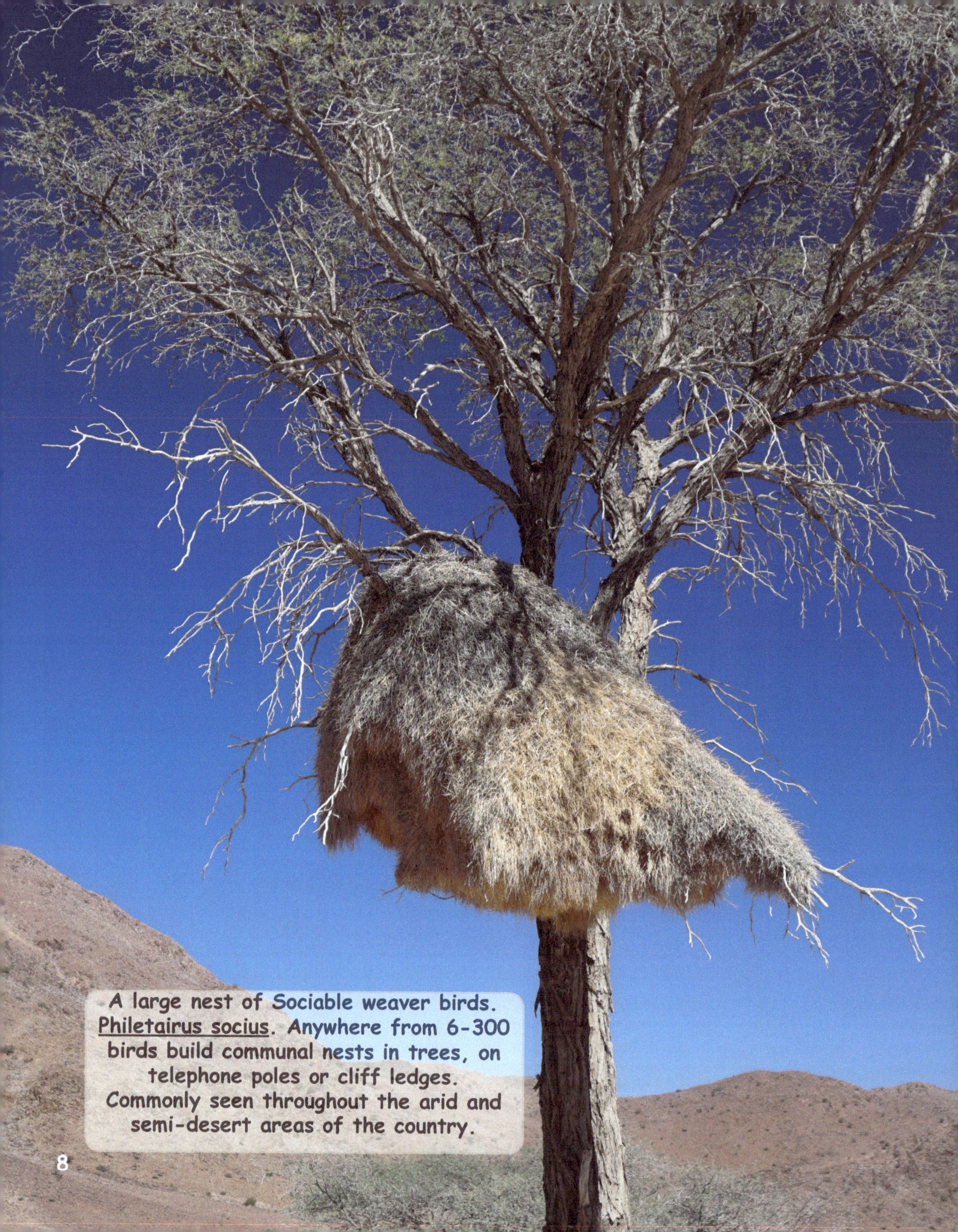

A large nest of Sociable weaver birds.
<u>Philetairus socius</u>. Anywhere from 6-300
birds build communal nests in trees, on
telephone poles or cliff ledges.
Commonly seen throughout the arid and
semi-desert areas of the country.

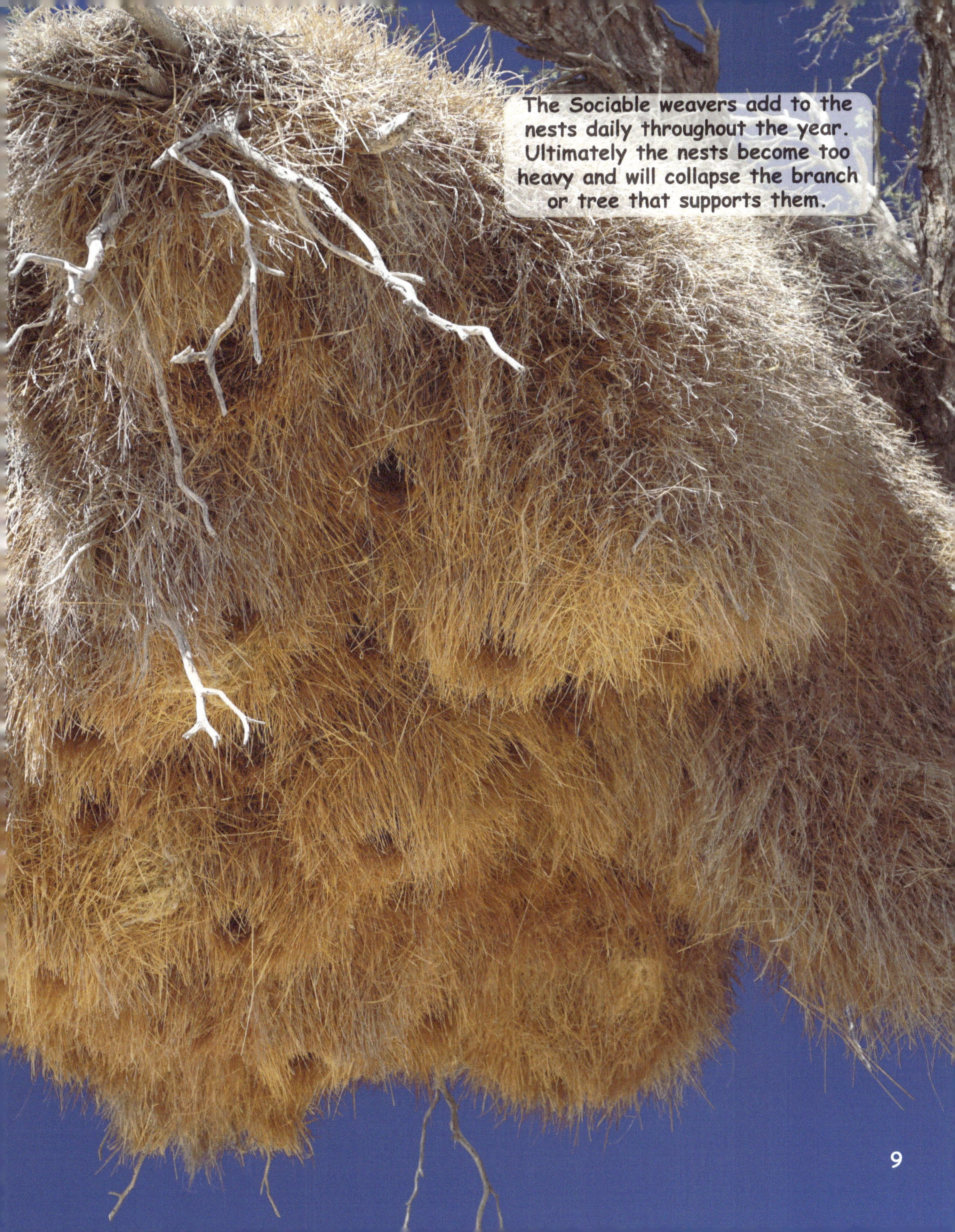
The Sociable weavers add to the
nests daily throughout the year.
Ultimately the nests become too
heavy and will collapse the branch
or tree that supports them.

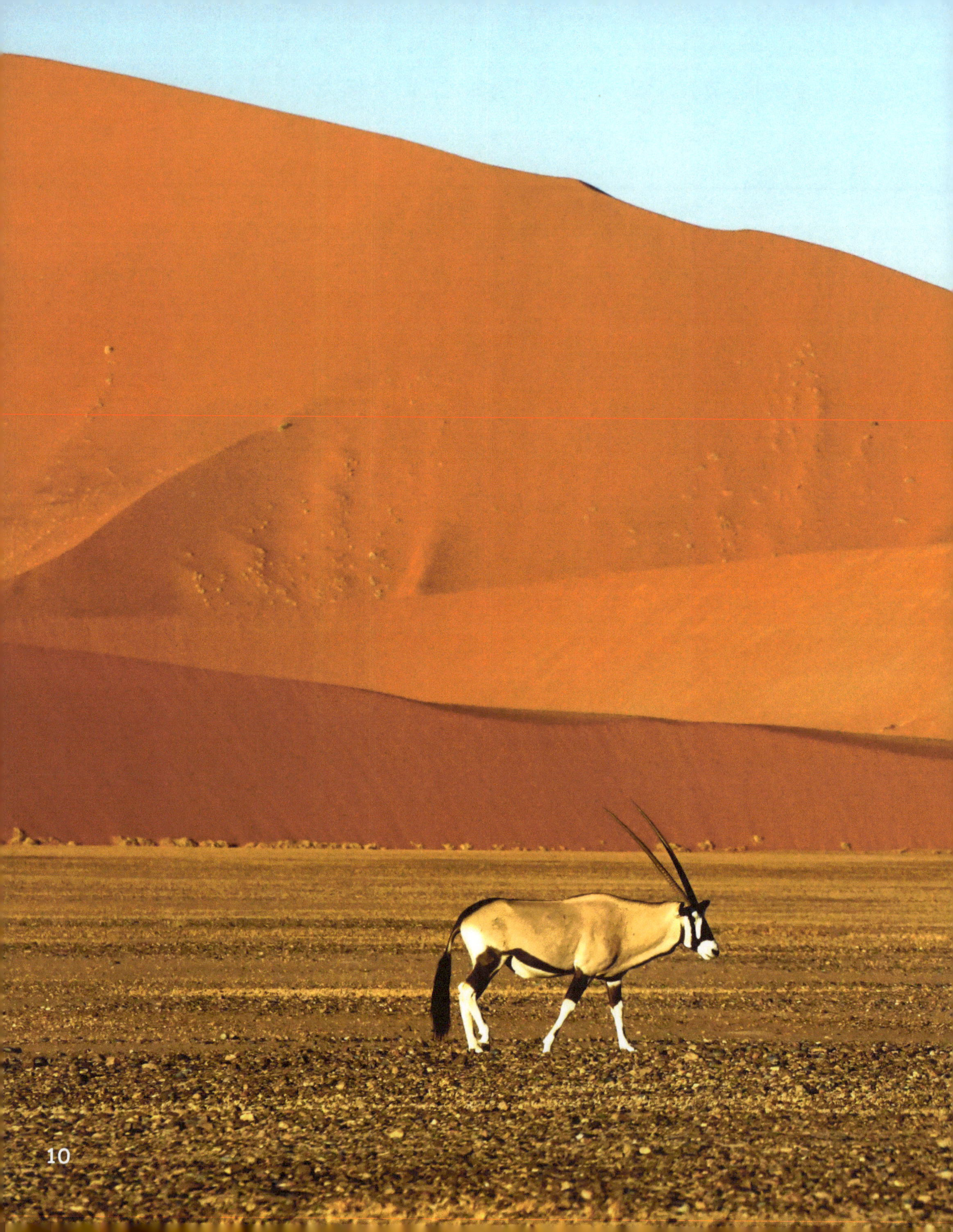

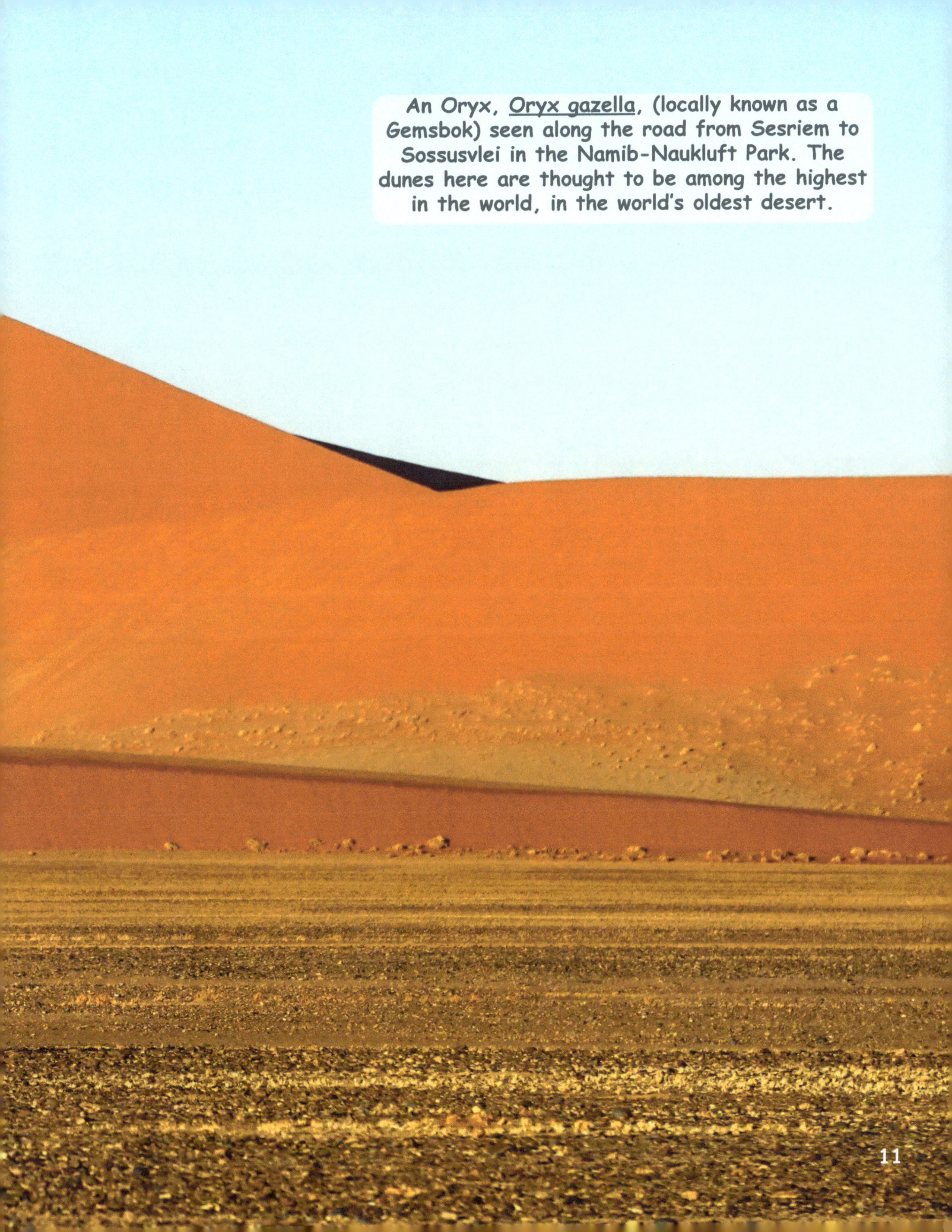

An Oryx, _Oryx gazella_, (locally known as a
Gemsbok) seen along the road from Sesriem to
Sossusvlei in the Namib-Naukluft Park. The
dunes here are thought to be among the highest
in the world, in the world's oldest desert.

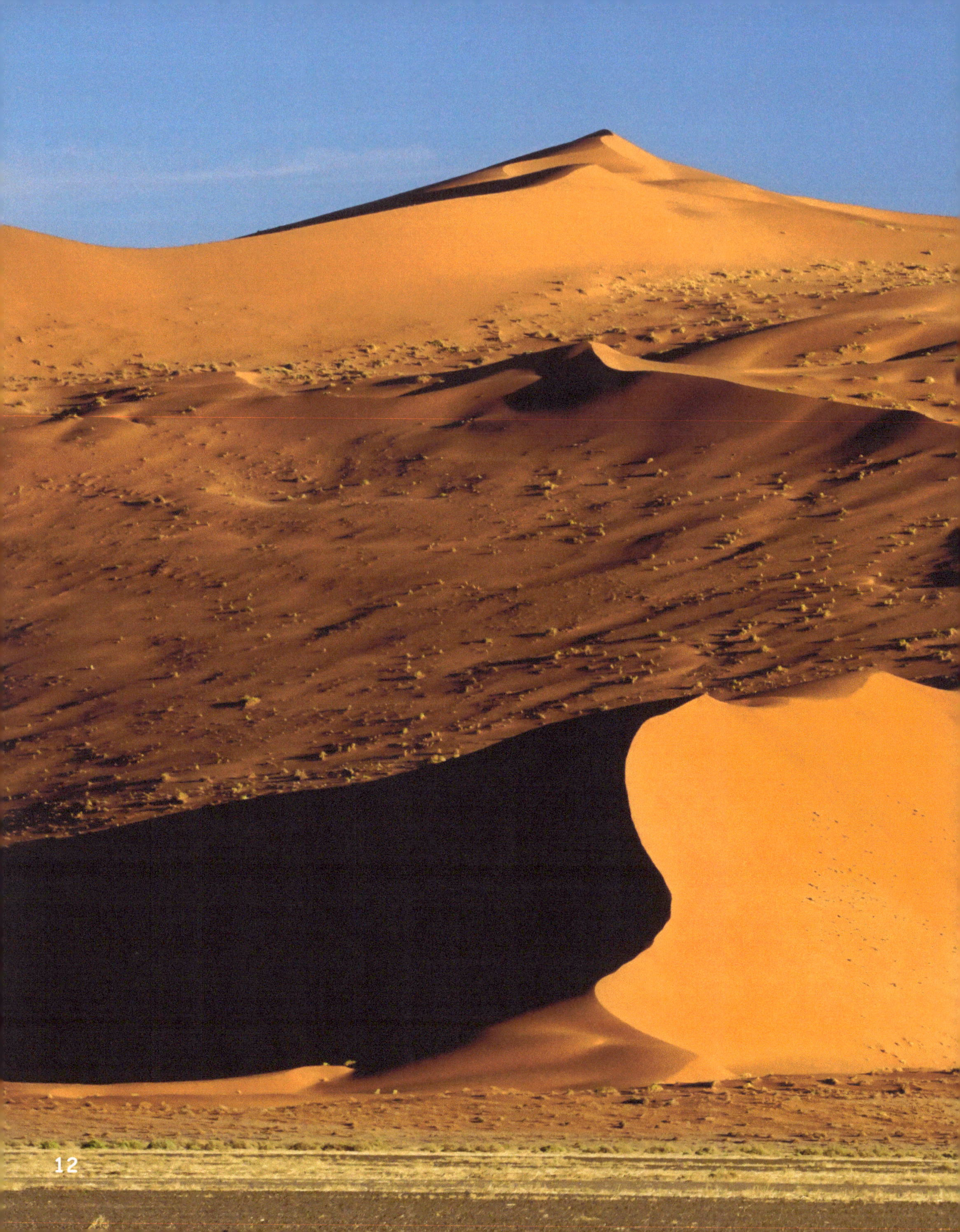

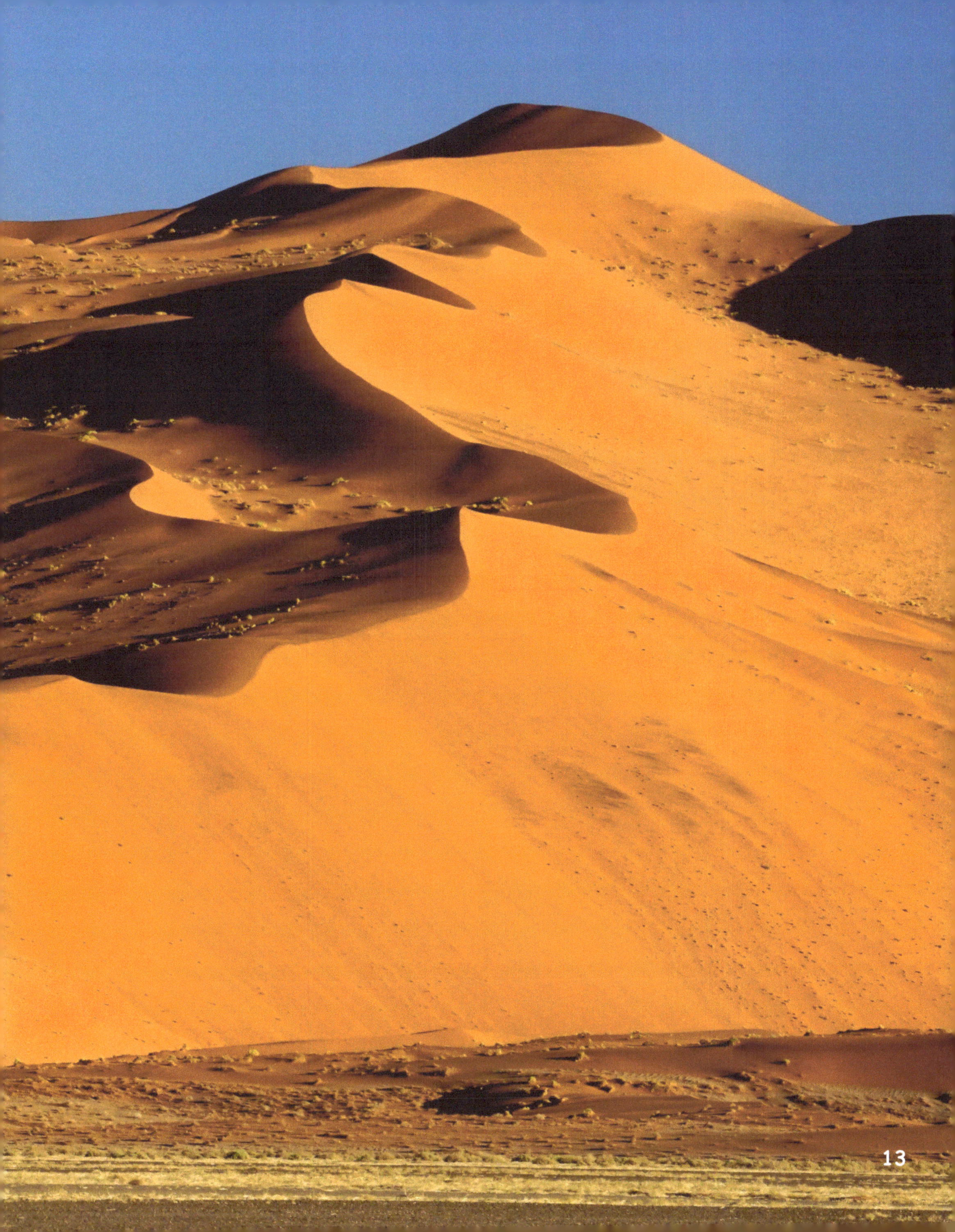

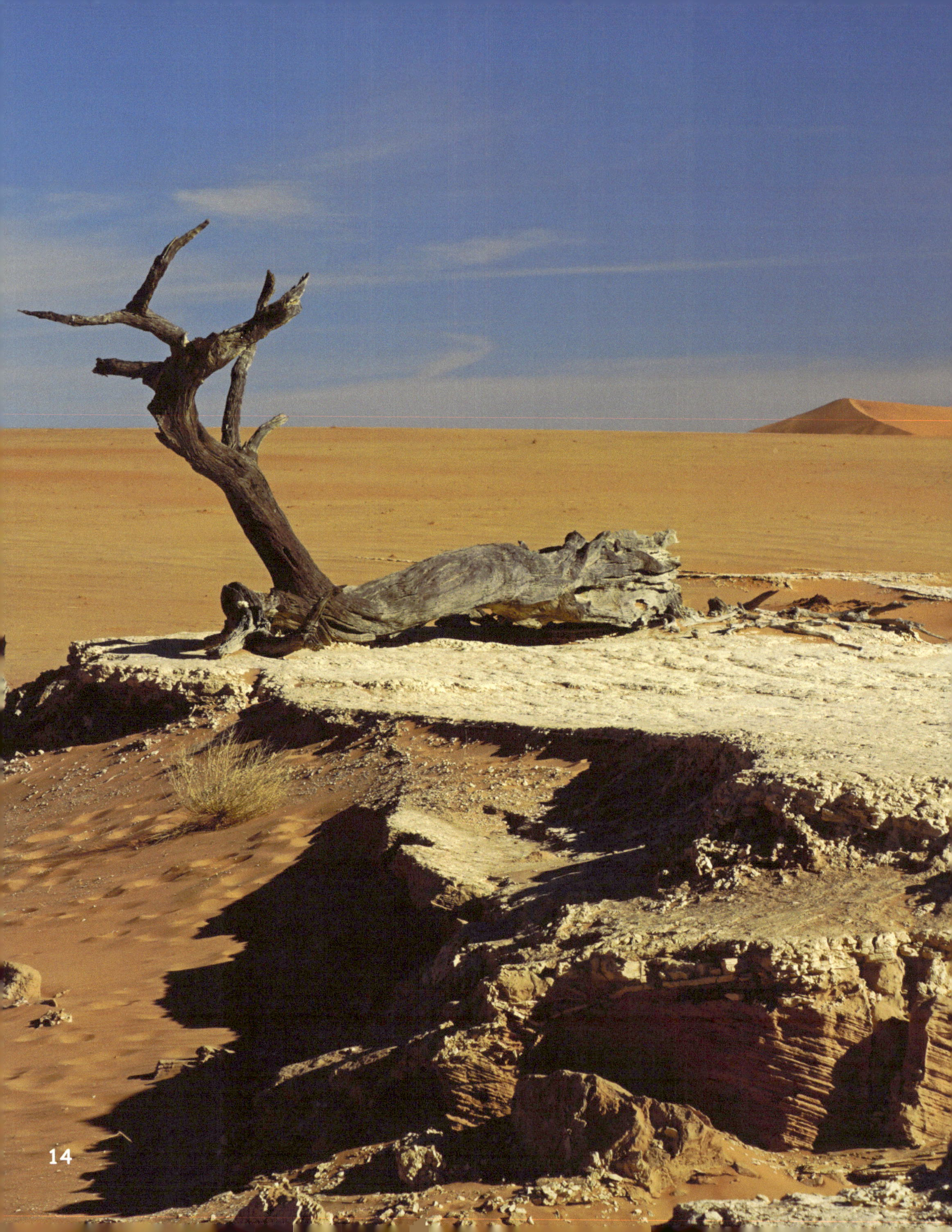

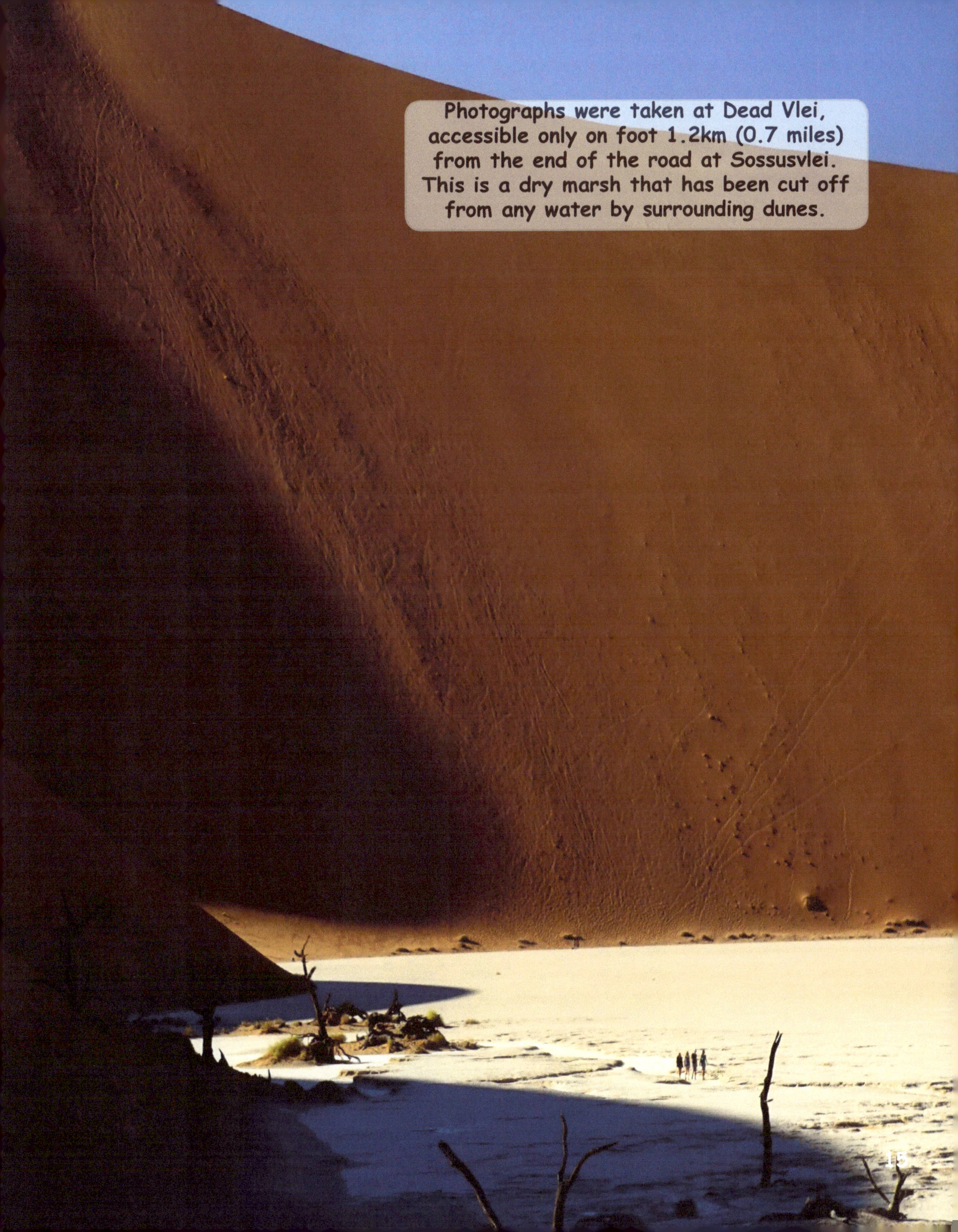

Photographs were taken at Dead Vlei, accessible only on foot 1.2km (0.7 miles) from the end of the road at Sossusvlei. This is a dry marsh that has been cut off from any water by surrounding dunes.

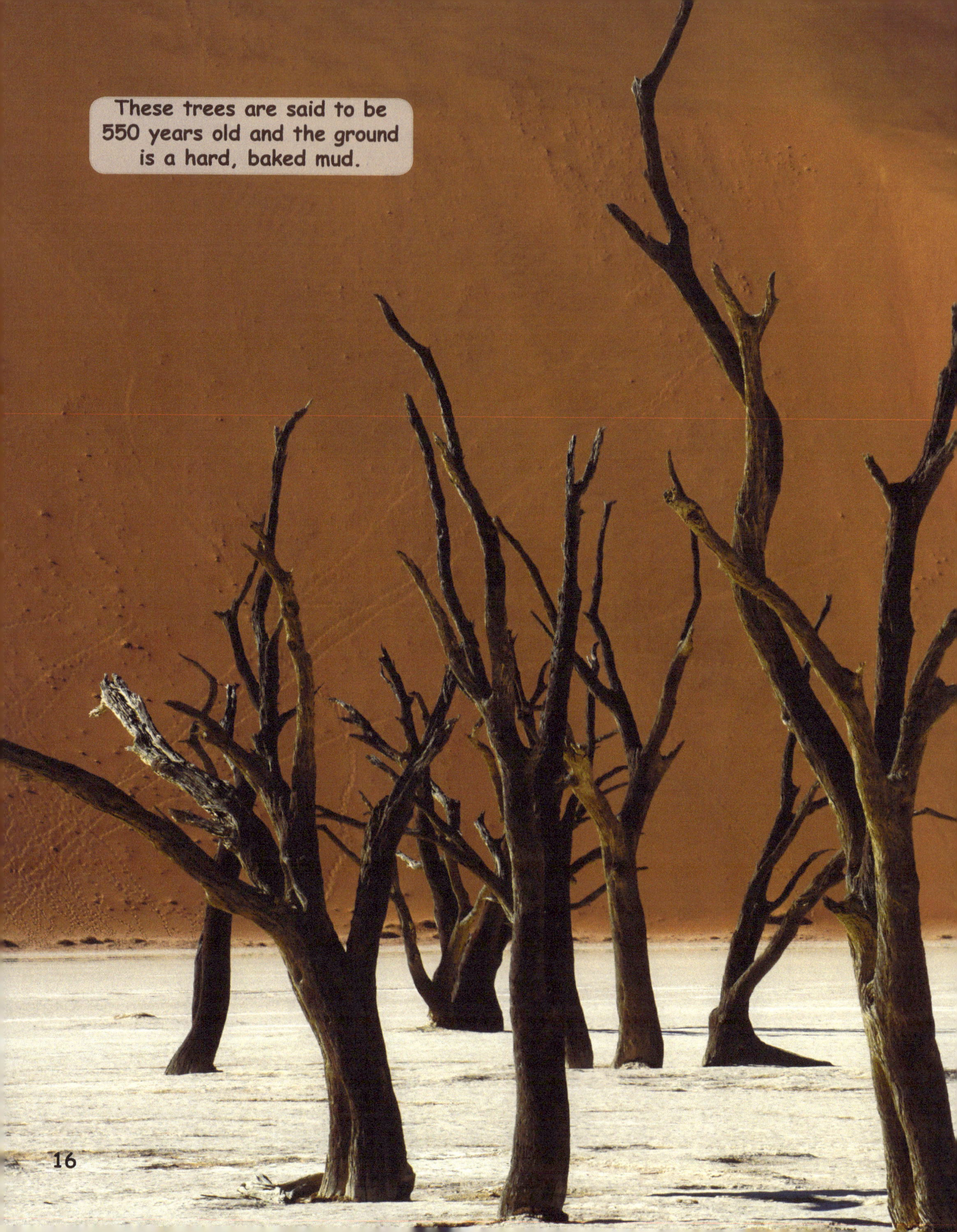
These trees are said to be 550 years old and the ground is a hard, baked mud.

16

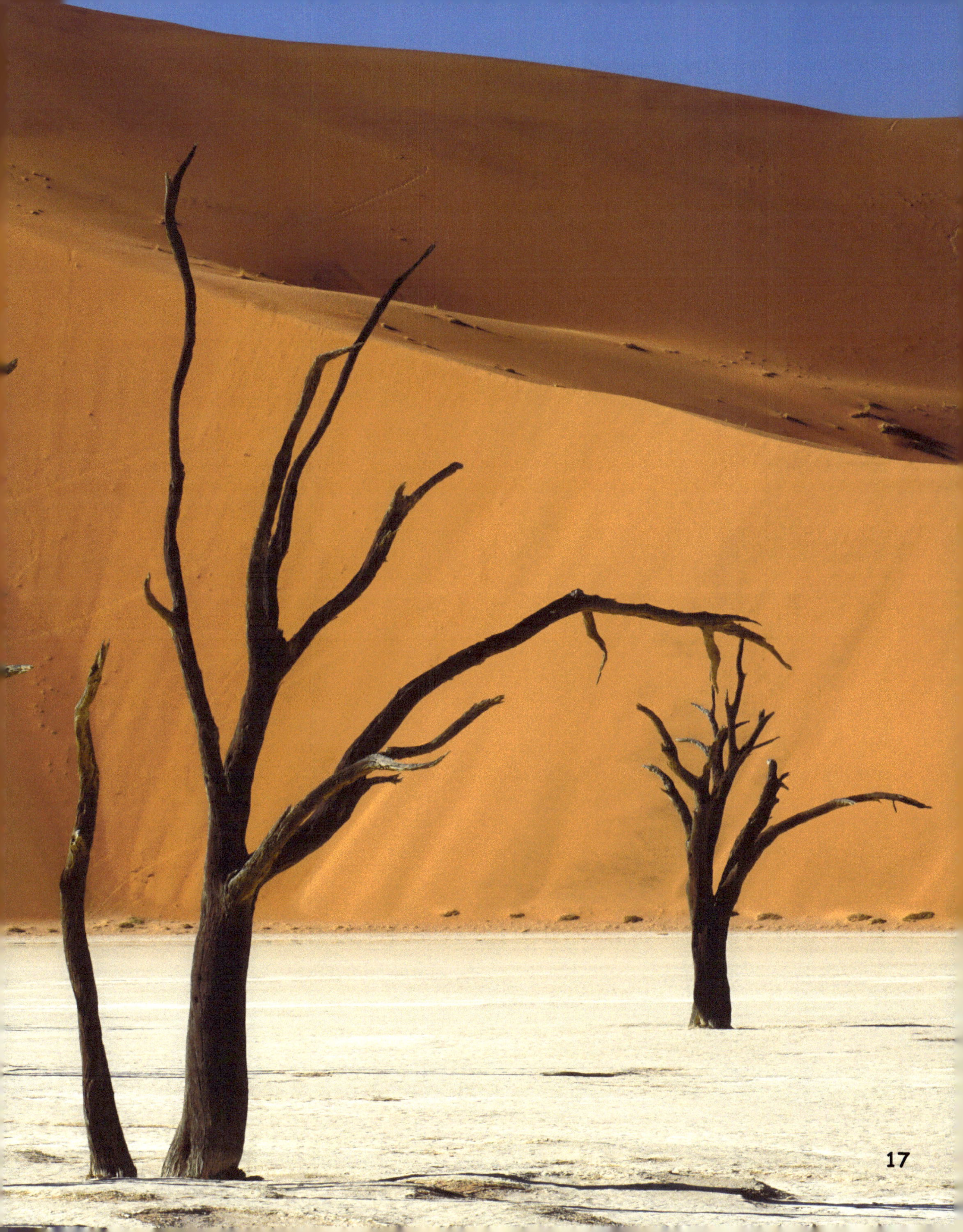

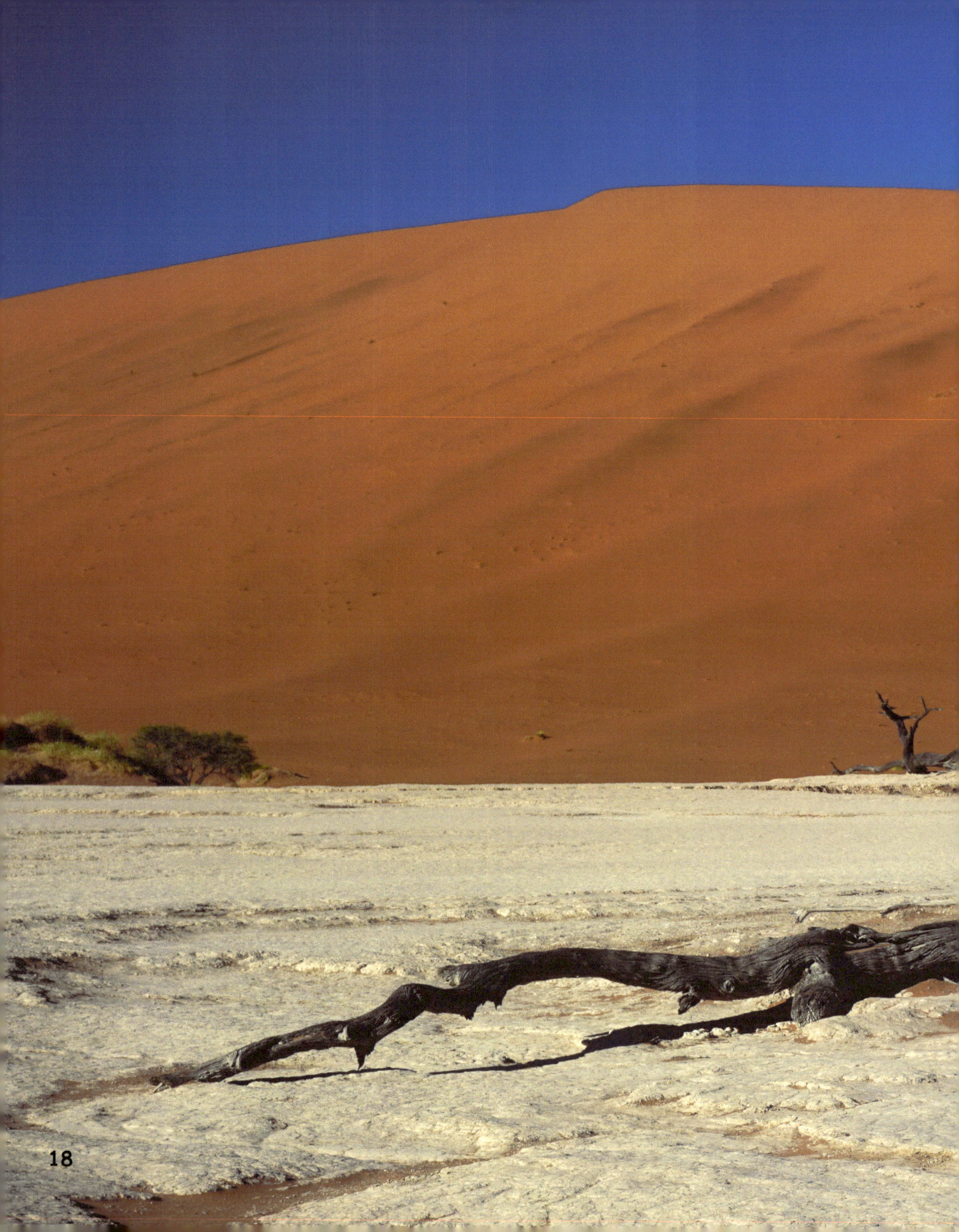

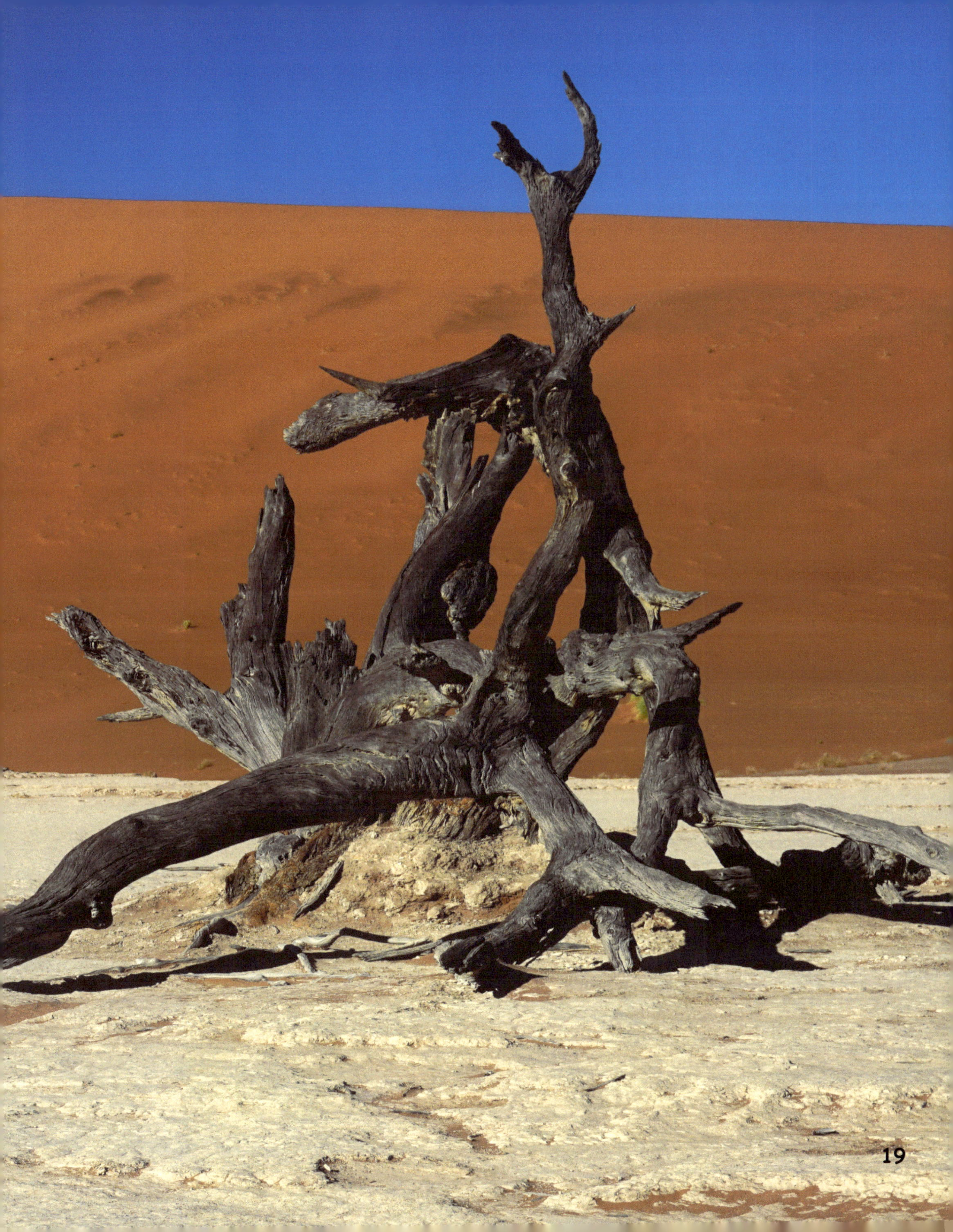

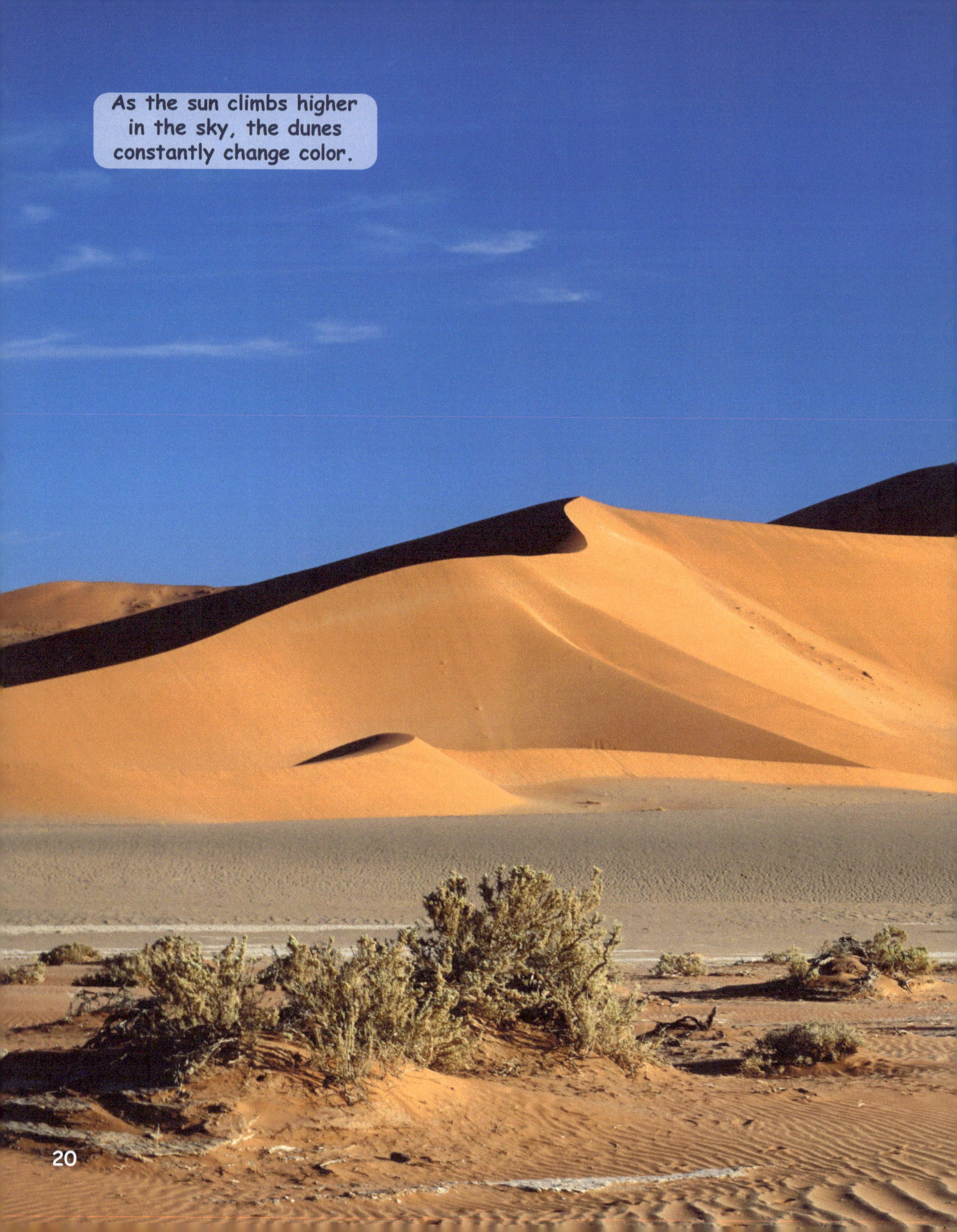
As the sun climbs higher in the sky, the dunes constantly change color.

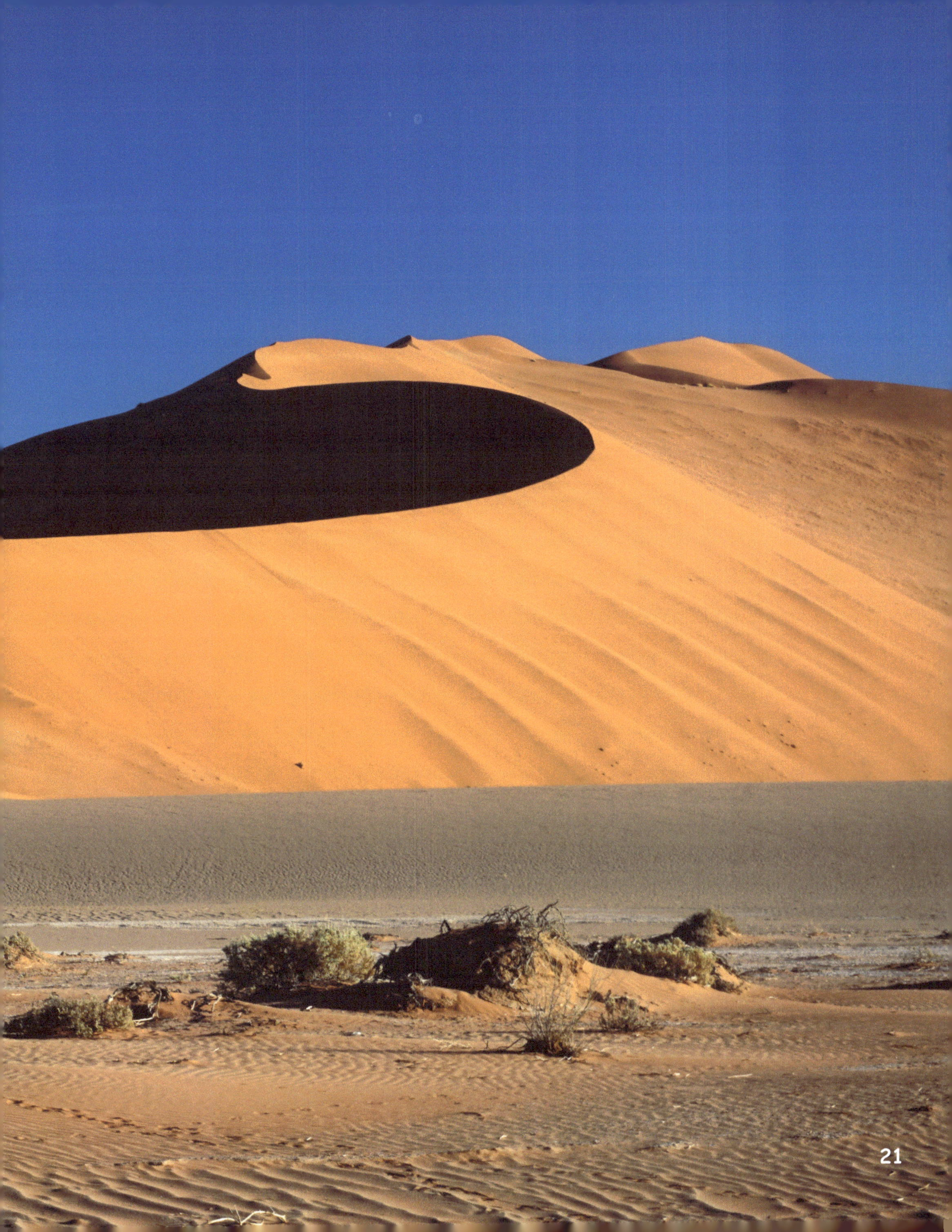

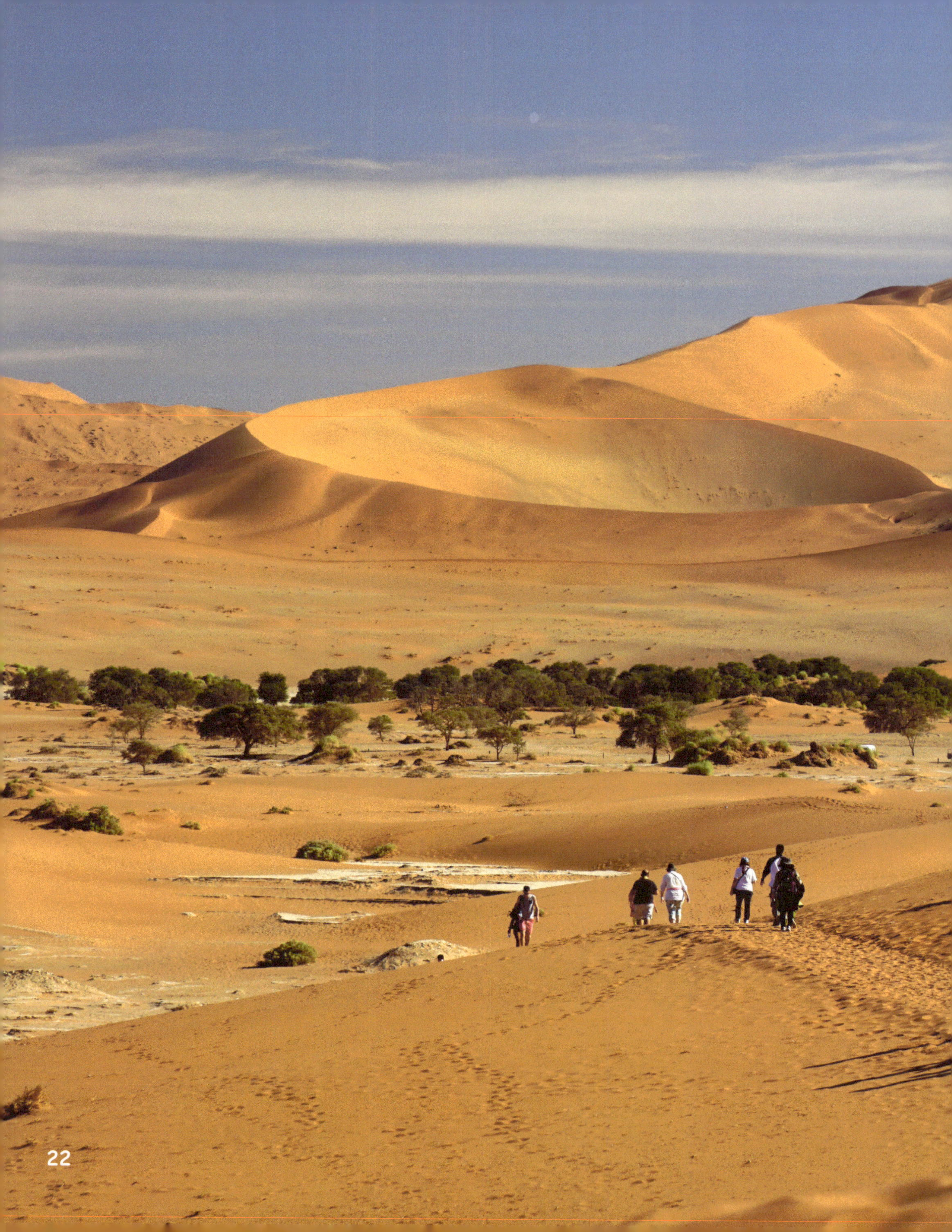

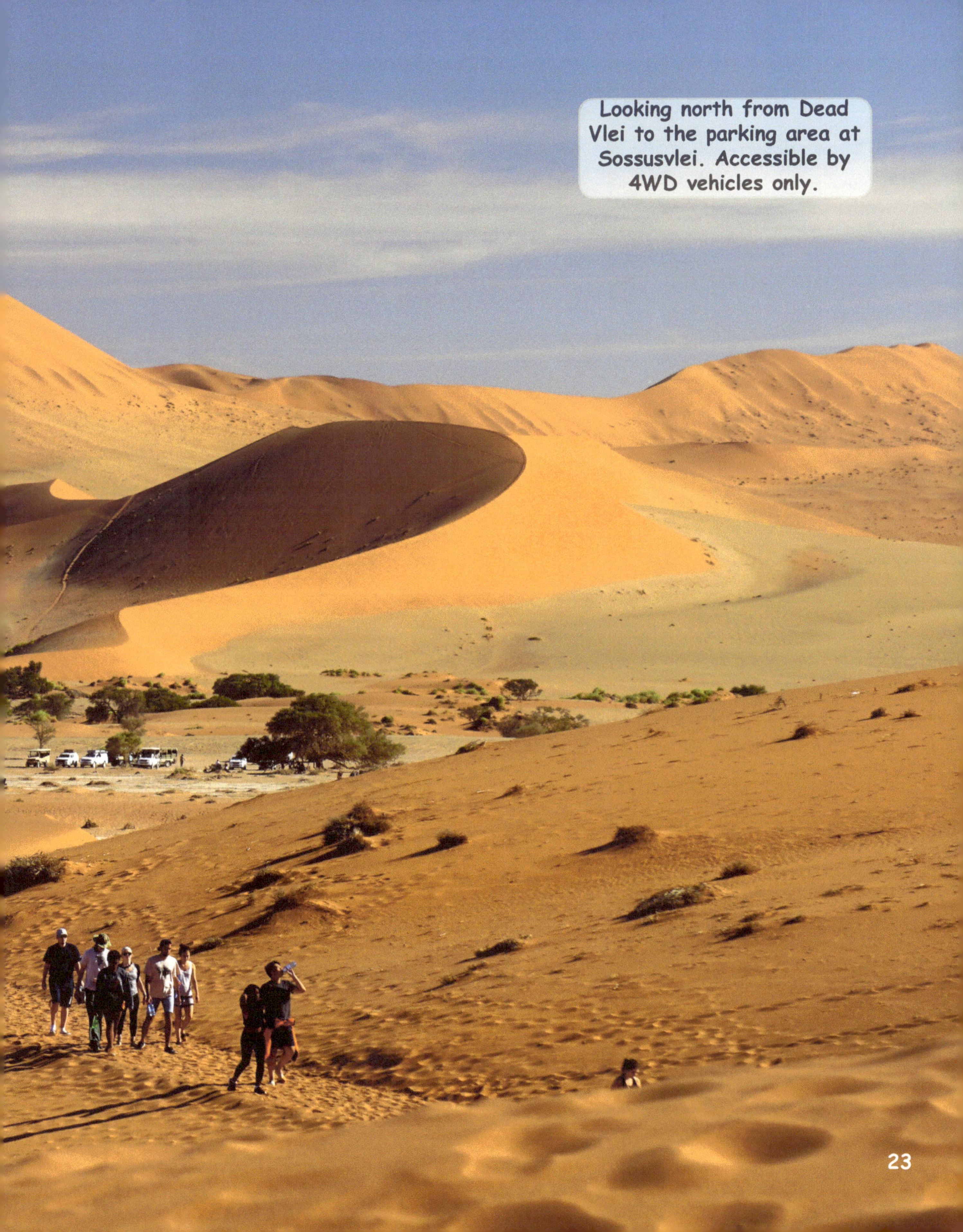

Looking north from Dead Vlei to the parking area at Sossusvlei. Accessible by 4WD vehicles only.

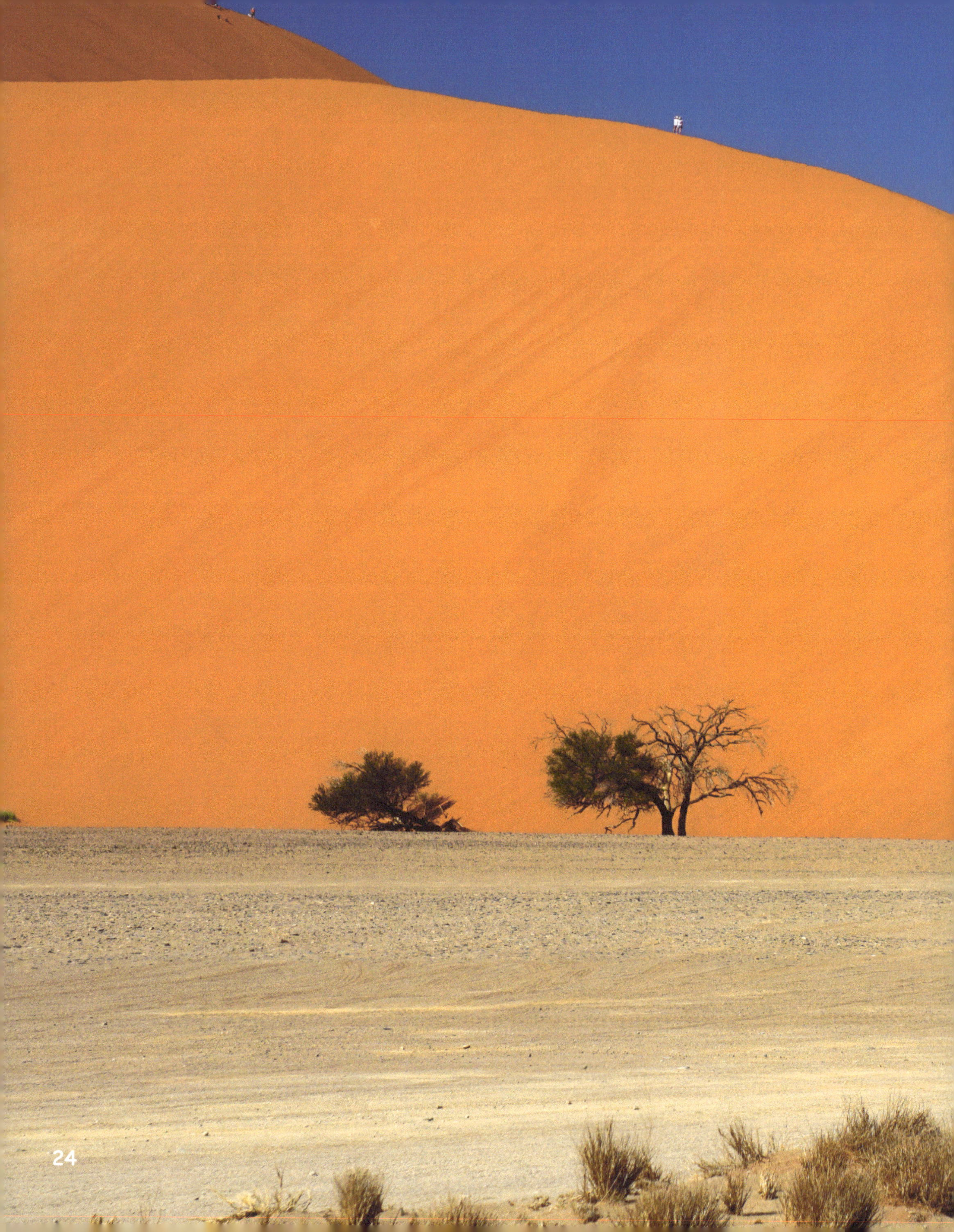

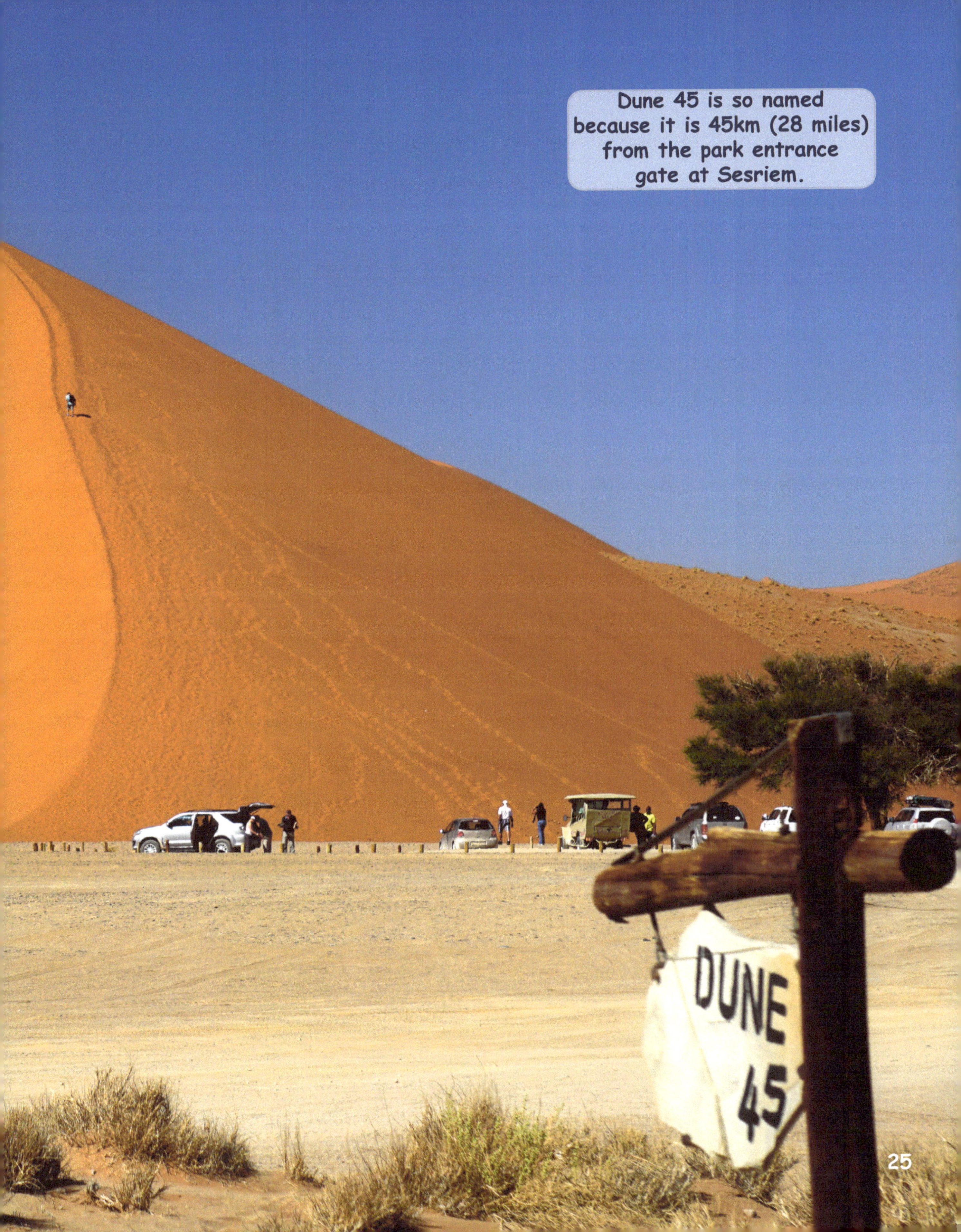

Dune 45 is so named because it is 45km (28 miles) from the park entrance gate at Sesriem.
DUNE 45

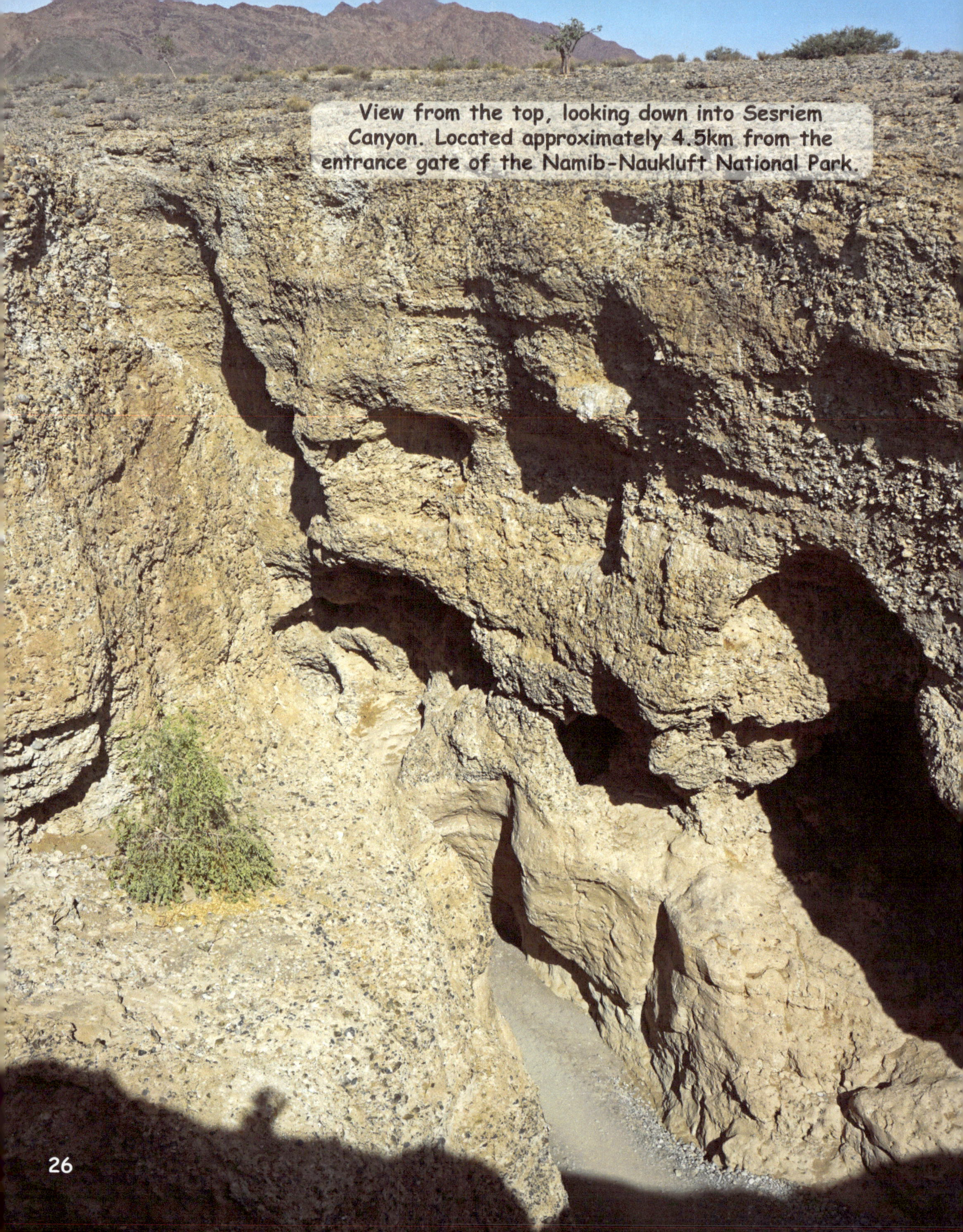

View from the top, looking down into Sesriem Canyon. Located approximately 4.5km from the entrance gate of the Namib-Naukluft National Park.

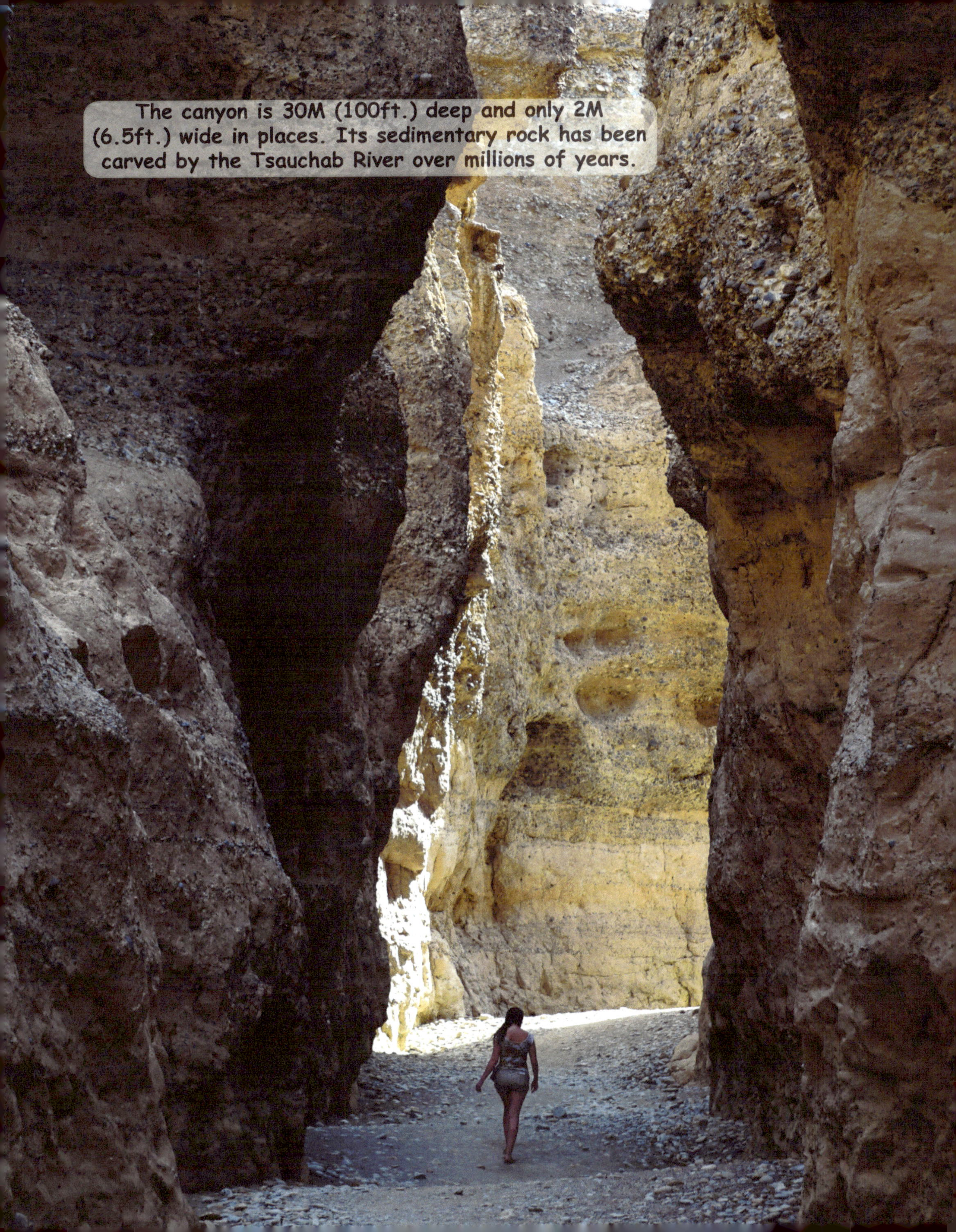

The canyon is 30M (100ft.) deep and only 2M (6.5ft.) wide in places. Its sedimentary rock has been carved by the Tsauchab River over millions of years.

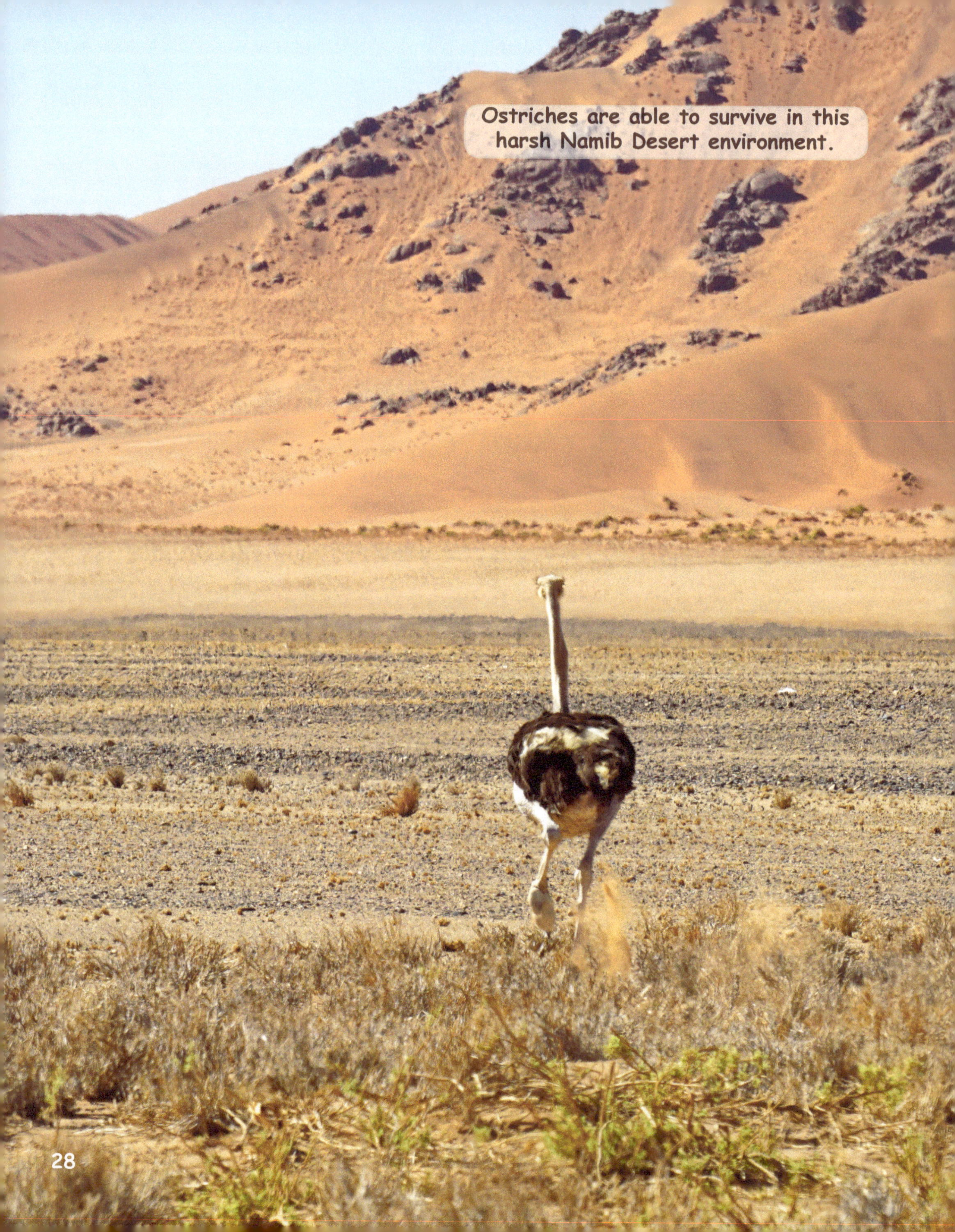
Ostriches are able to survive in this harsh Namib Desert environment.

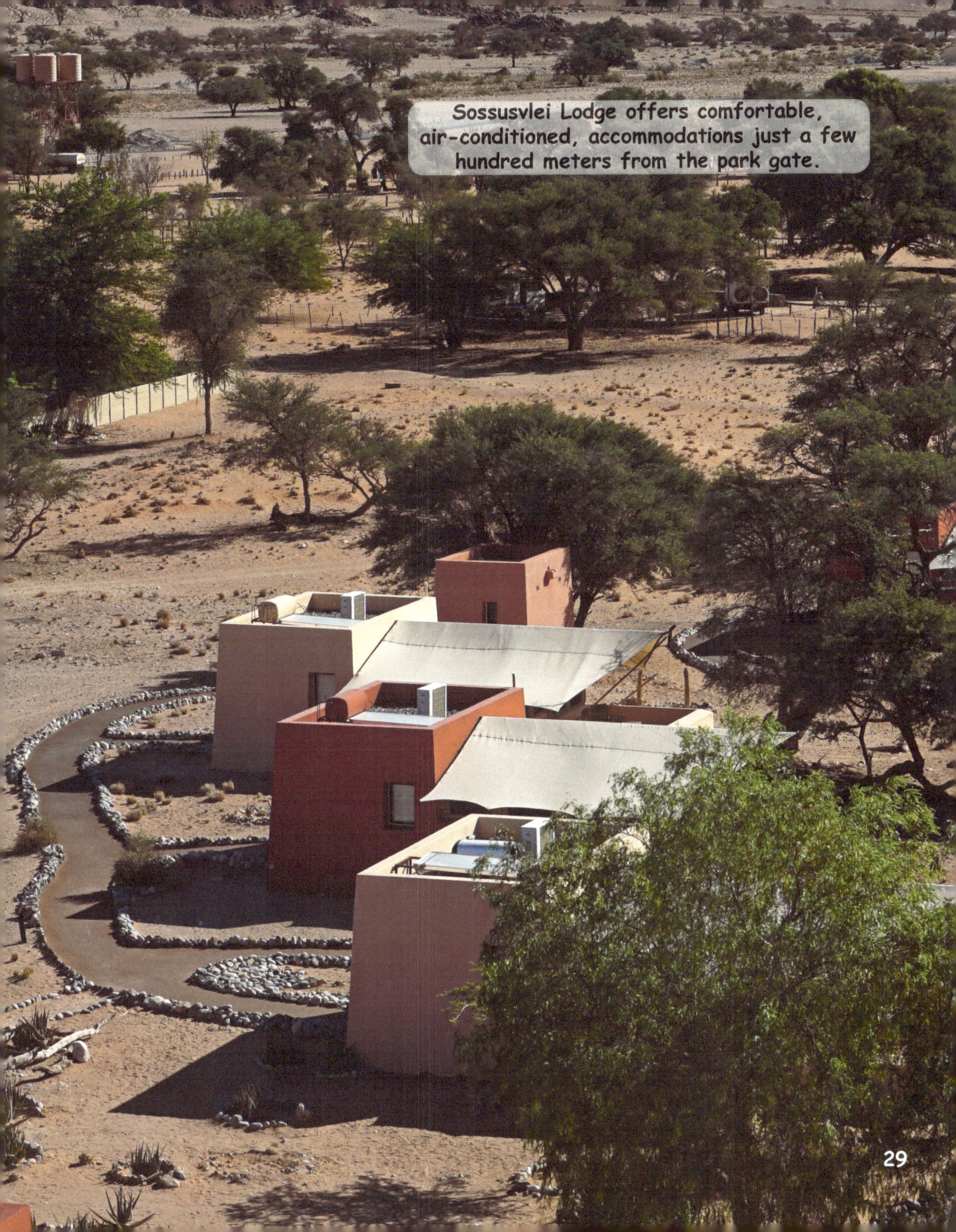

Sossusvlei Lodge offers comfortable, air-conditioned, accommodations just a few hundred meters from the park gate.

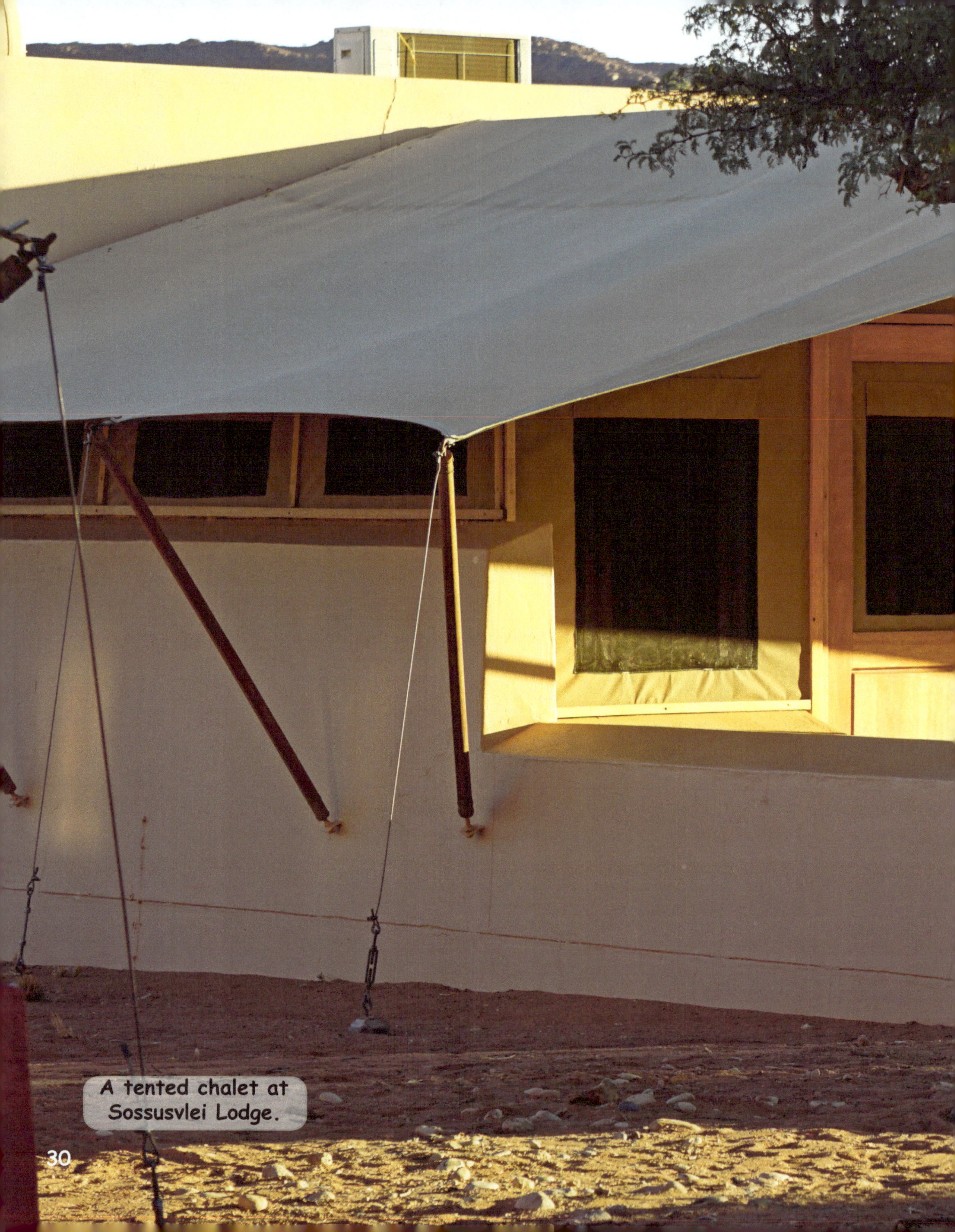

A tented chalet at Sossusvlei Lodge.

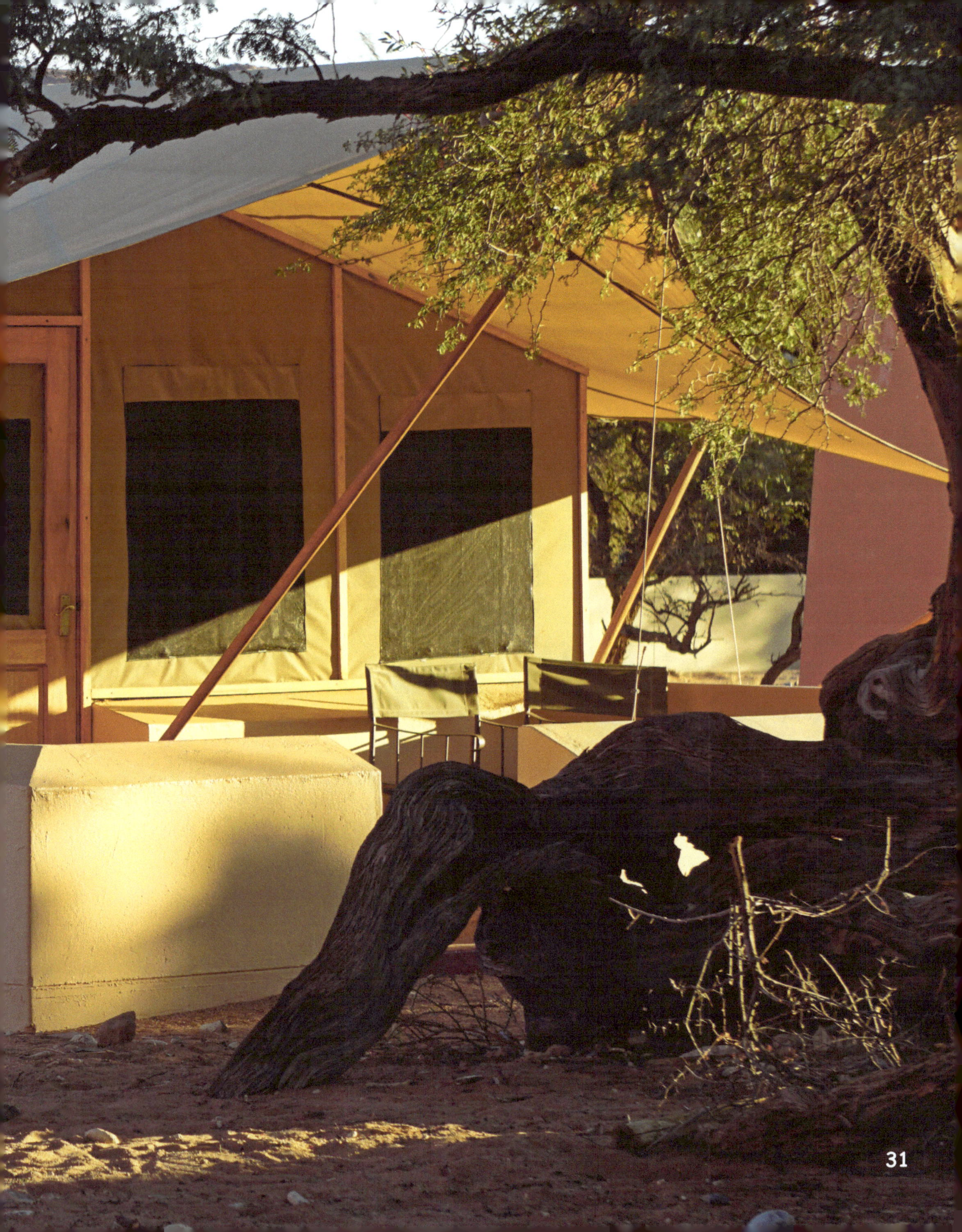

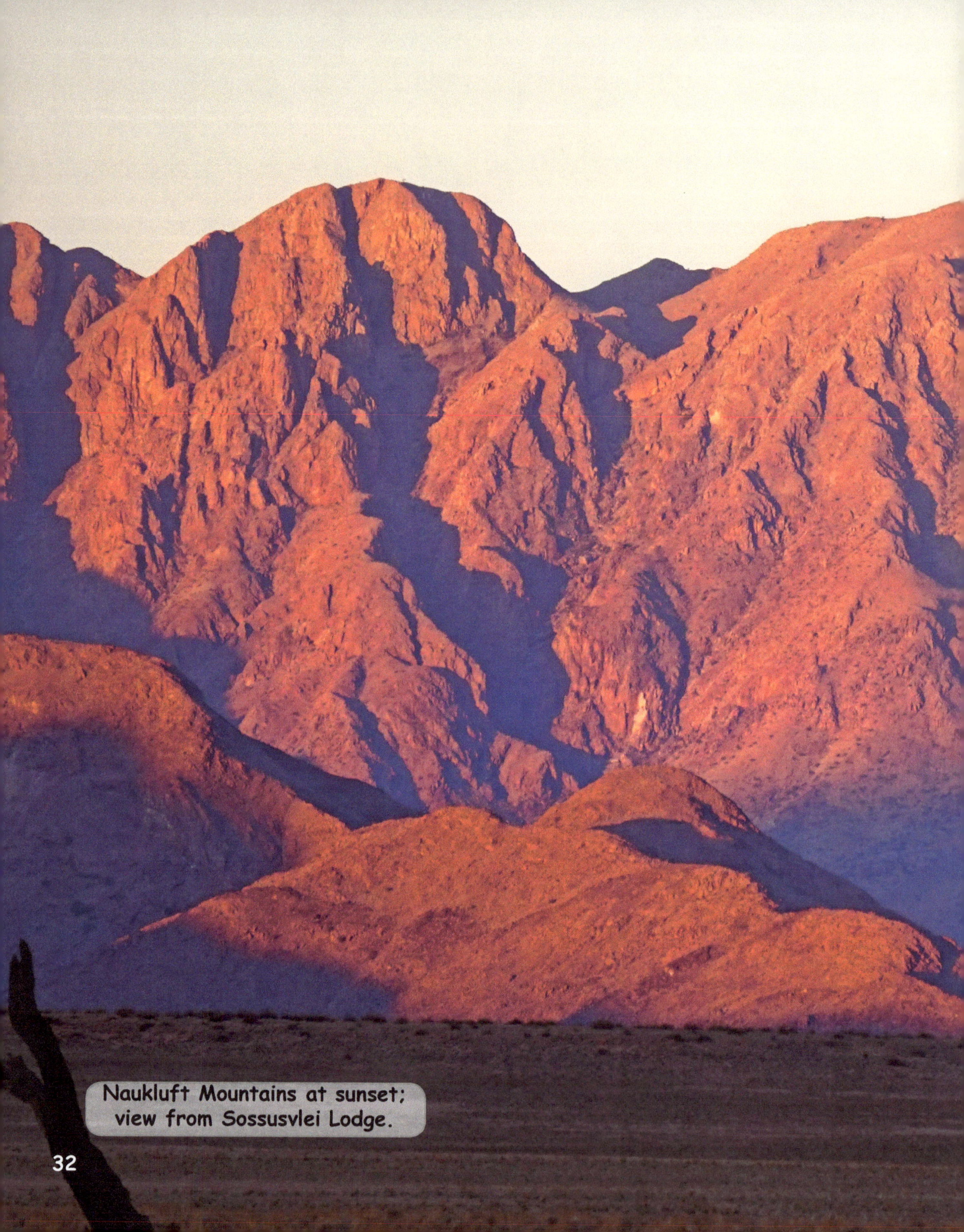

Naukluft Mountains at sunset;
view from Sossusvlei Lodge.

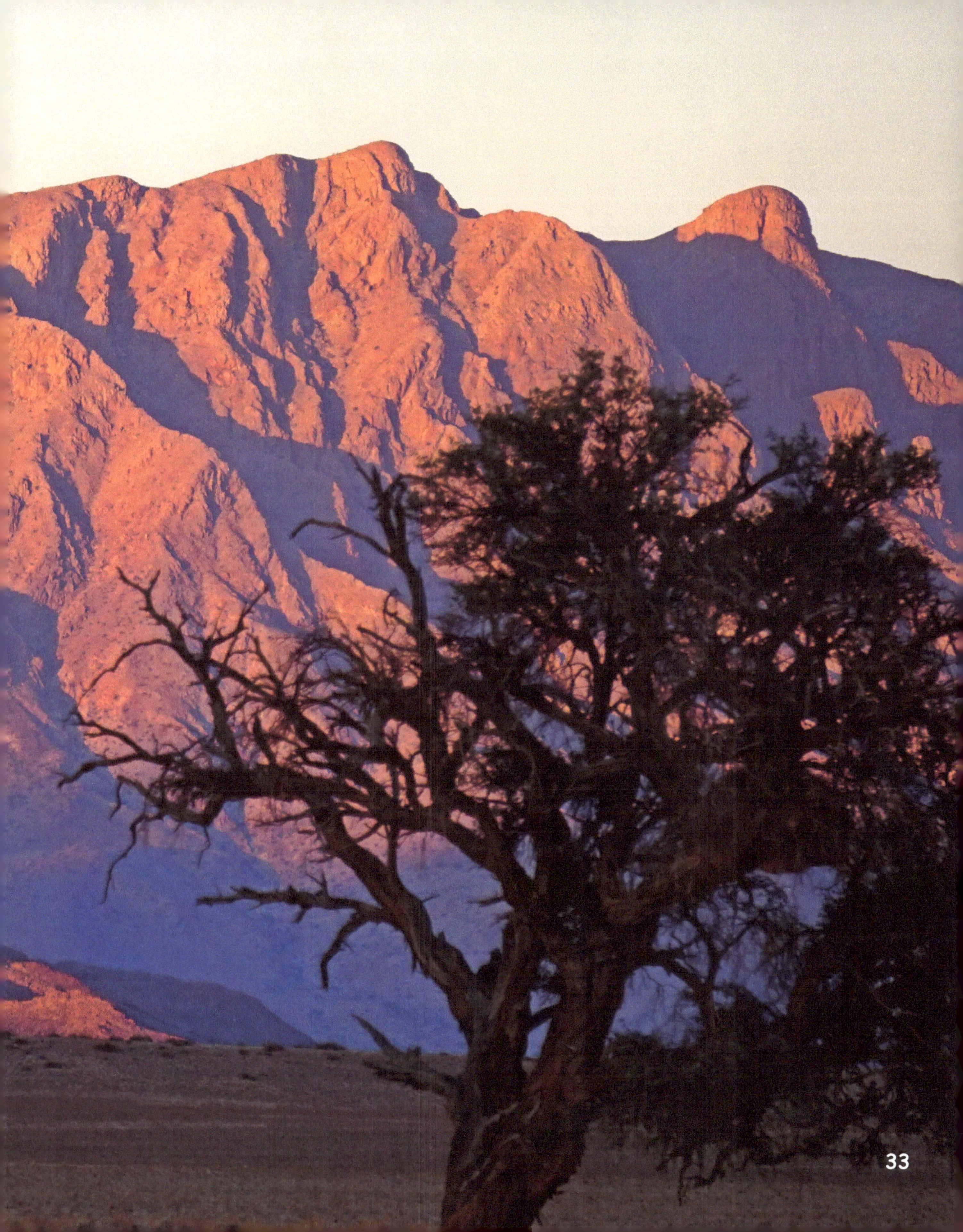

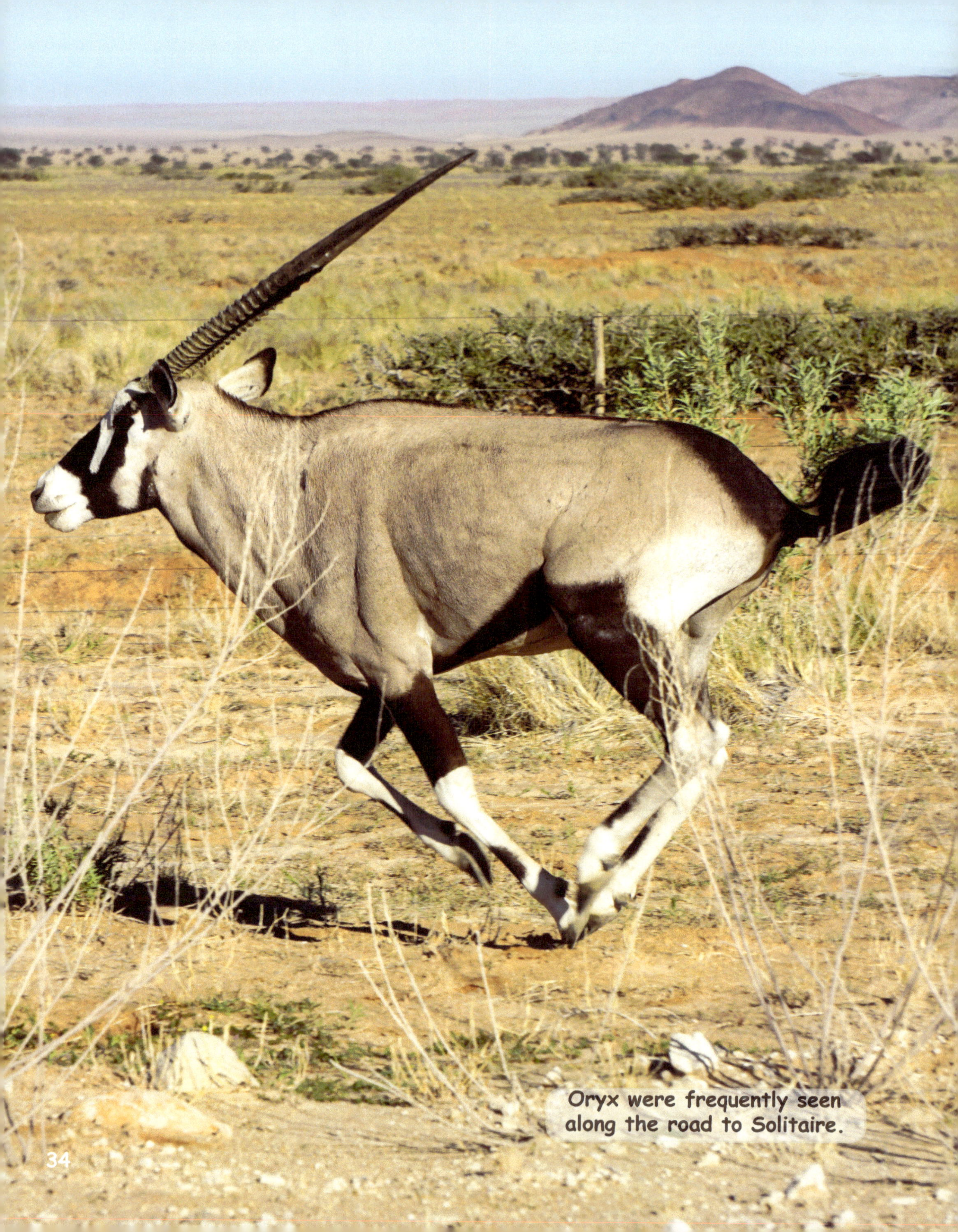

Oryx were frequently seen
along the road to Solitaire.

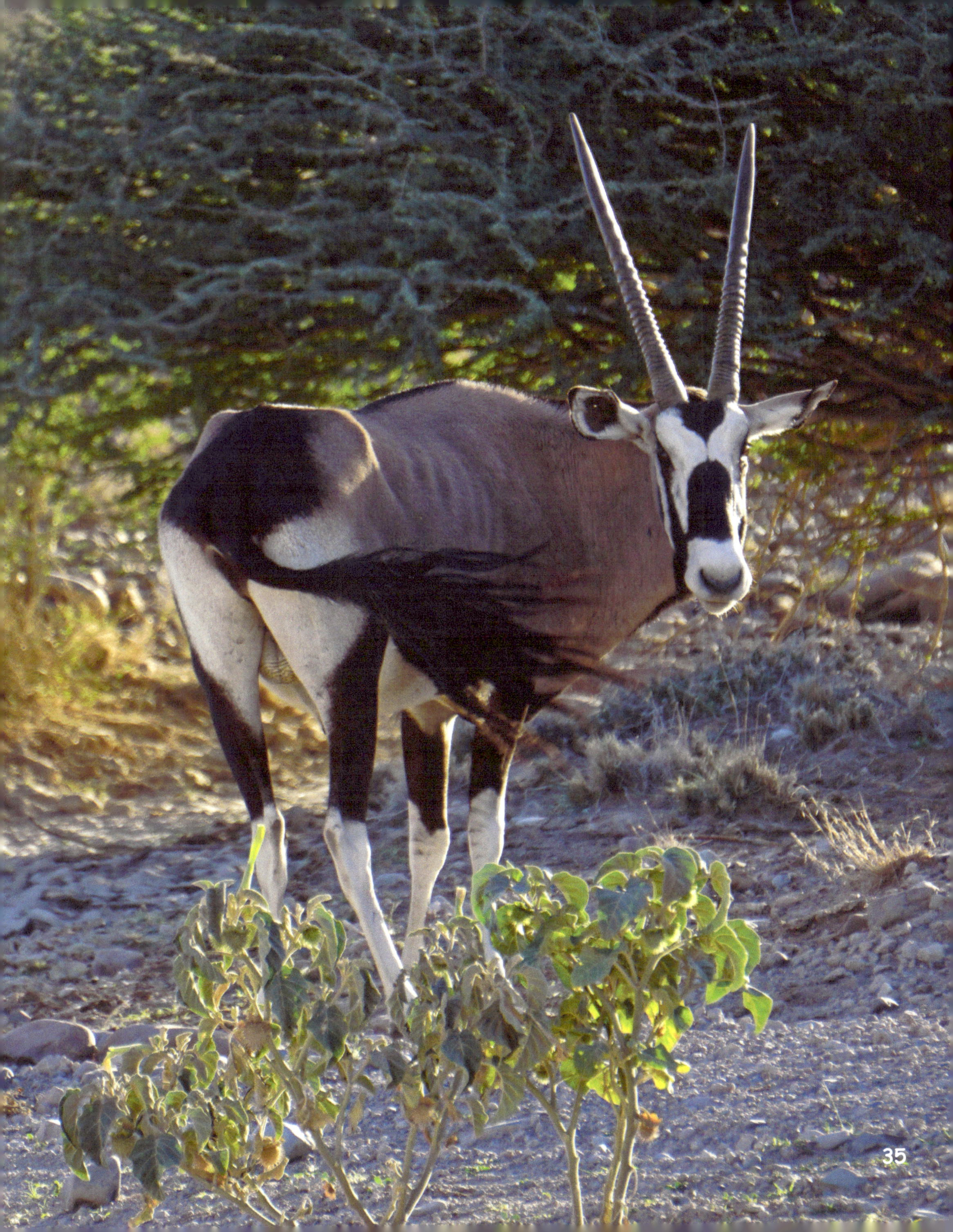

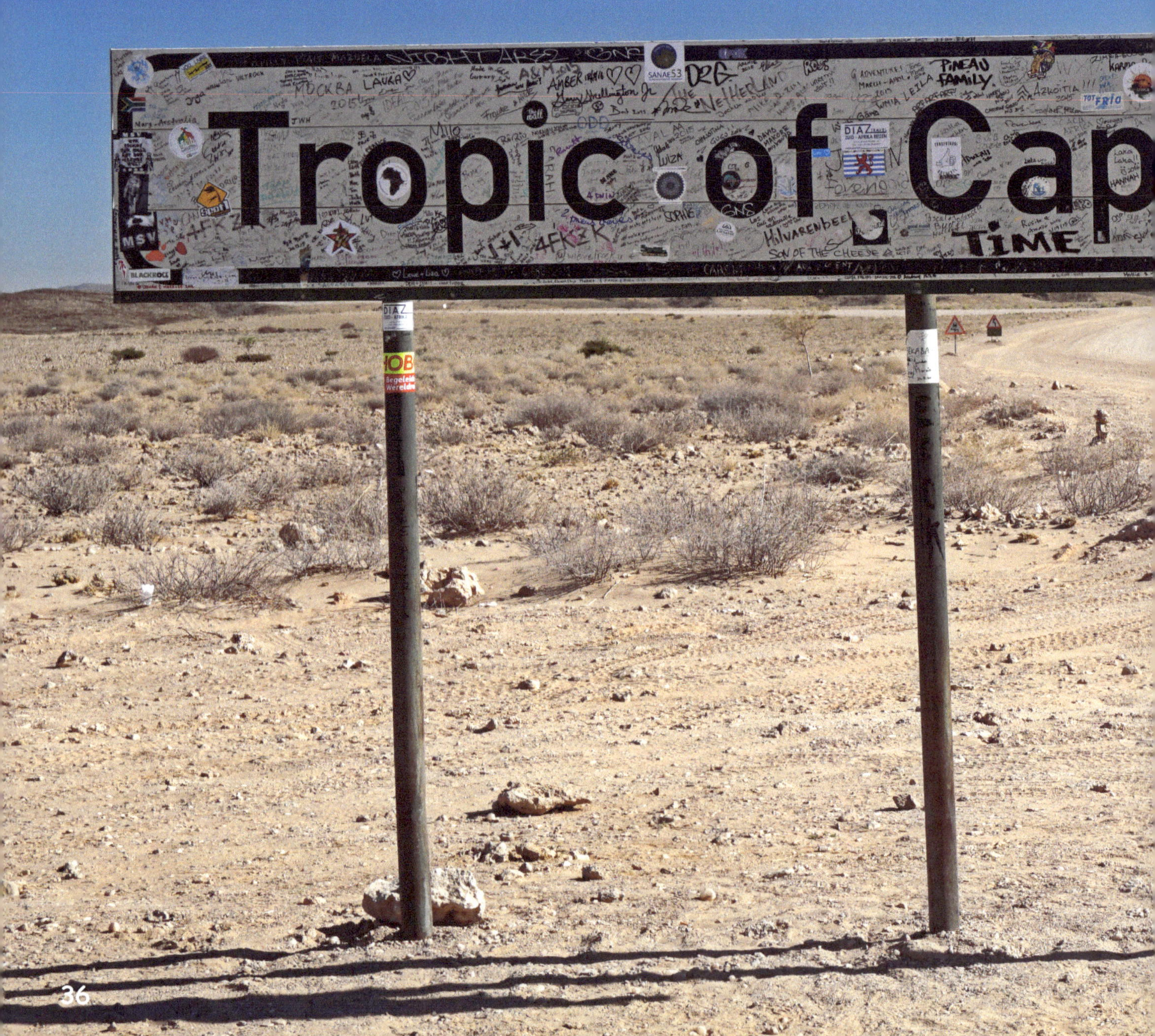

Tropic of Cap
TIME

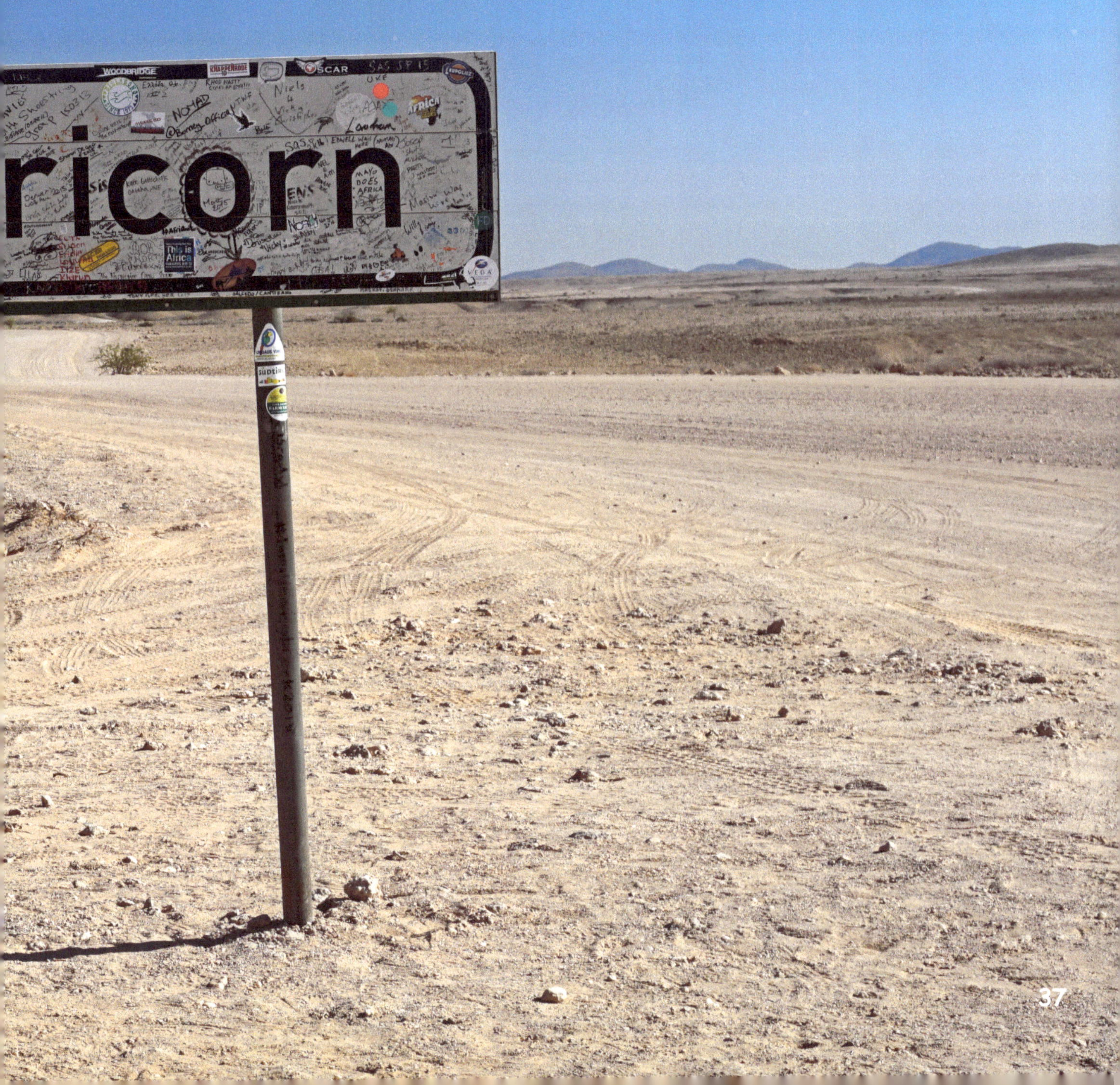

Crossing the Tropic of Capricorn on road C14 from Solitaire to Walvis Bay. Latitude 23°26'13.8" (or 23.43716°) south of the equator. It moves approximately 15M (48.75ft.) northward each year.

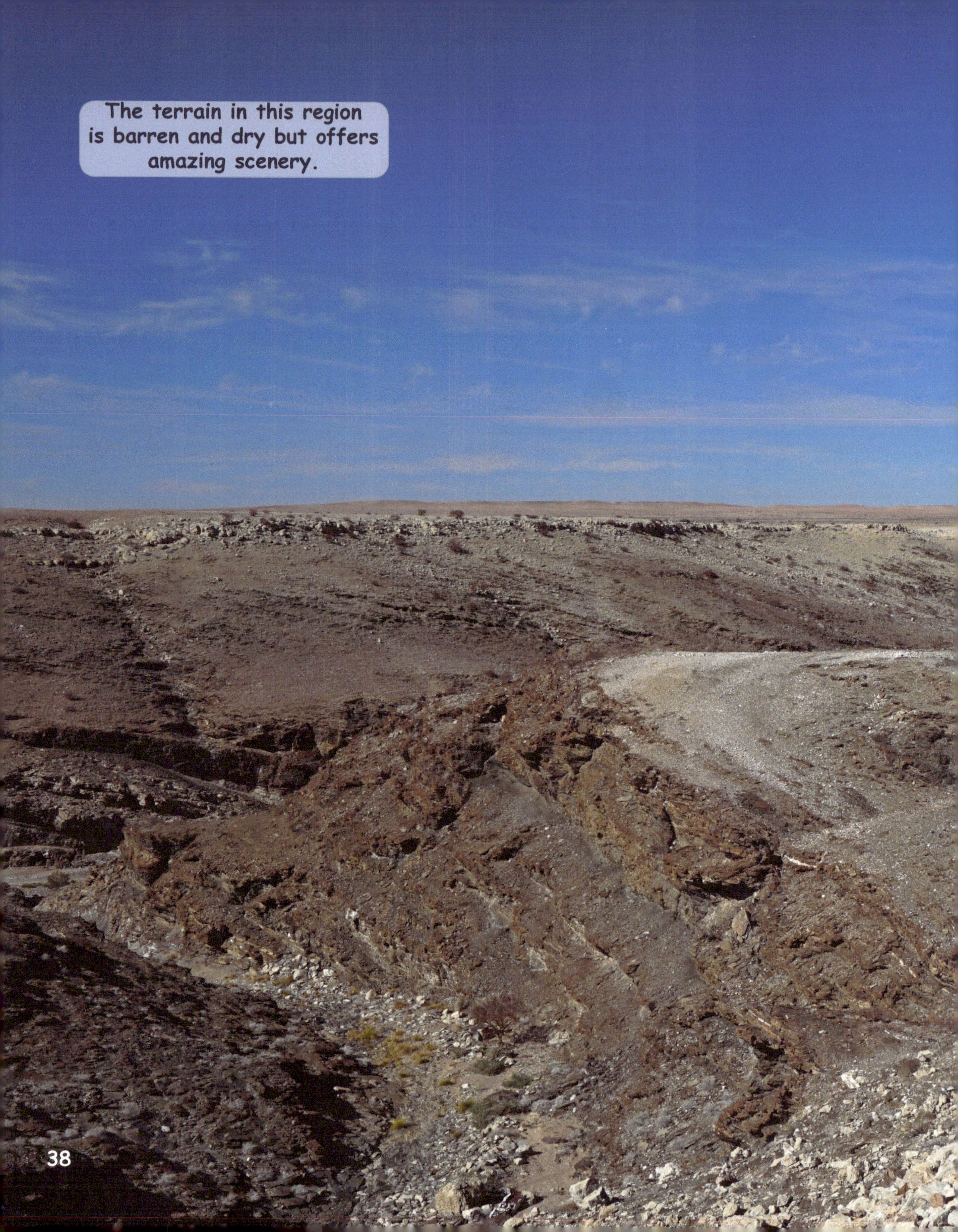
The terrain in this region is barren and dry but offers amazing scenery.

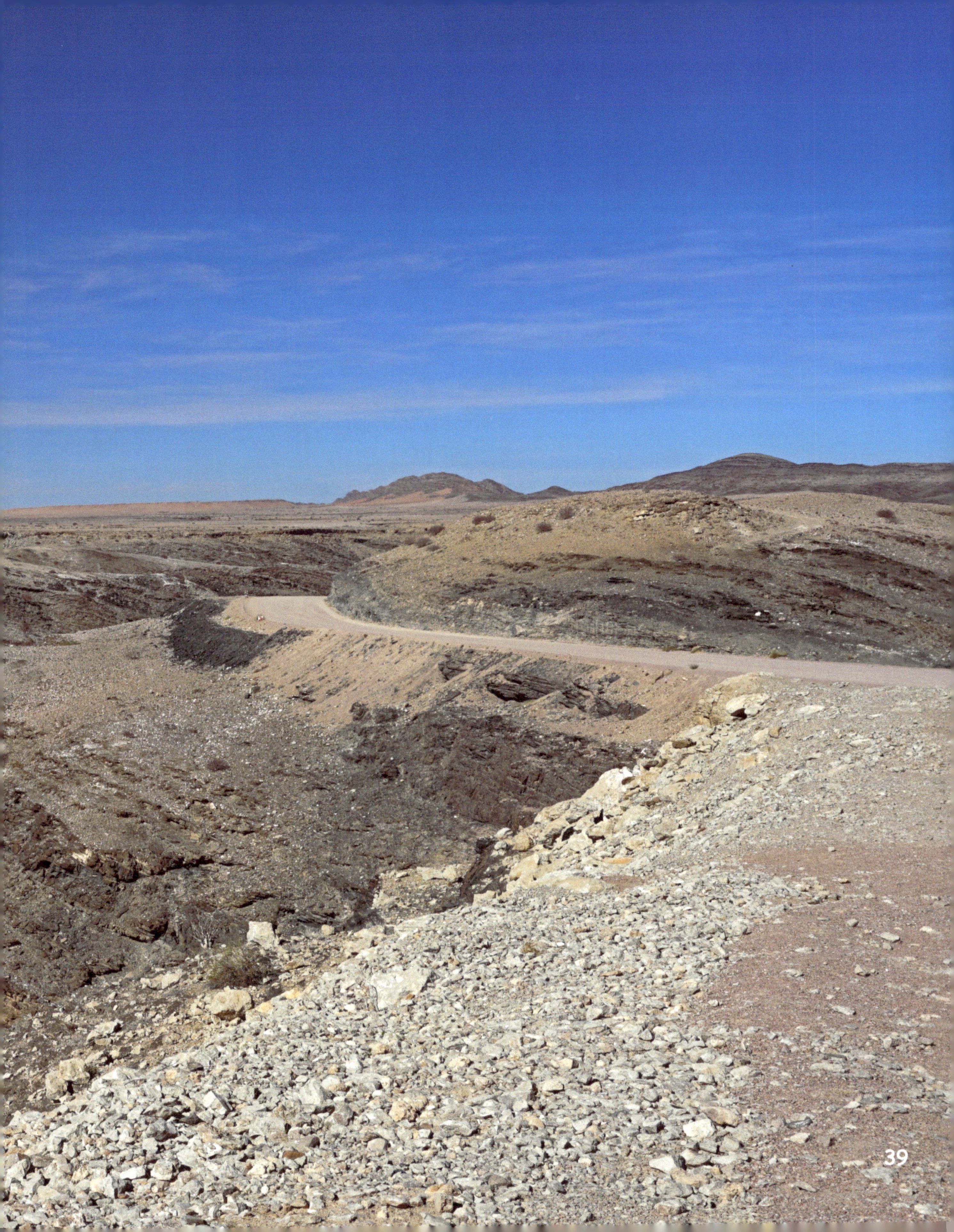

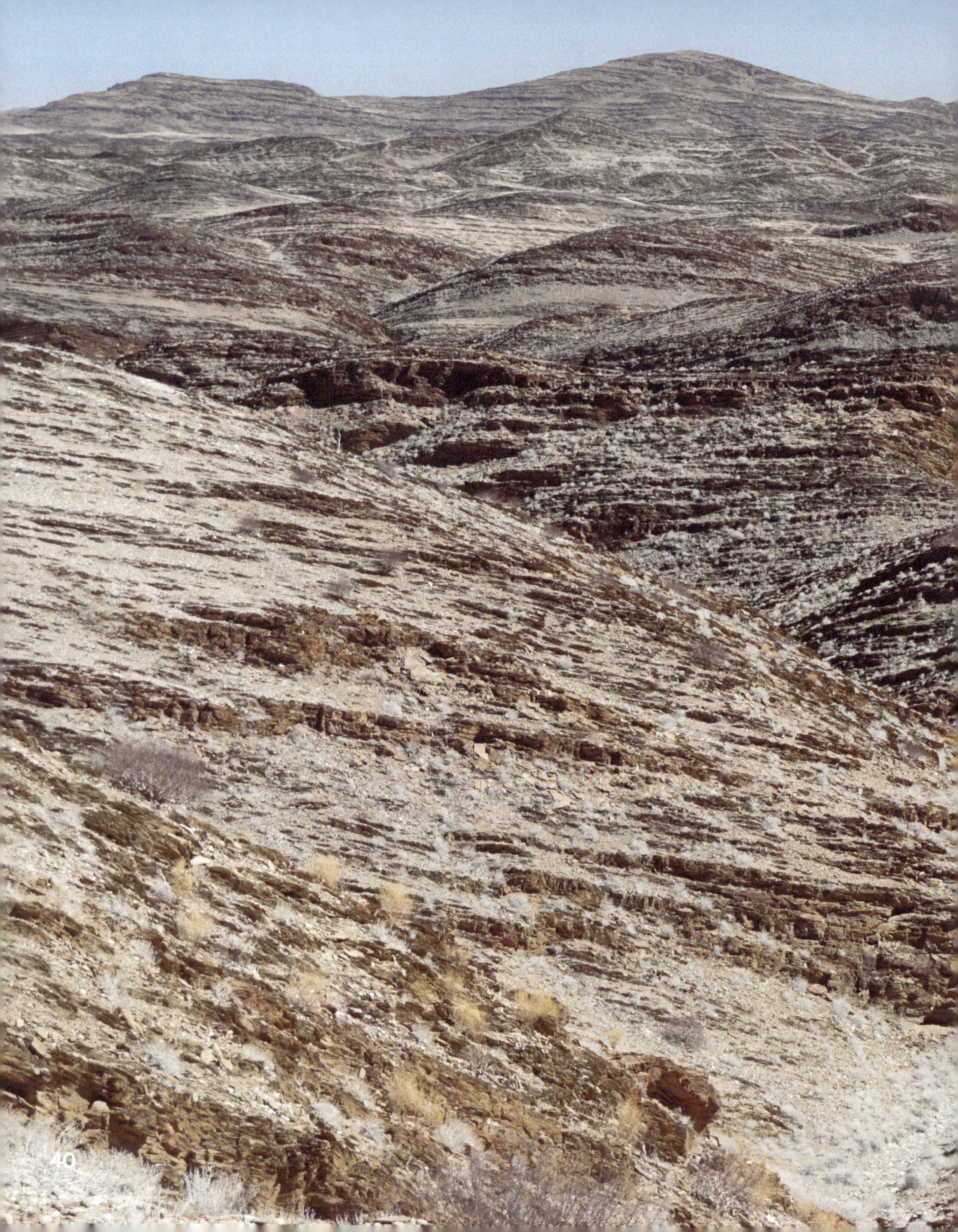

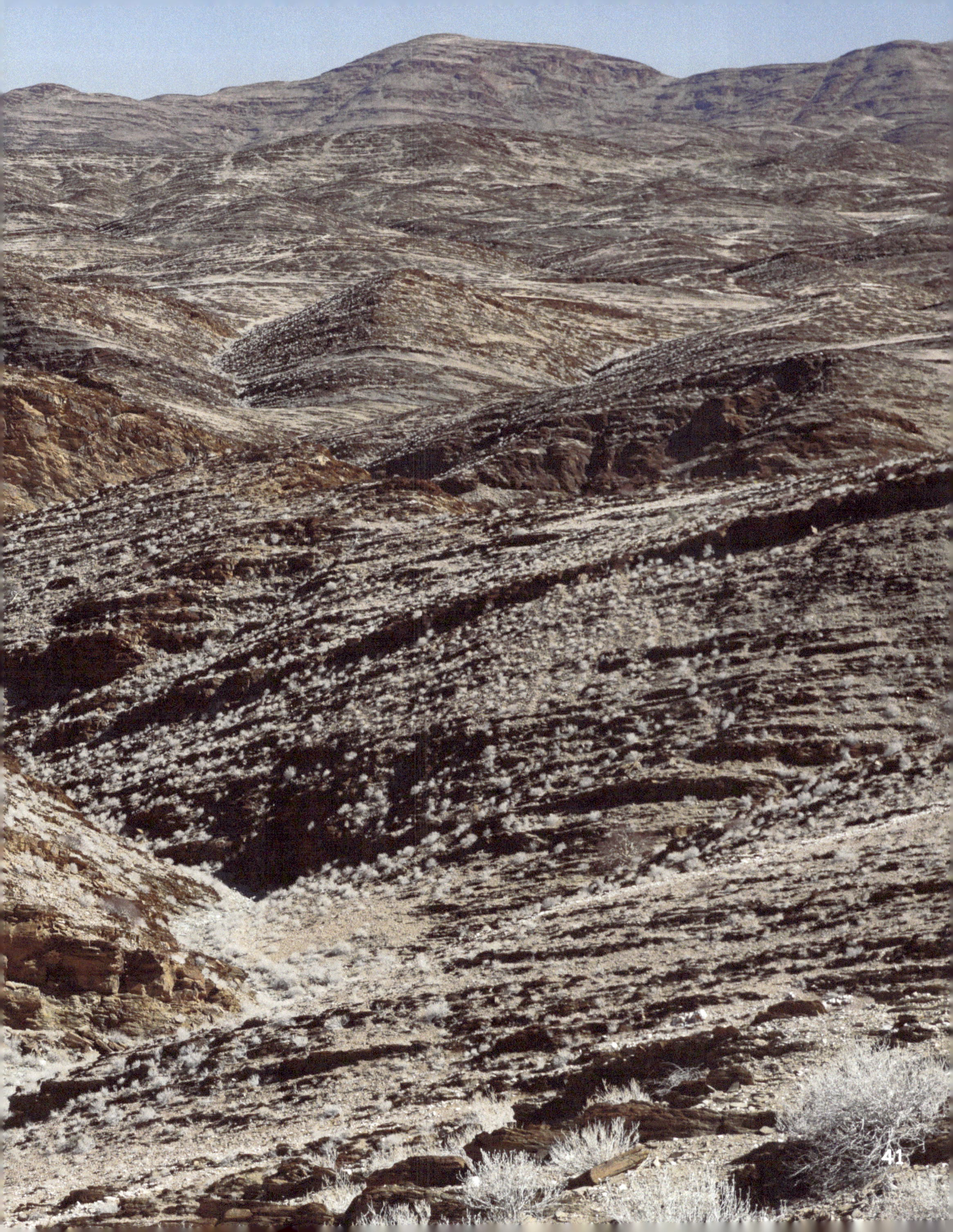

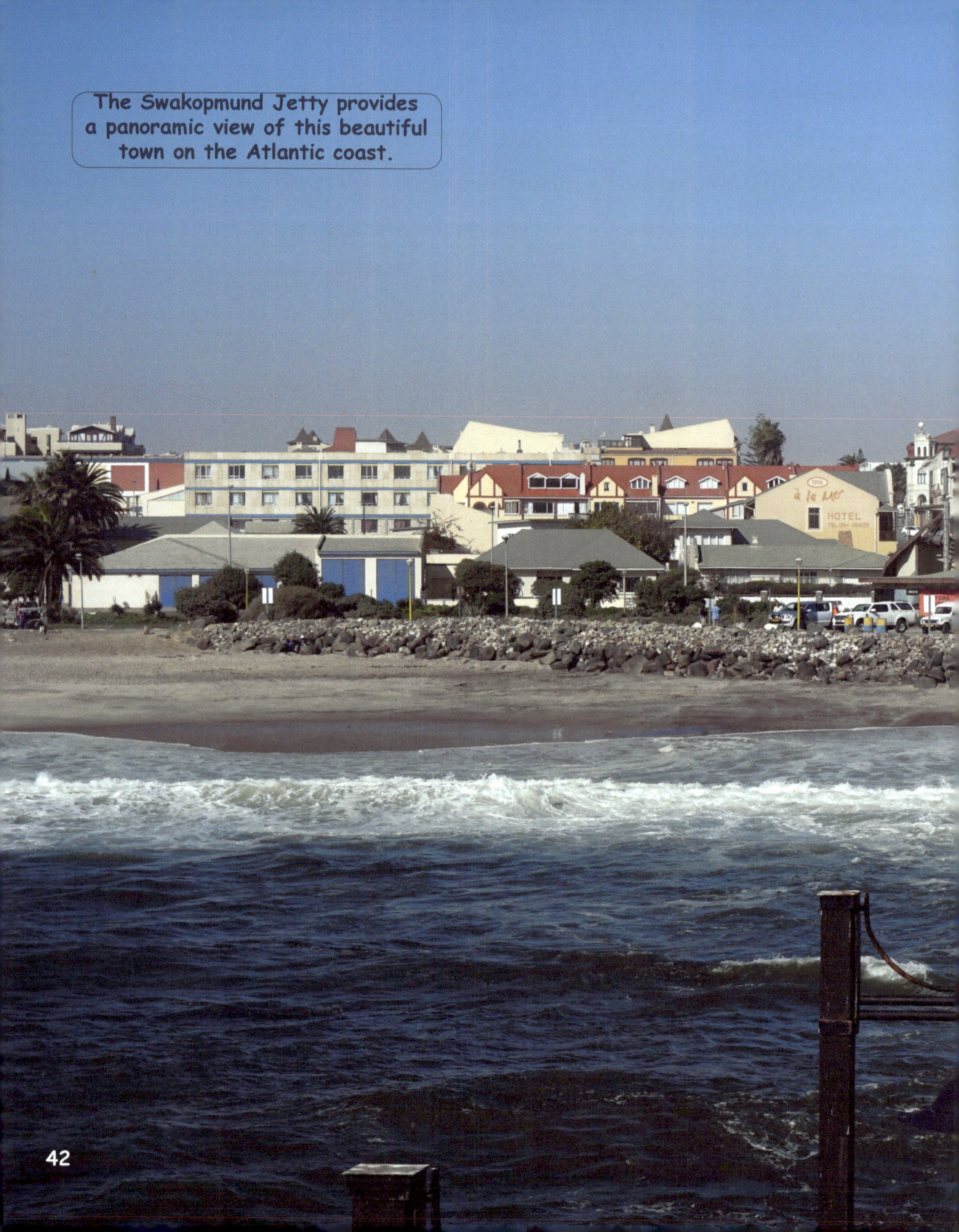

The Swakopmund Jetty provides a panoramic view of this beautiful town on the Atlantic coast.

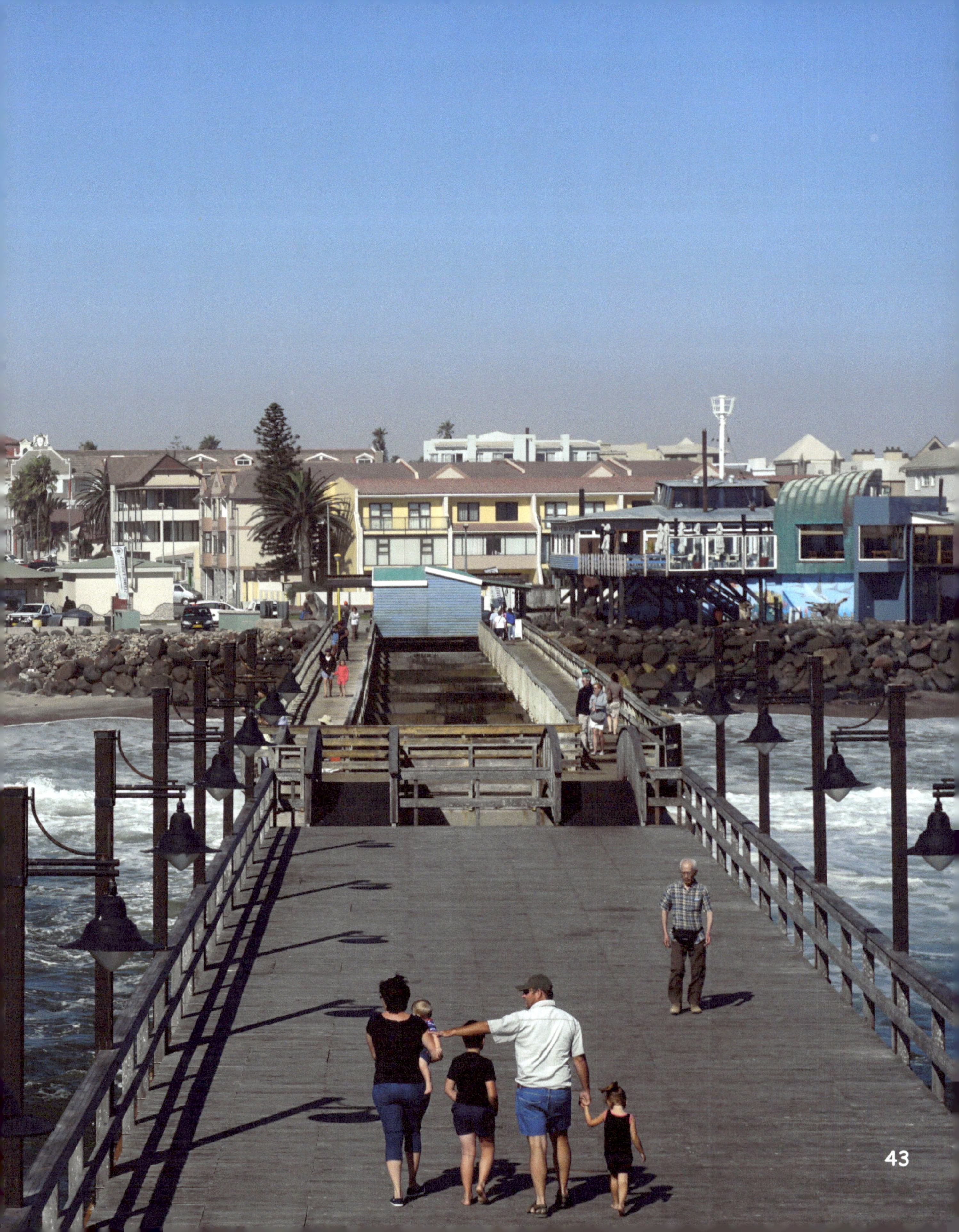

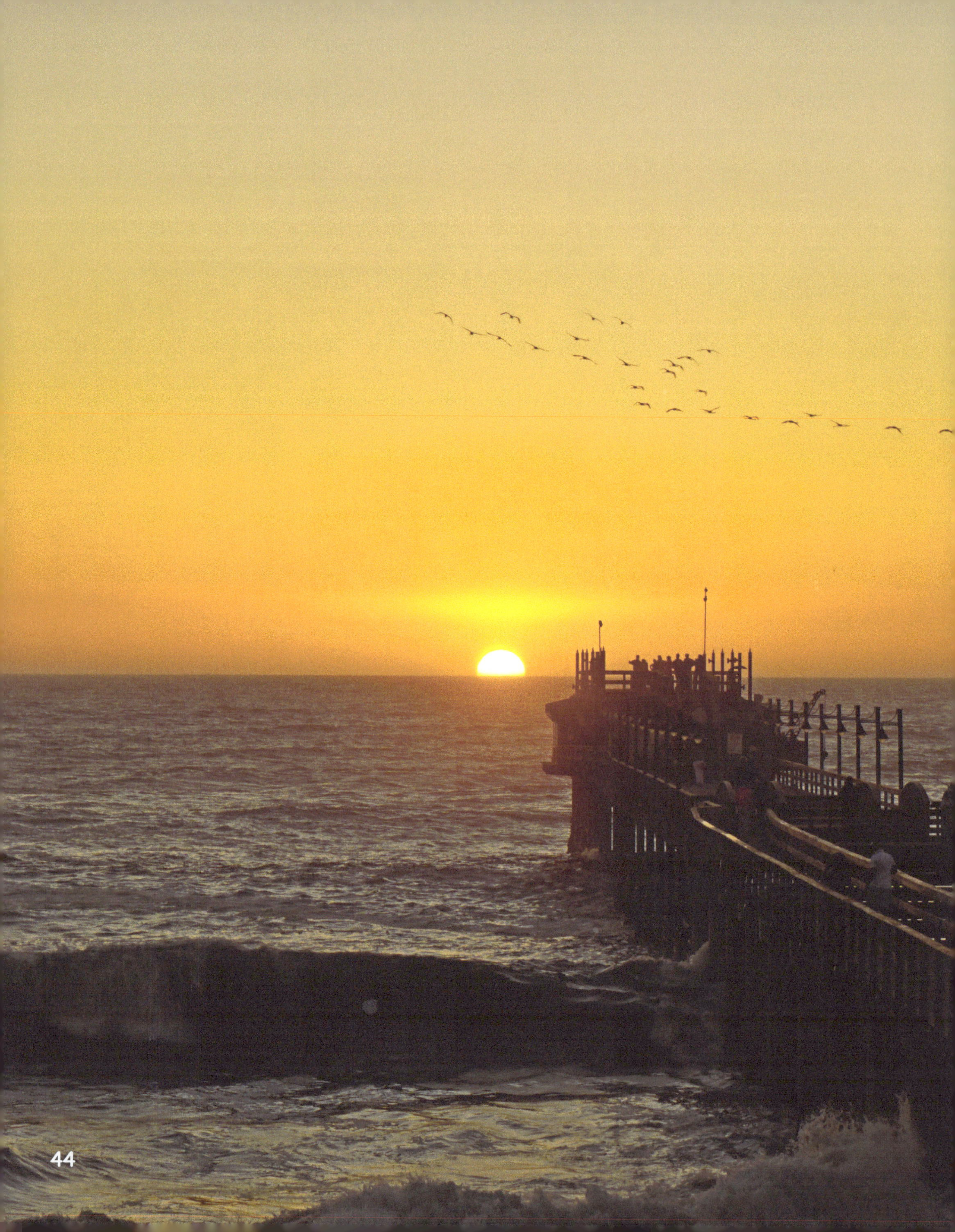

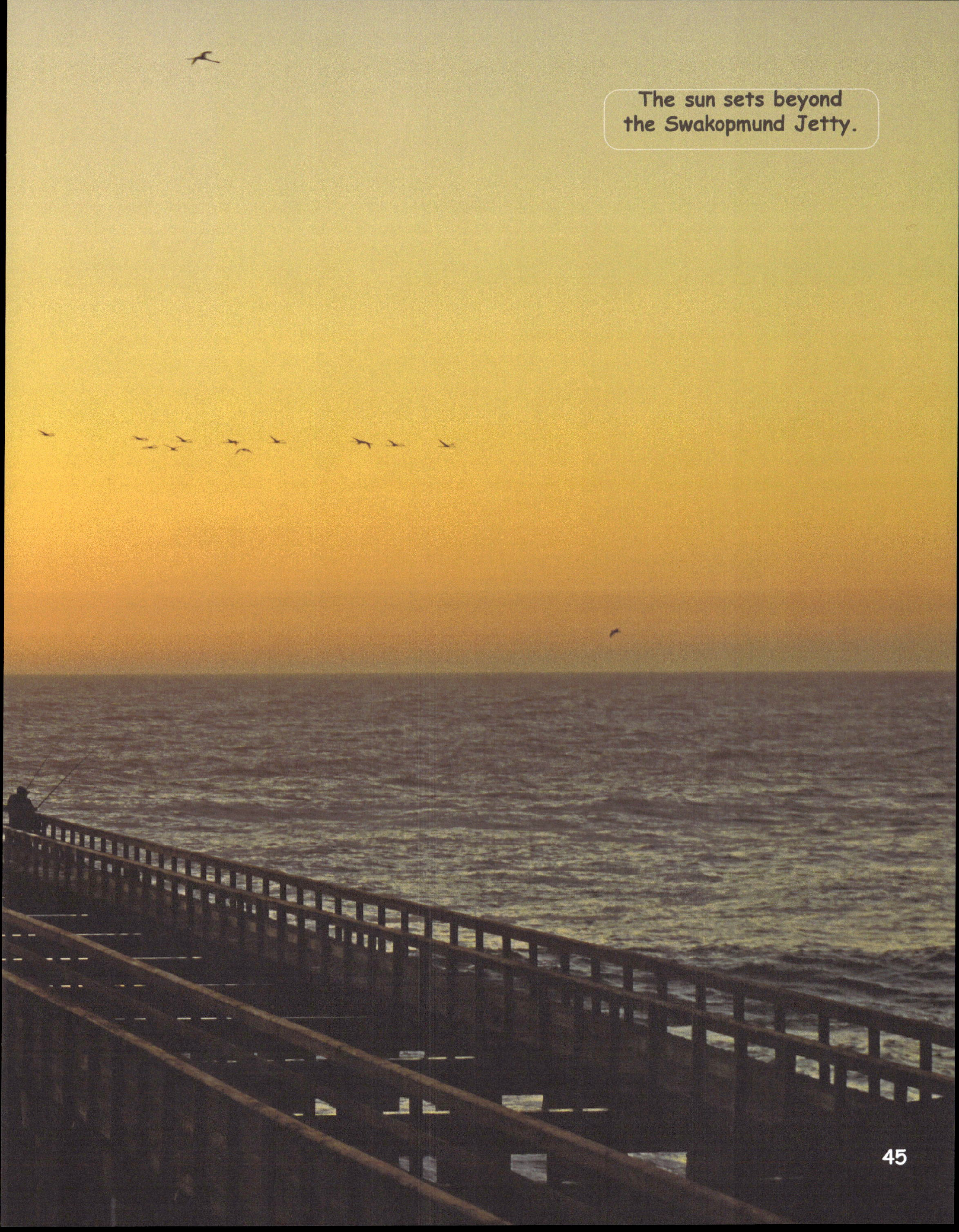

The sun sets beyond
the Swakopmund Jetty.

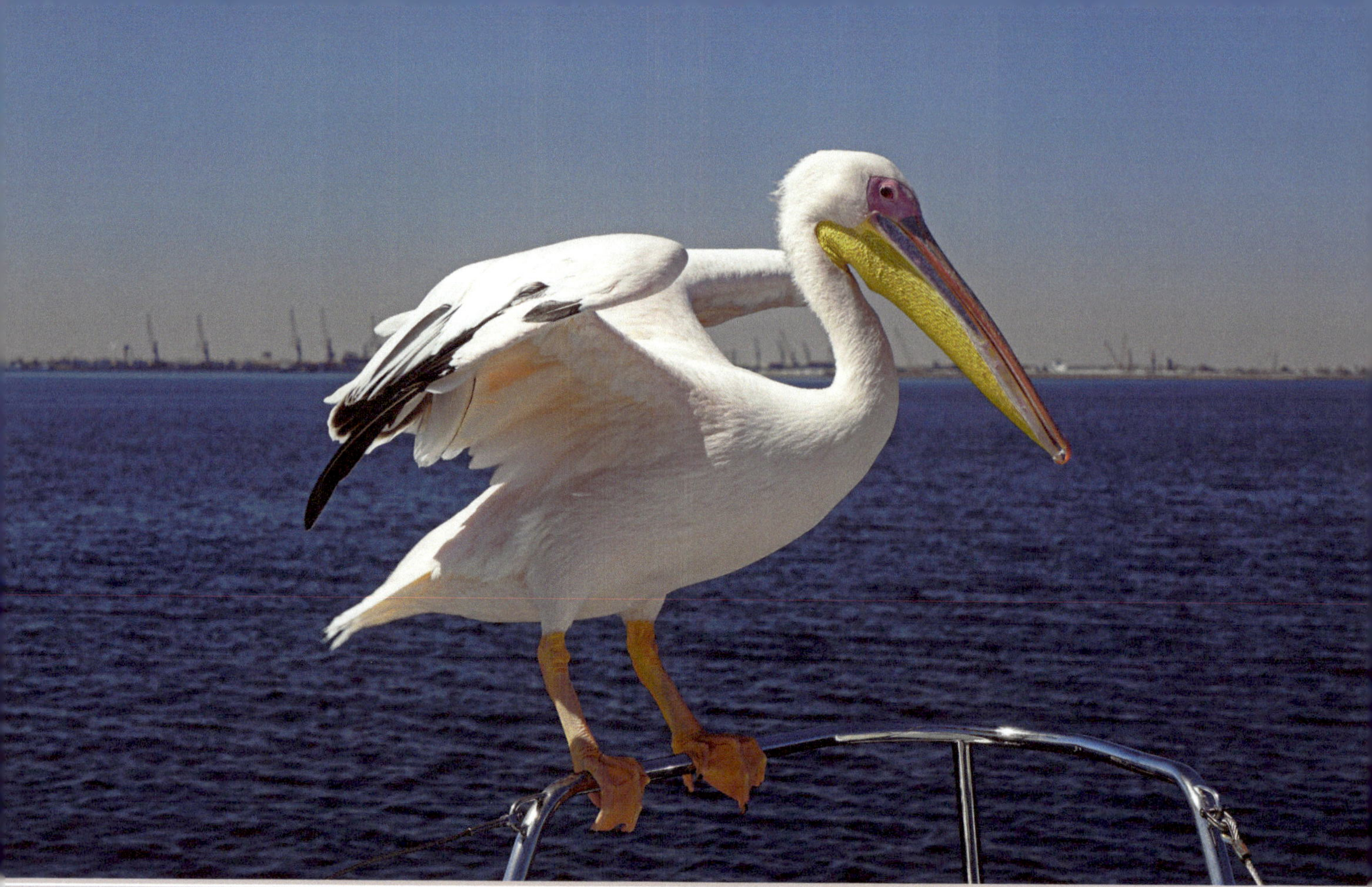

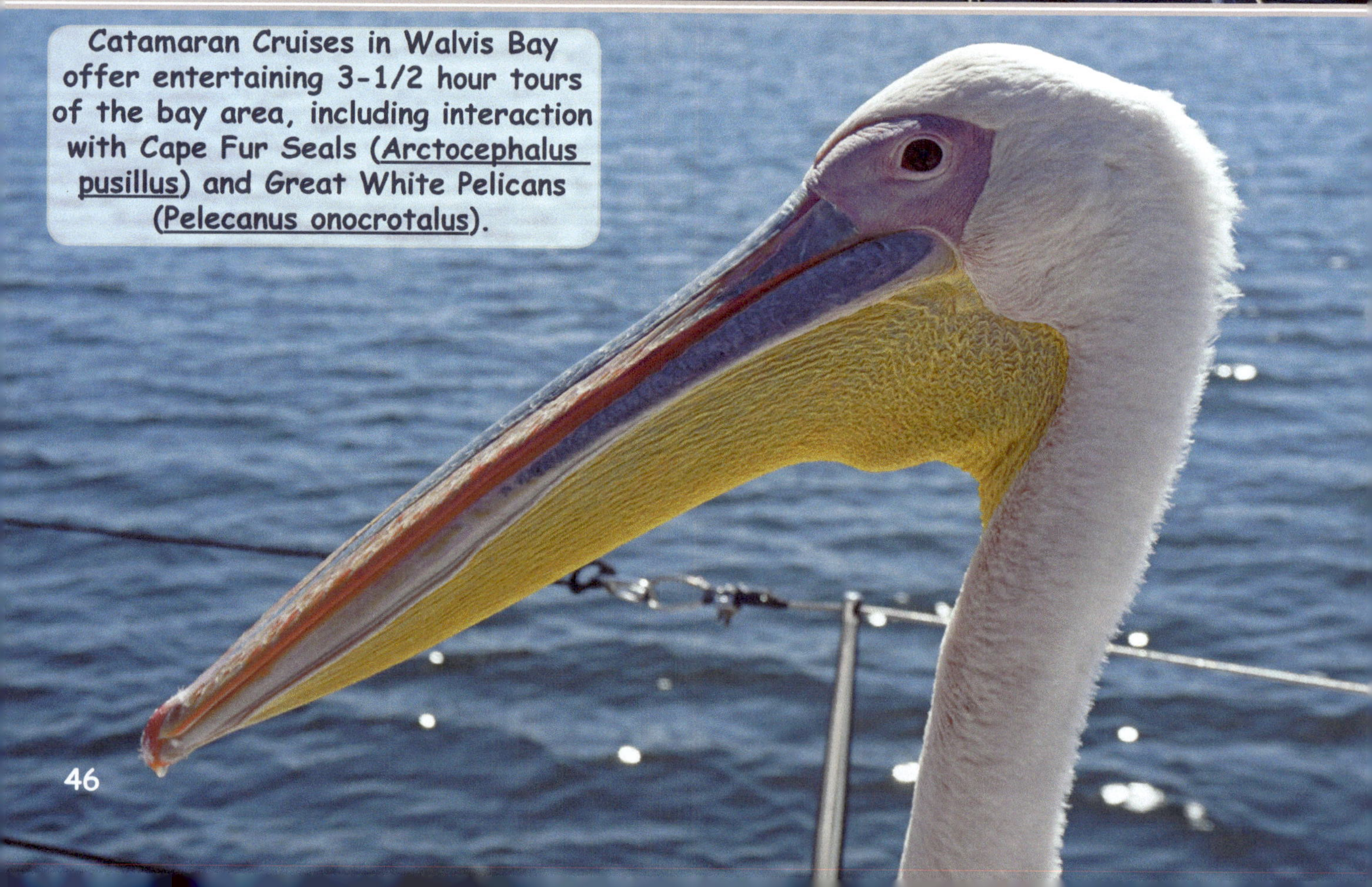

Catamaran Cruises in Walvis Bay offer entertaining 3-1/2 hour tours of the bay area, including interaction with Cape Fur Seals (<u>Arctocephalus pusillus</u>) and Great White Pelicans (<u>Pelecanus onocrotalus</u>).

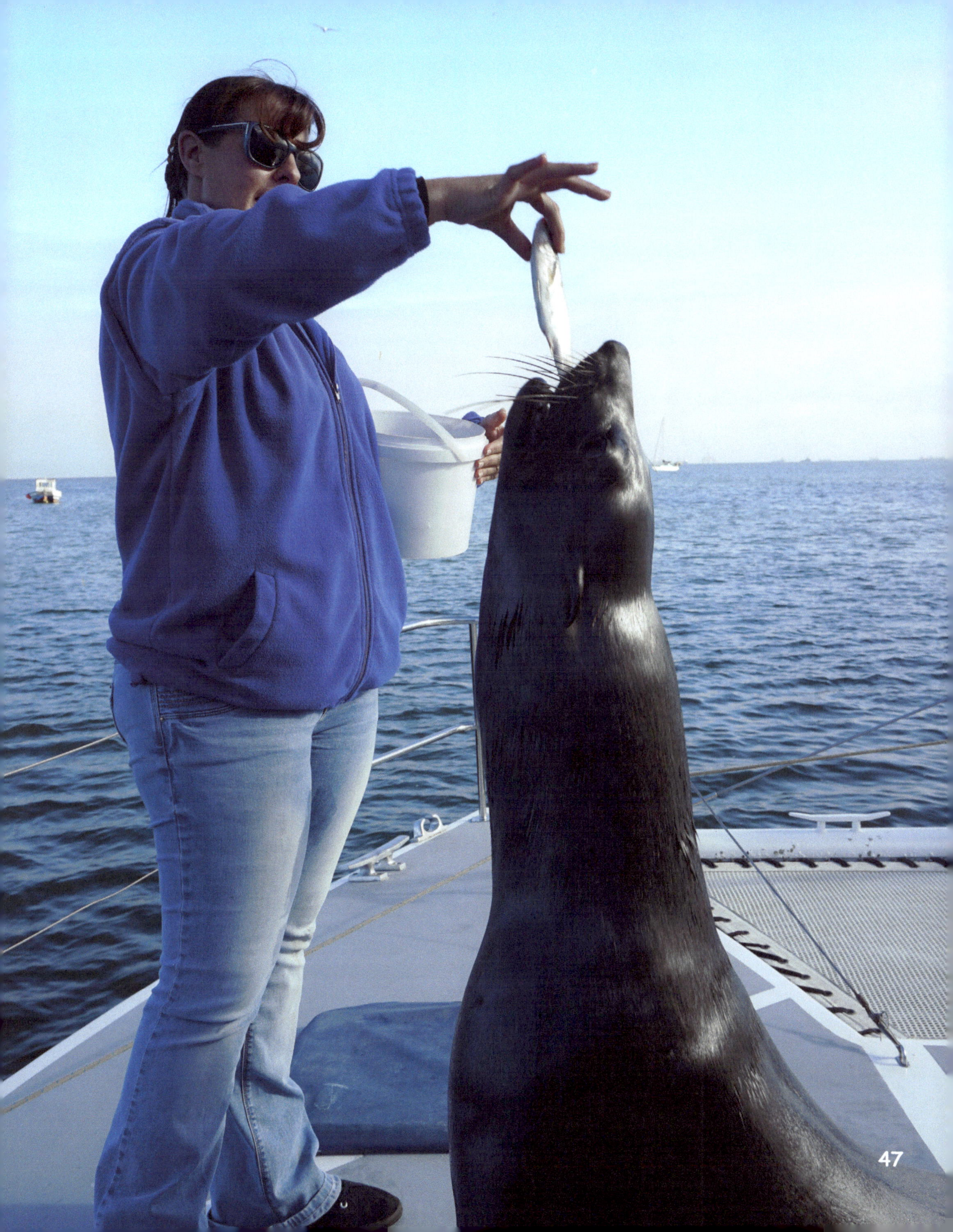

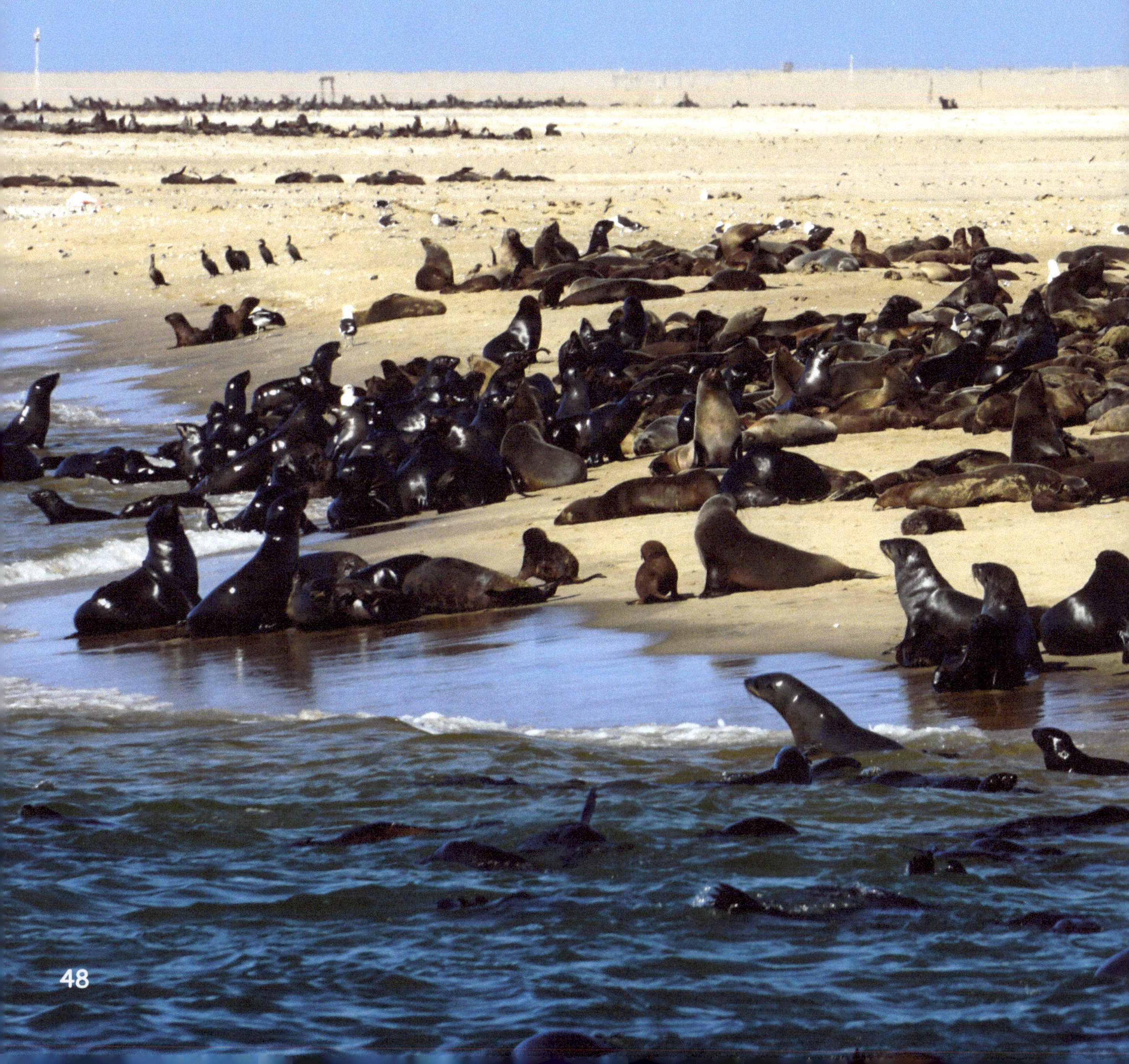

Thousands of Cape Fur Seals in the seal colony at Pelican Point. The cold ocean currents here provide rich food sources for a great variety of sea life.

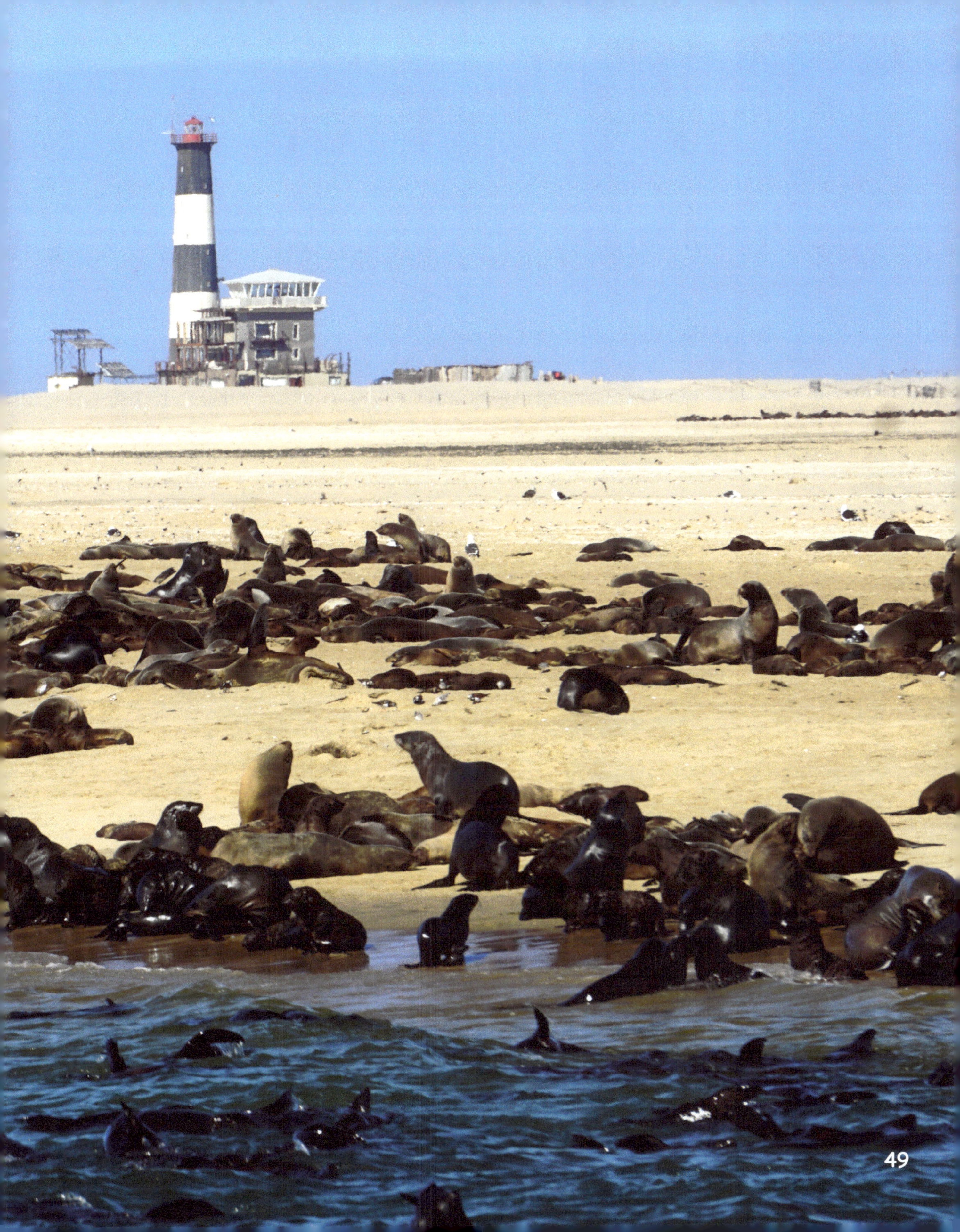

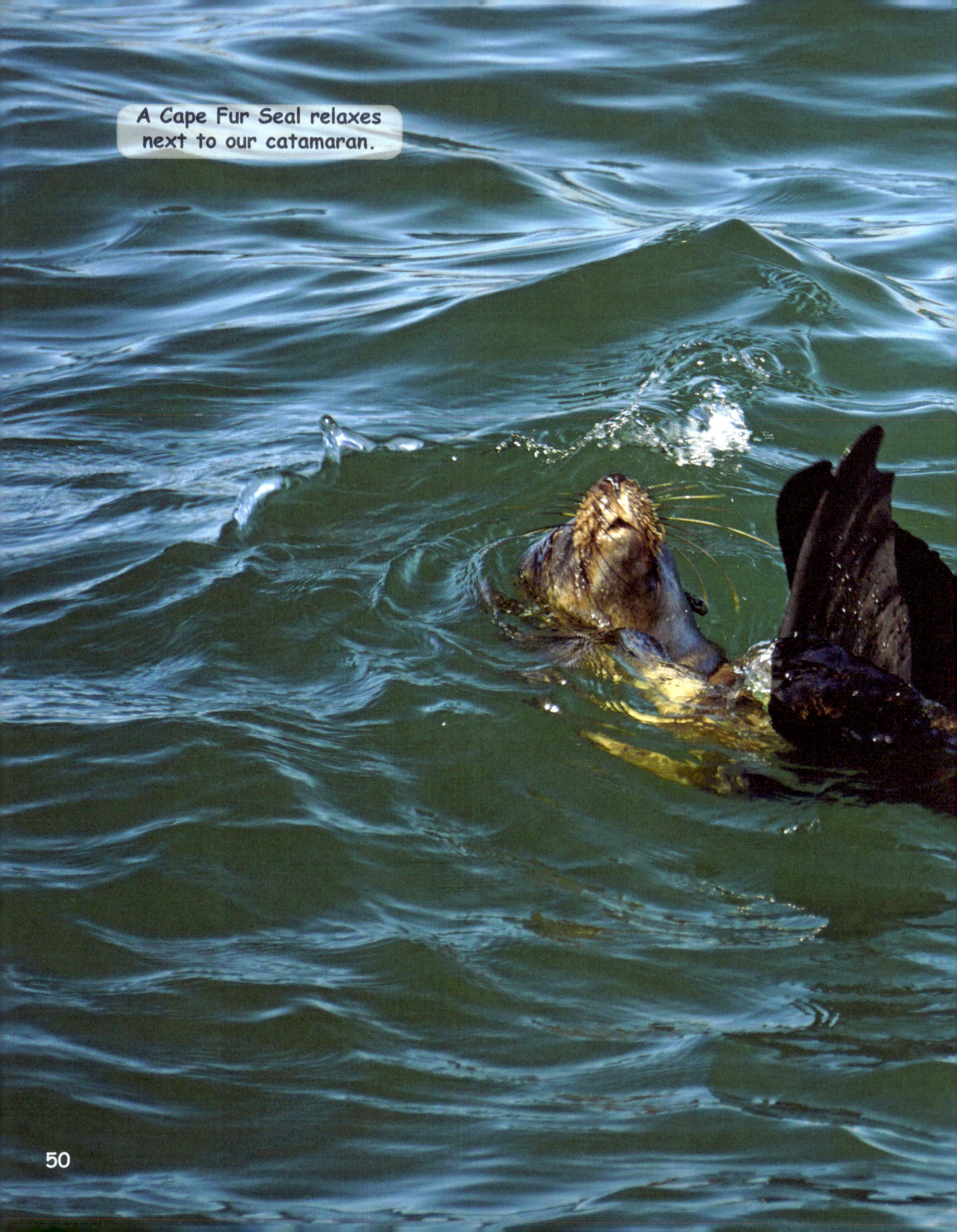

50

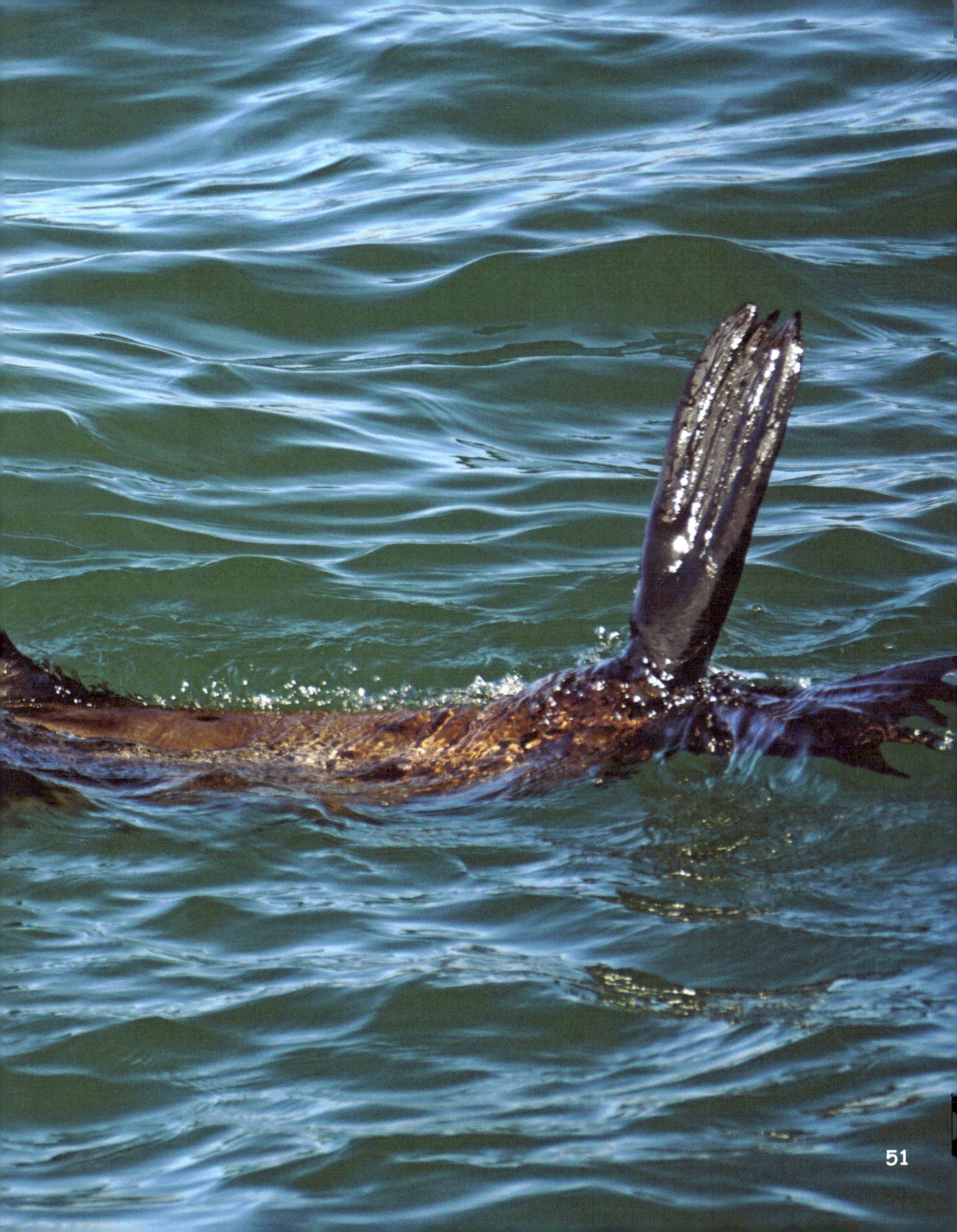

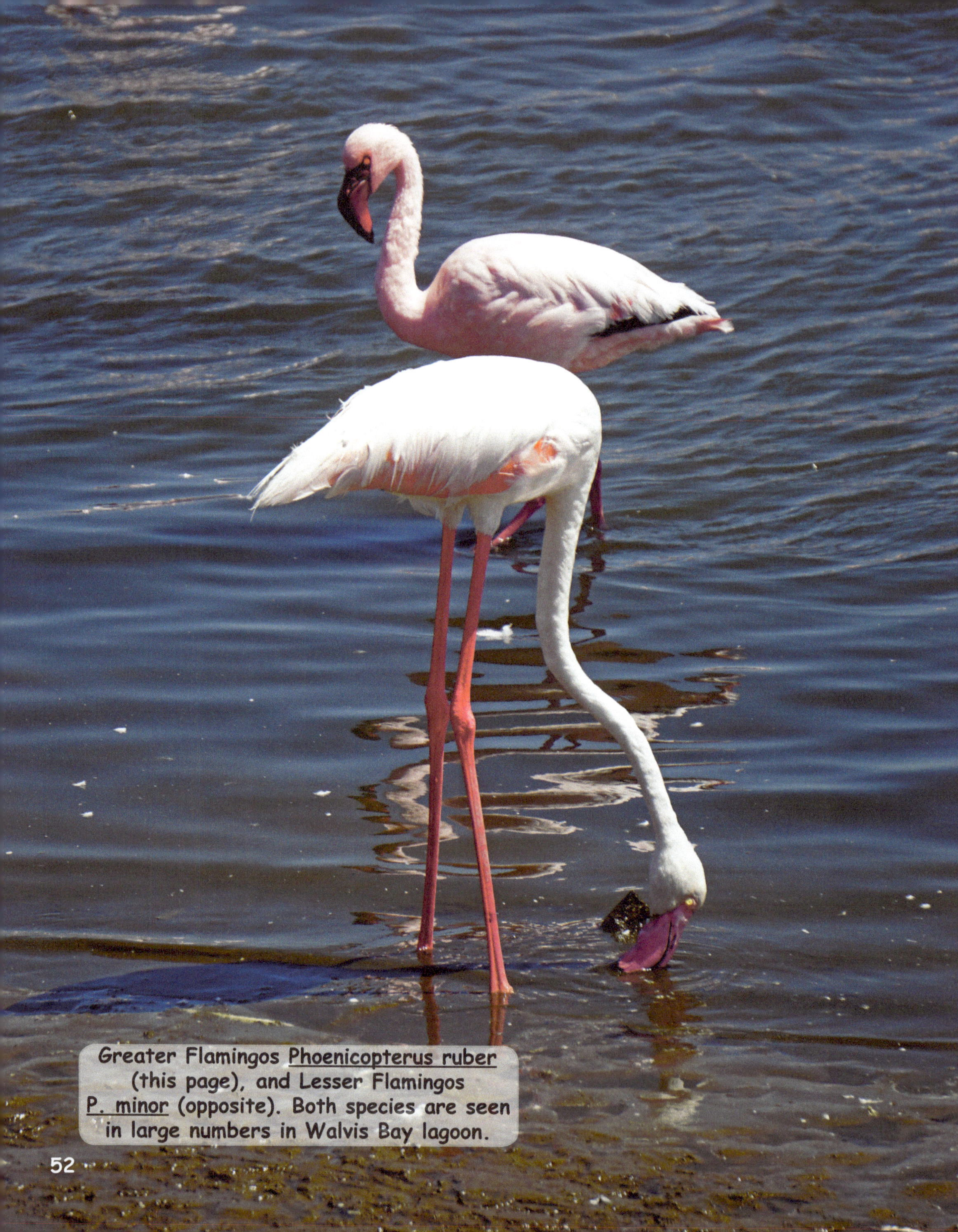

Greater Flamingos <u>Phoenicopterus ruber</u>
(this page), and Lesser Flamingos
<u>P. minor</u> (opposite). Both species are seen
in large numbers in Walvis Bay lagoon.

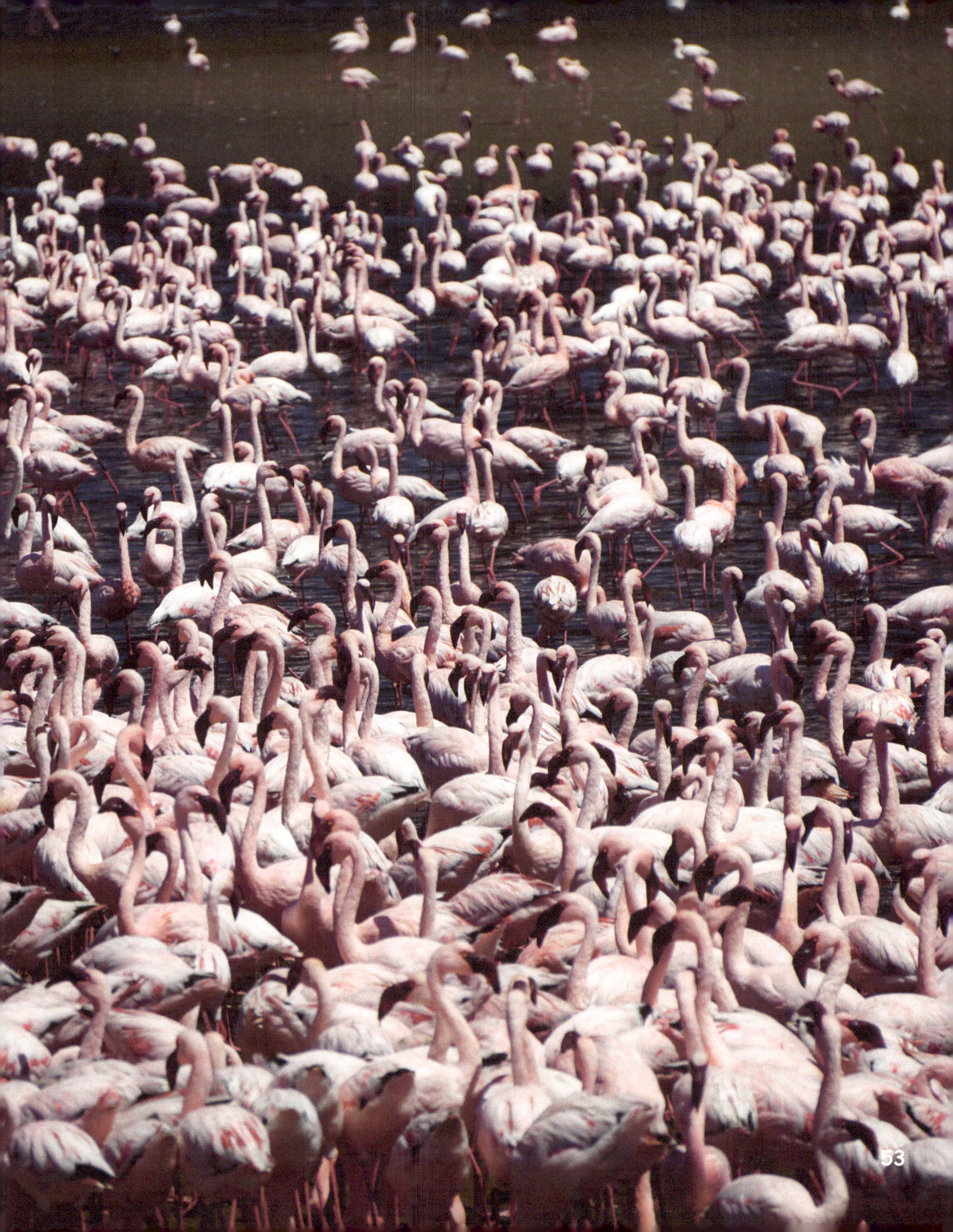

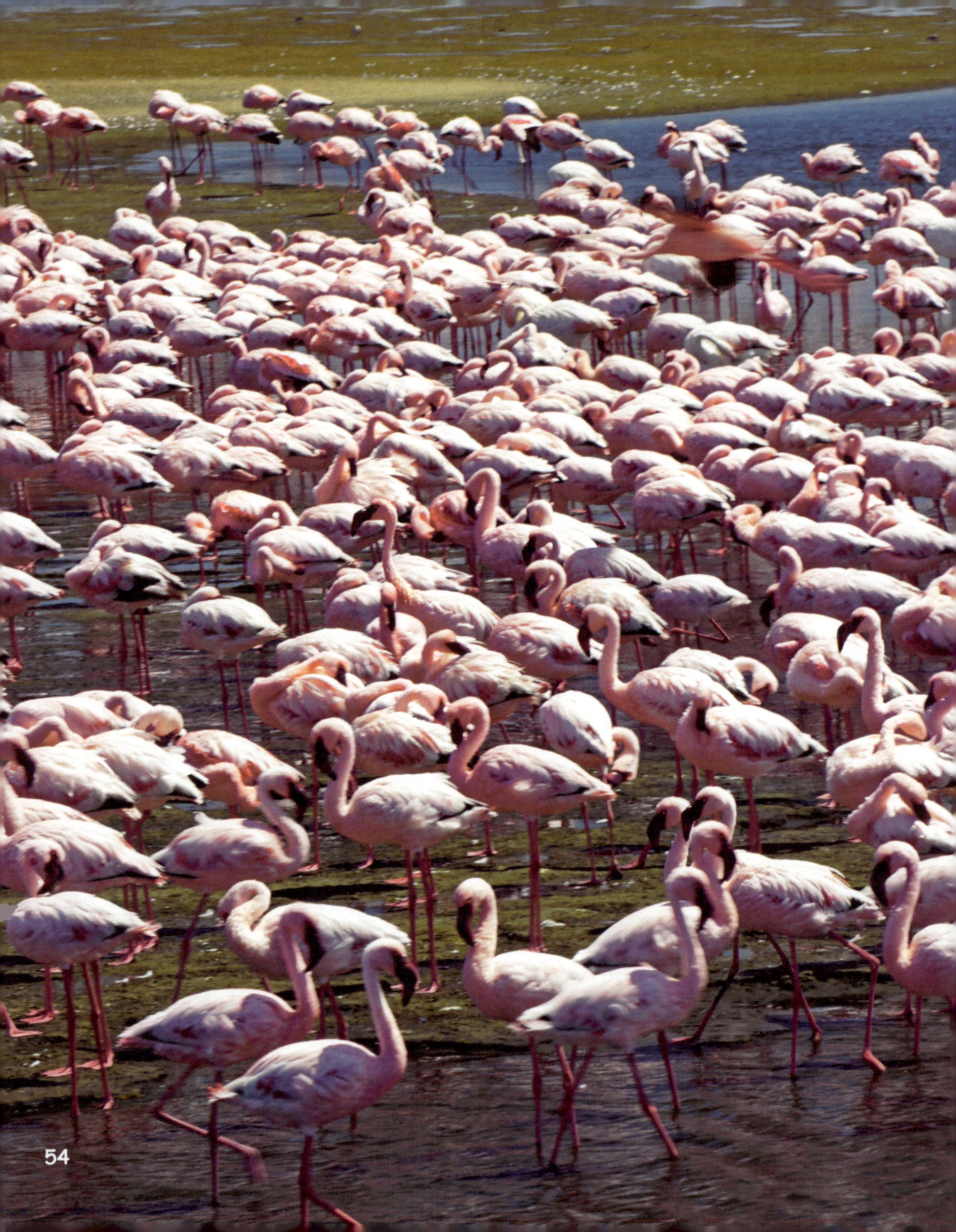

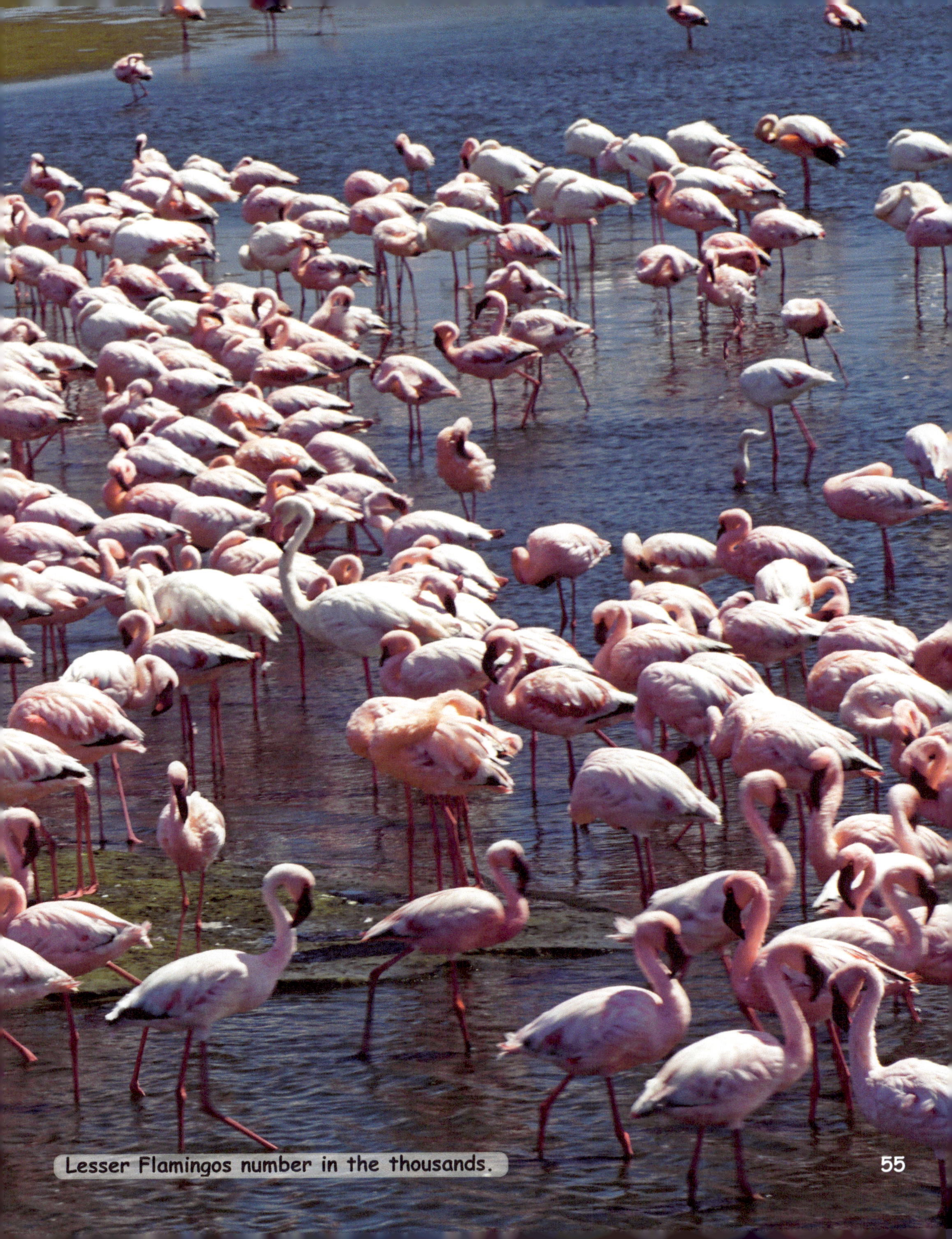

Lesser Flamingos number in the thousands.

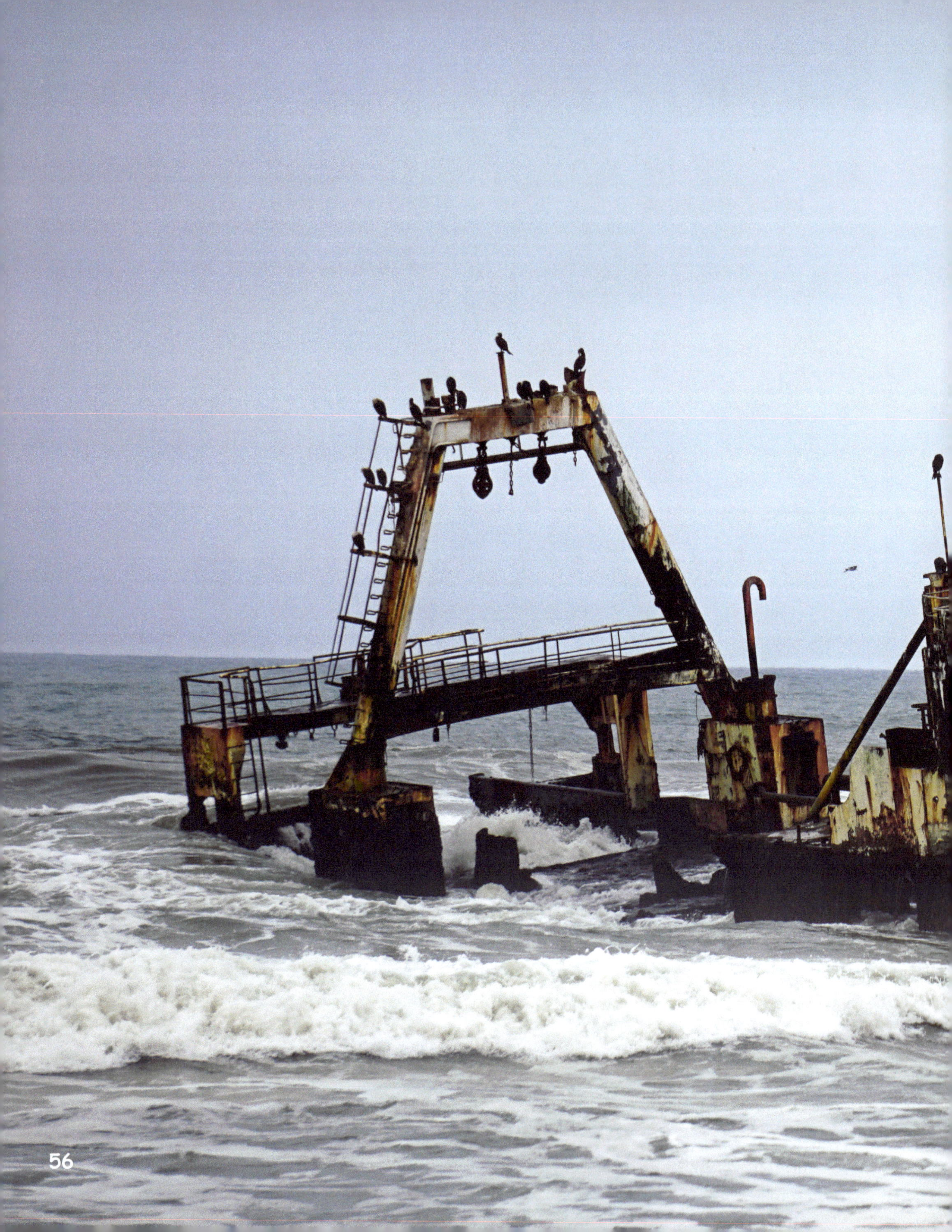

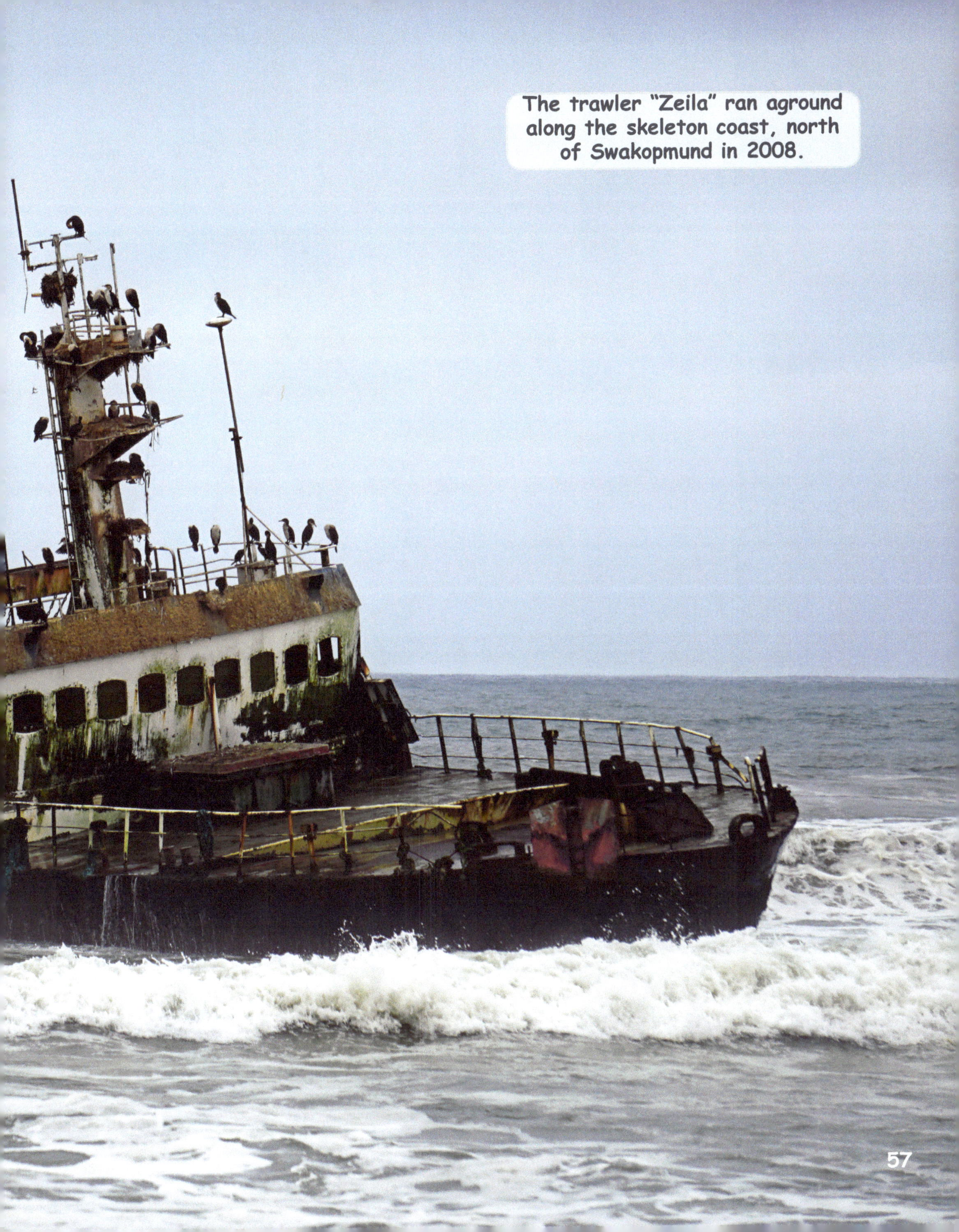

The trawler "Zeila" ran aground along the skeleton coast, north of Swakopmund in 2008.

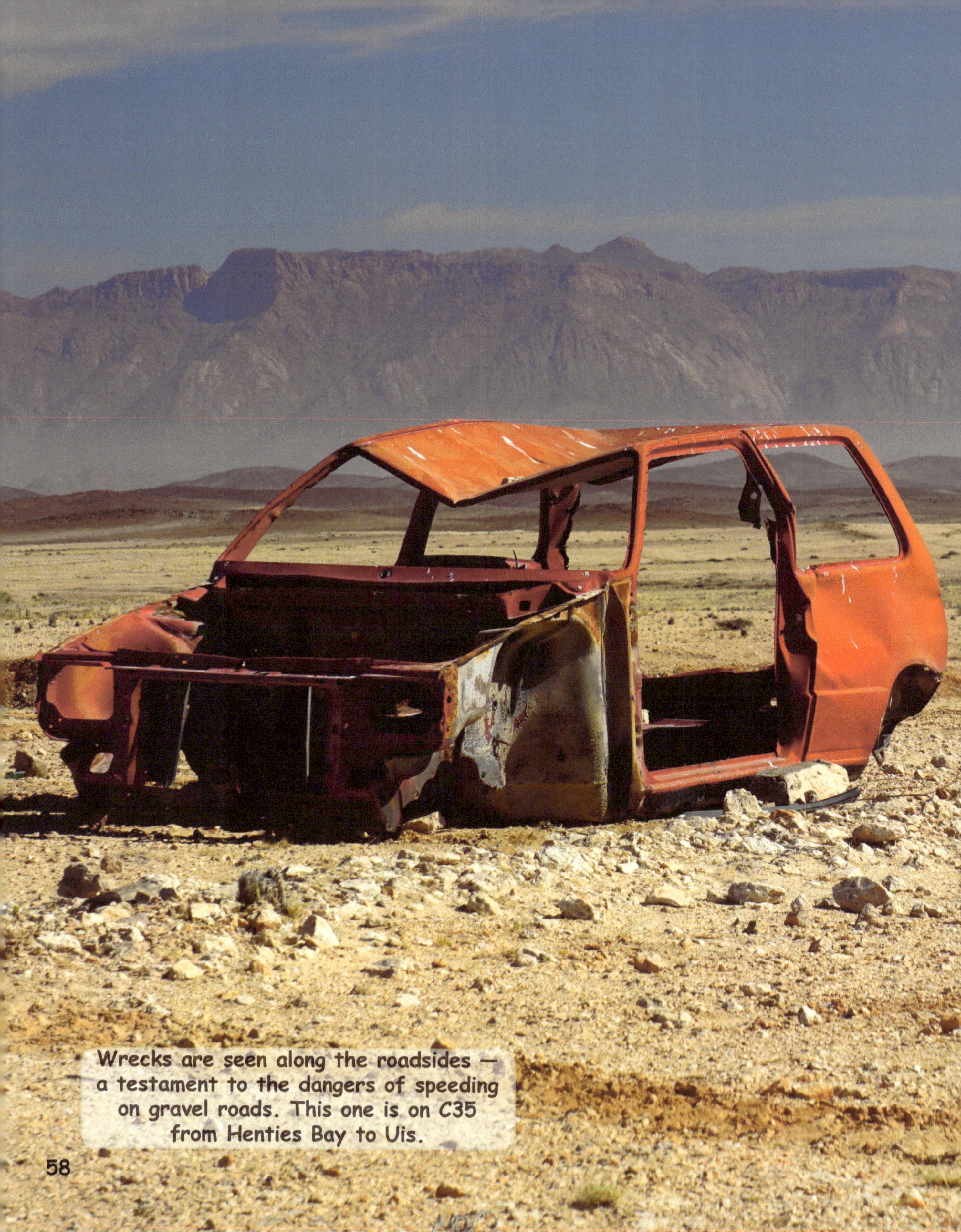

Wrecks are seen along the roadsides —
a testament to the dangers of speeding
on gravel roads. This one is on C35
from Henties Bay to Uis.

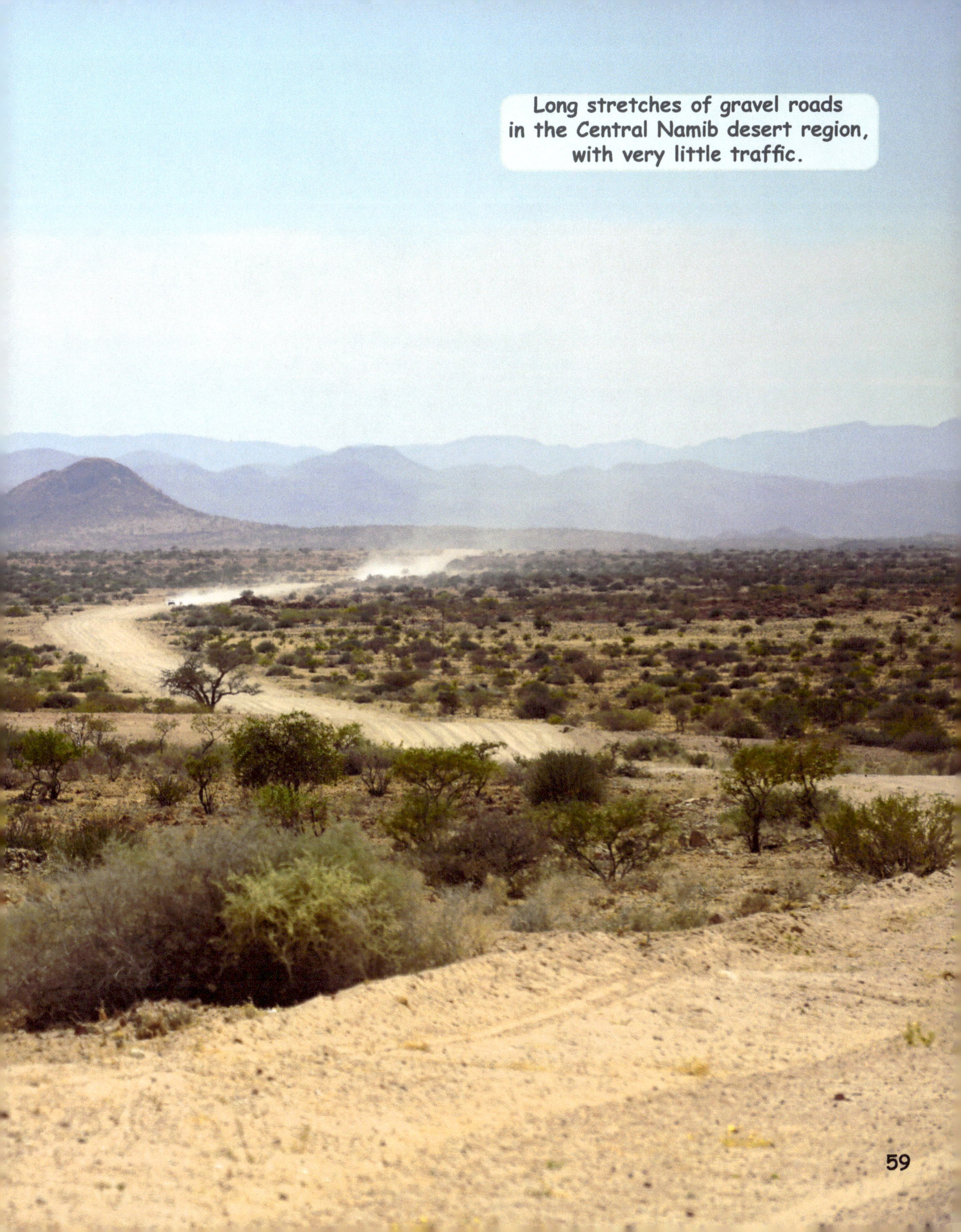

Long stretches of gravel roads
in the Central Namib desert region,
with very little traffic.

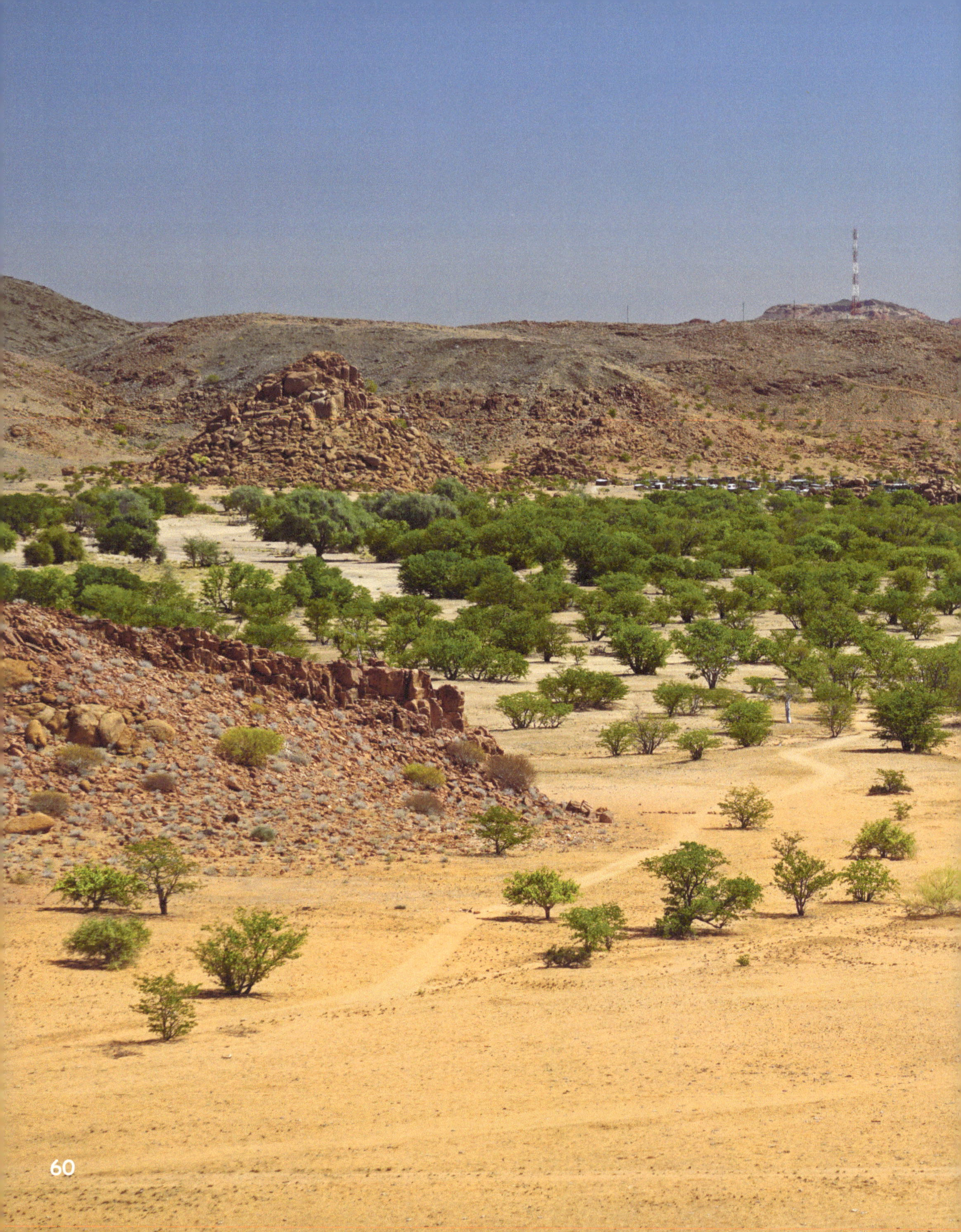

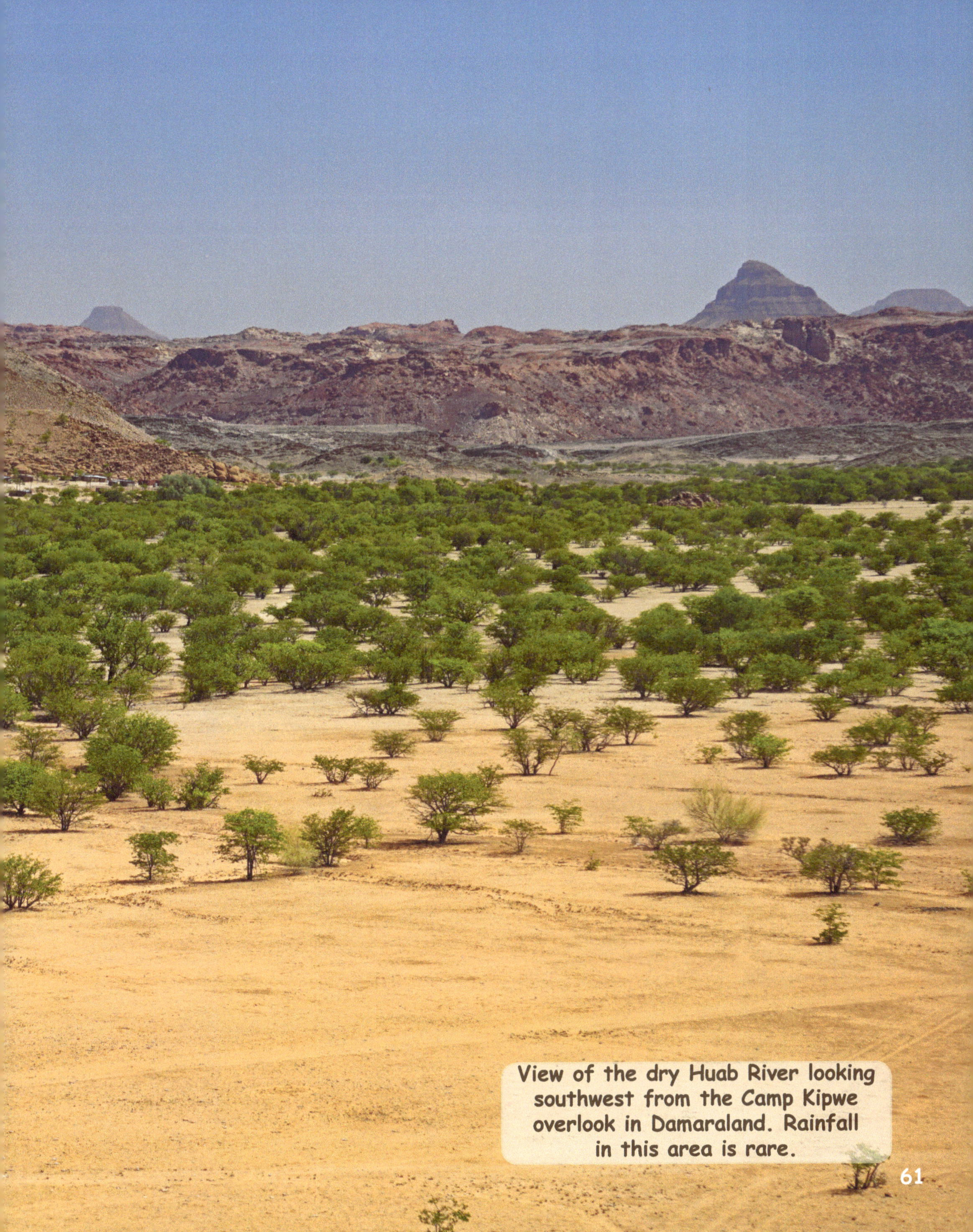

View of the dry Huab River looking
southwest from the Camp Kipwe
overlook in Damaraland. Rainfall
in this area is rare.

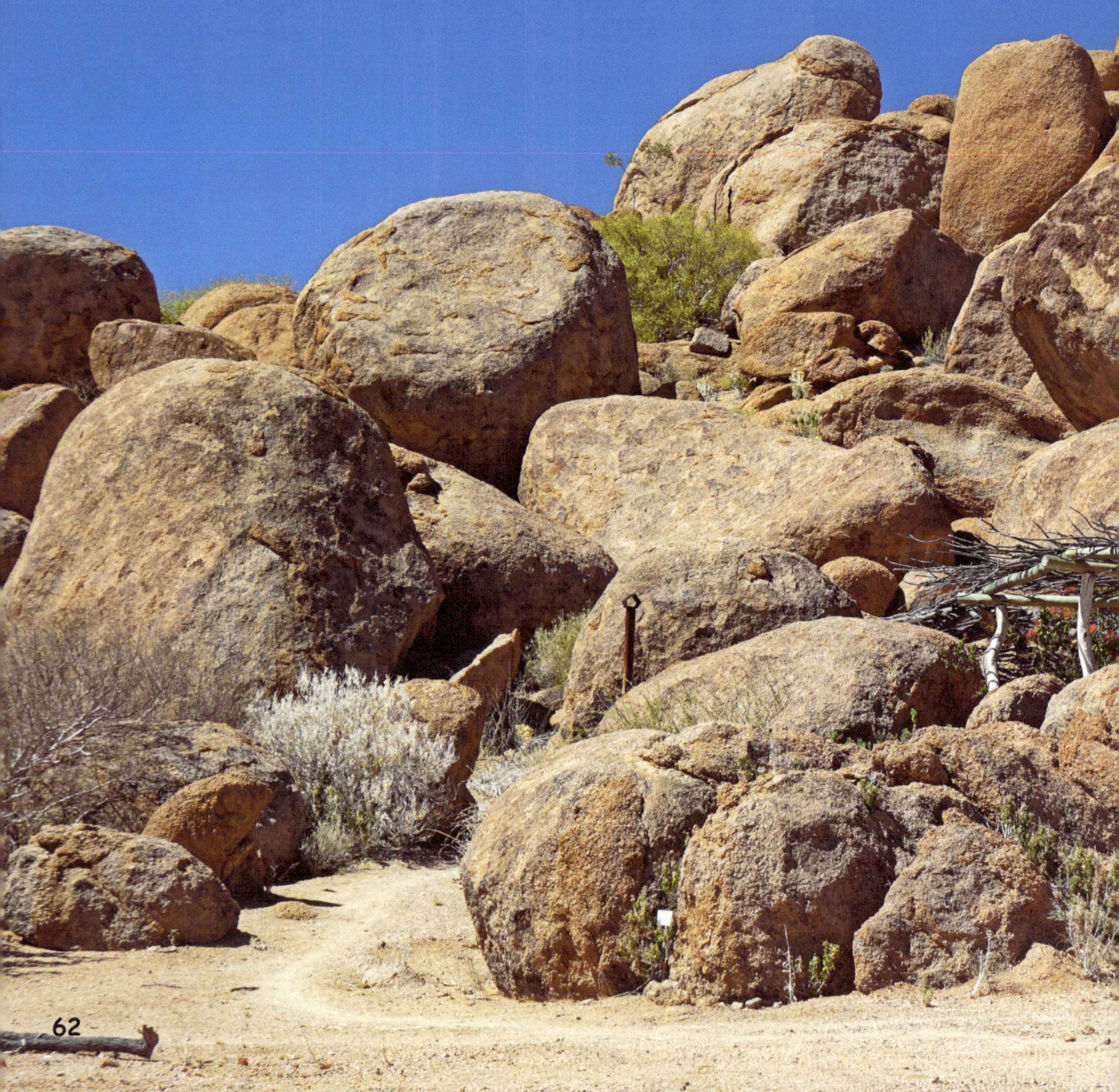
The beehive-style chalets at
Camp Kipwe are nestled among the
picturesque rocks, offering exceptional
privacy and panoramic views.

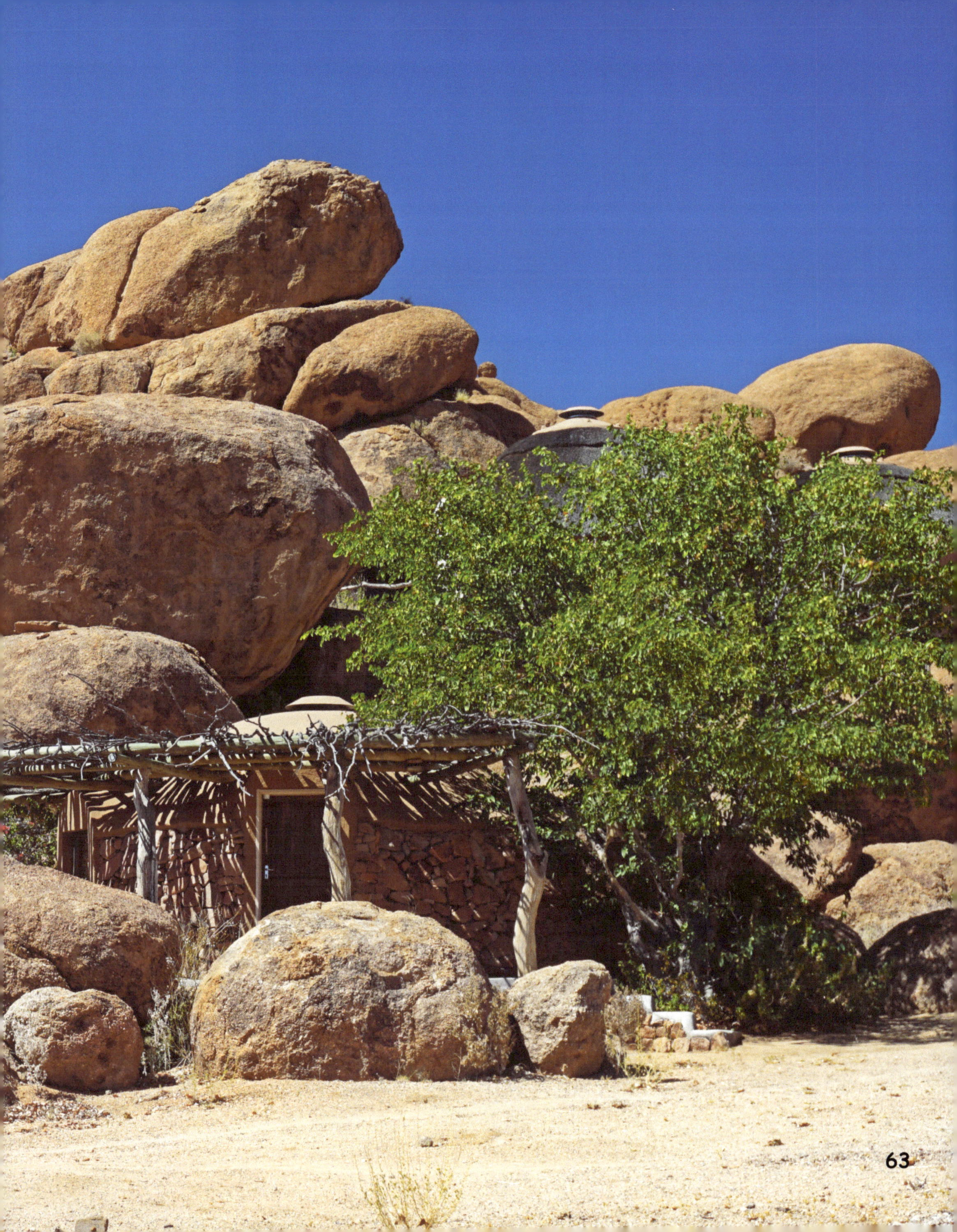

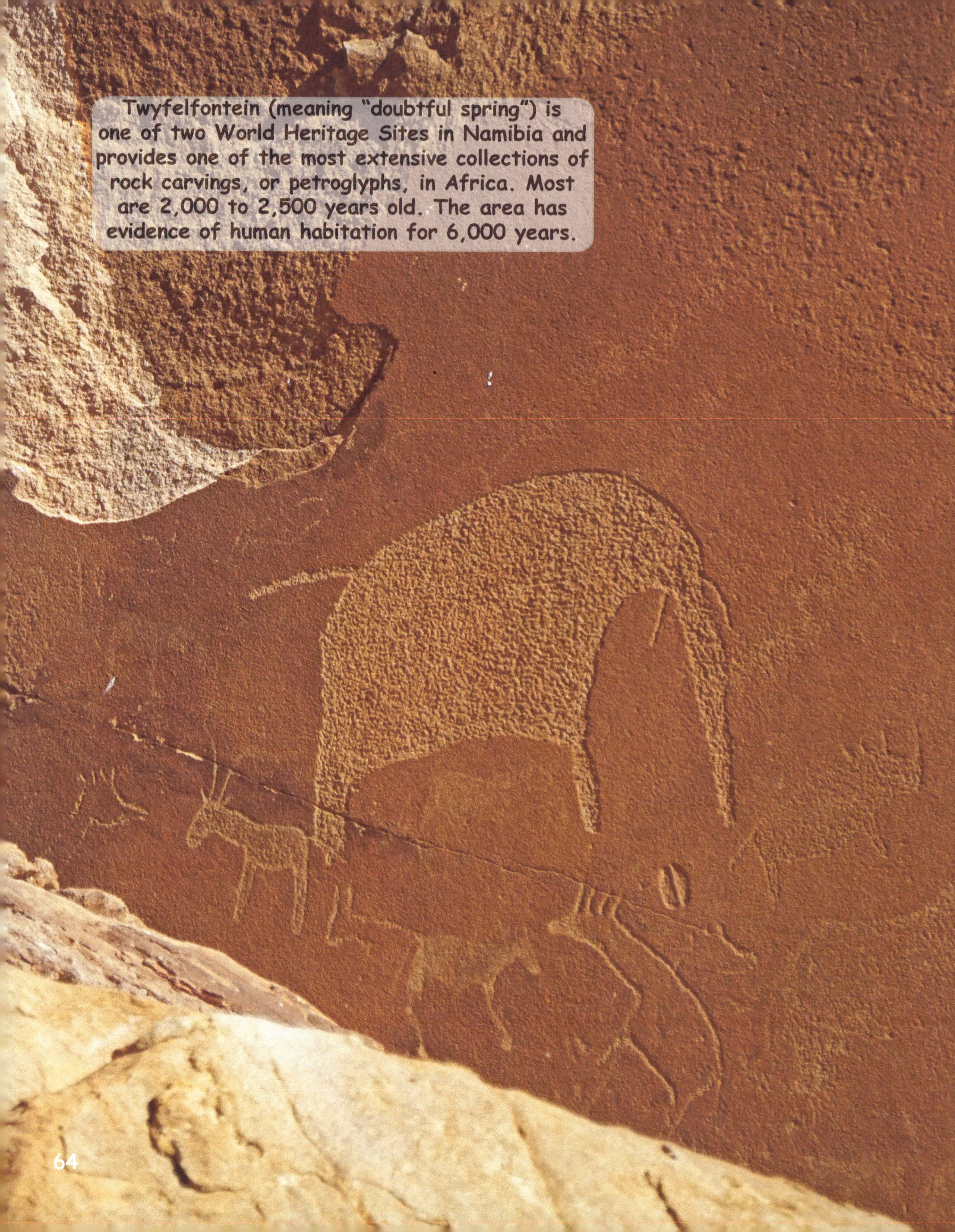

Twyfelfontein (meaning "doubtful spring") is one of two World Heritage Sites in Namibia and provides one of the most extensive collections of rock carvings, or petroglyphs, in Africa. Most are 2,000 to 2,500 years old. The area has evidence of human habitation for 6,000 years.

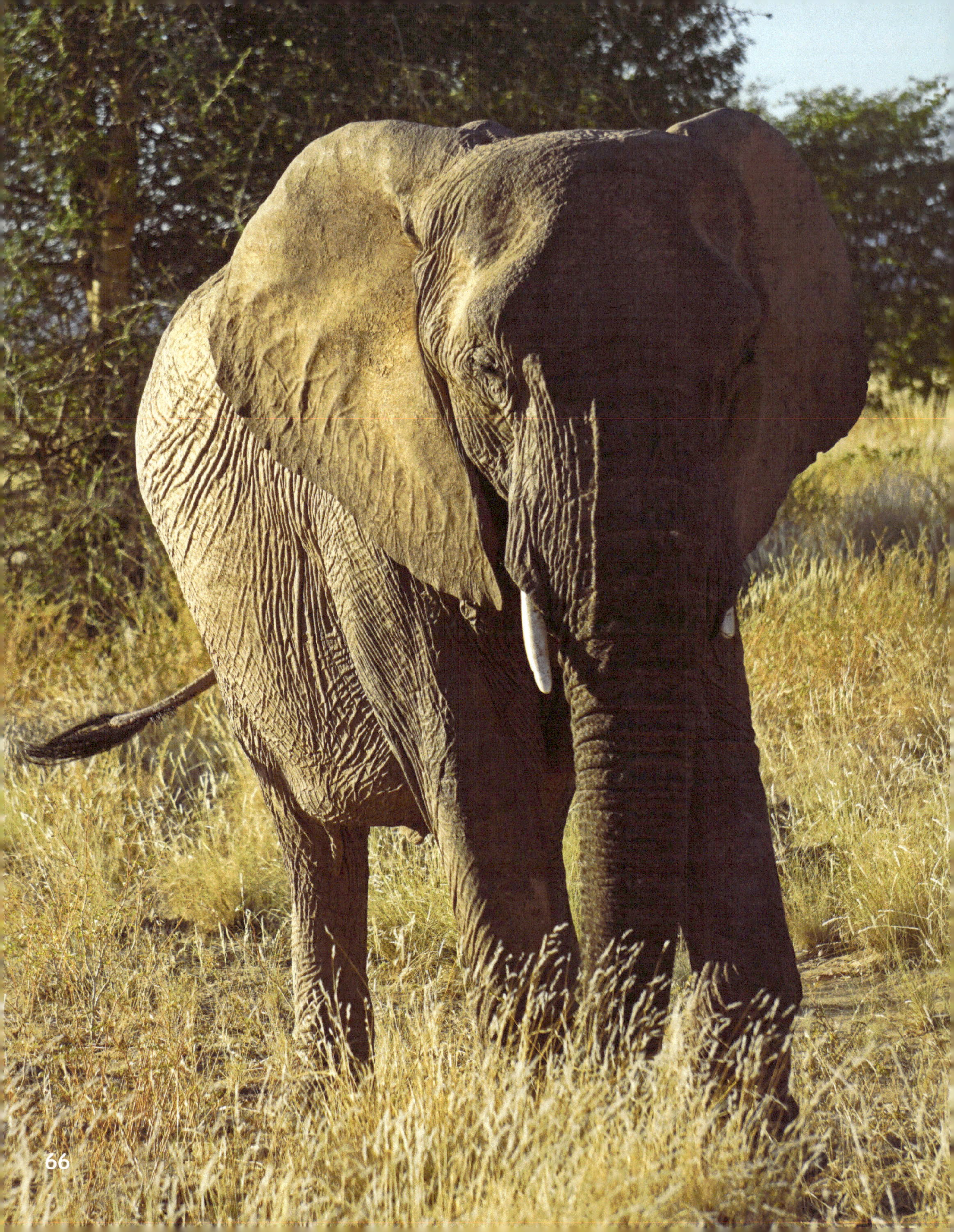

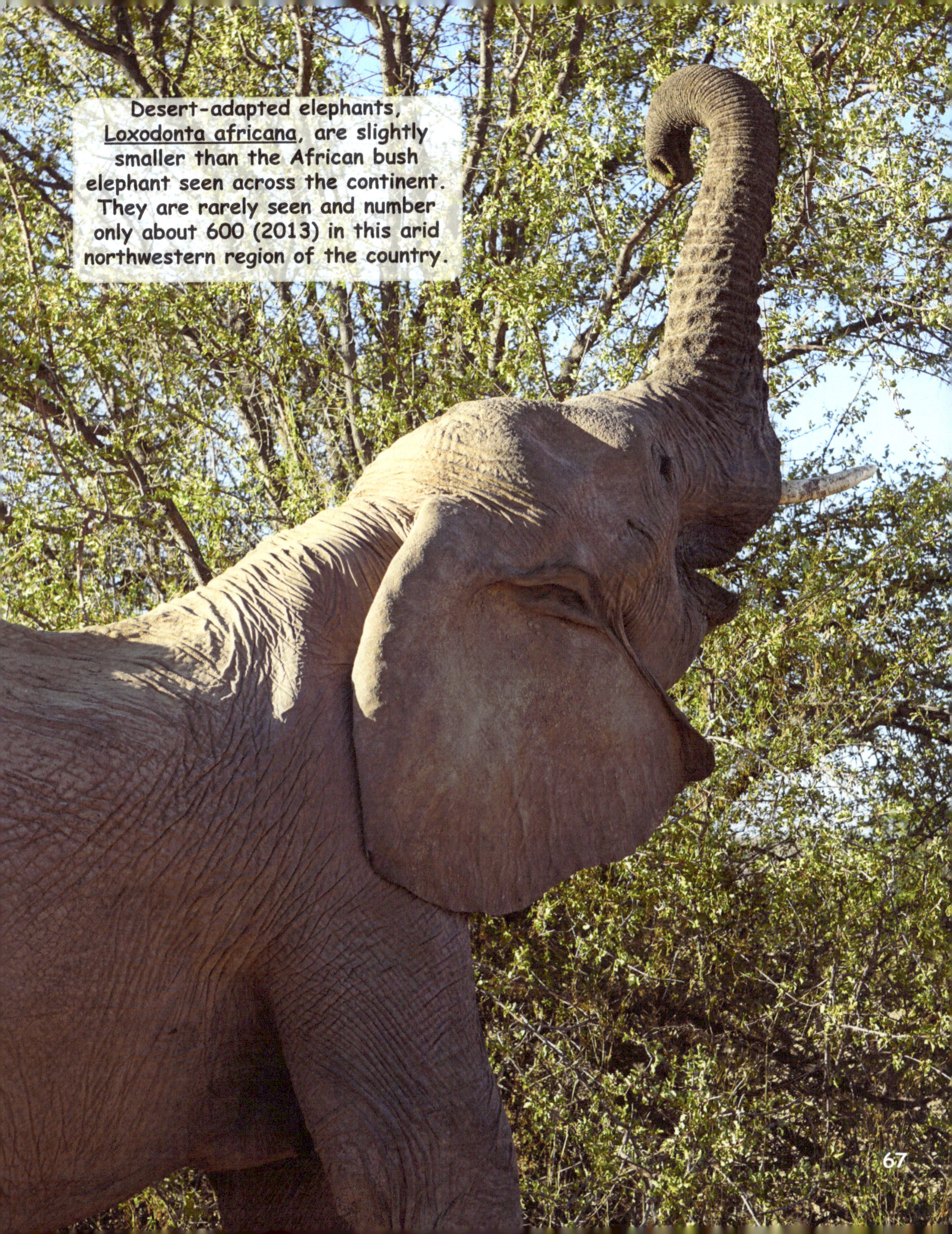

Desert-adapted elephants, Loxodonta africana, are slightly smaller than the African bush elephant seen across the continent. They are rarely seen and number only about 600 (2013) in this arid northwestern region of the country.

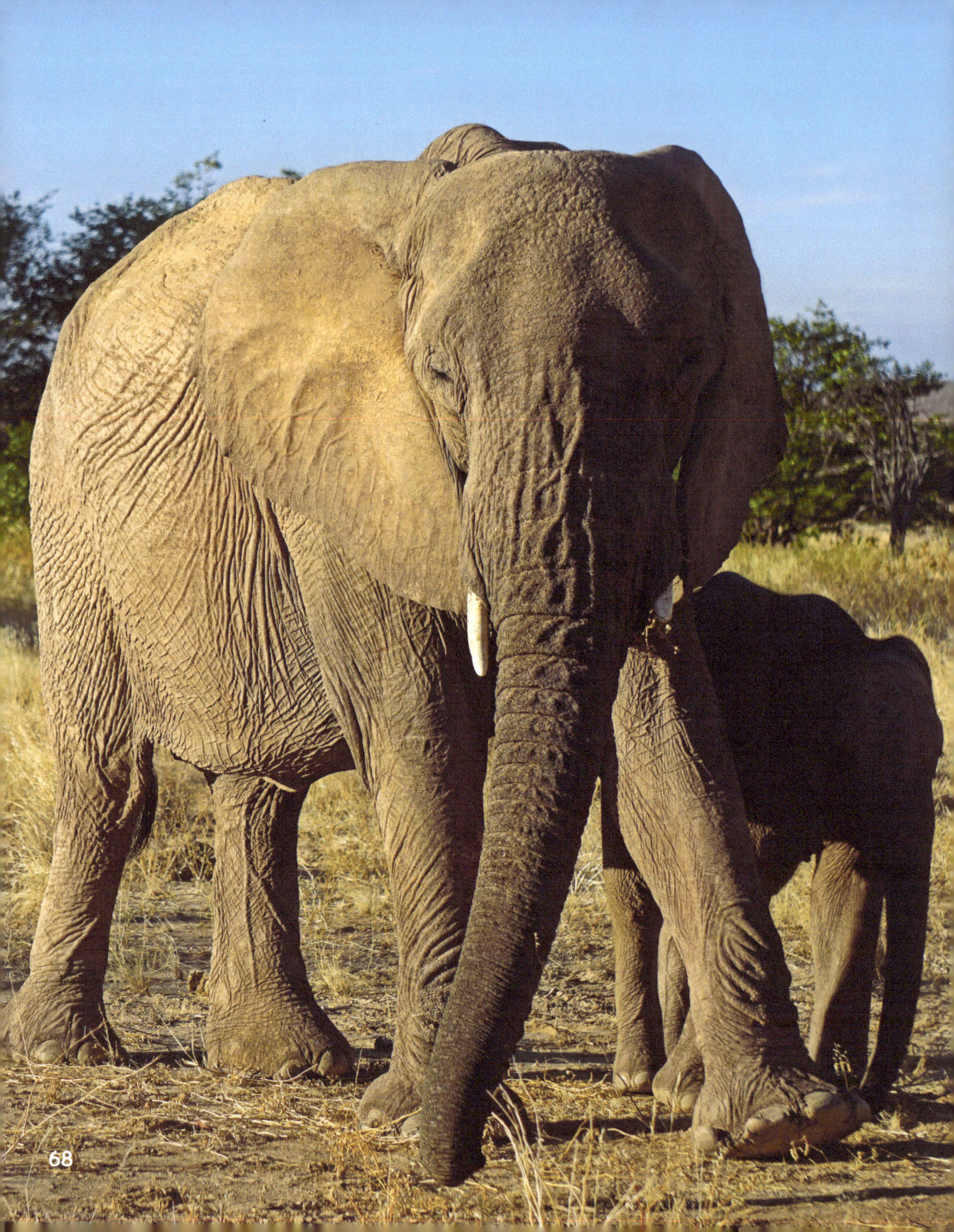

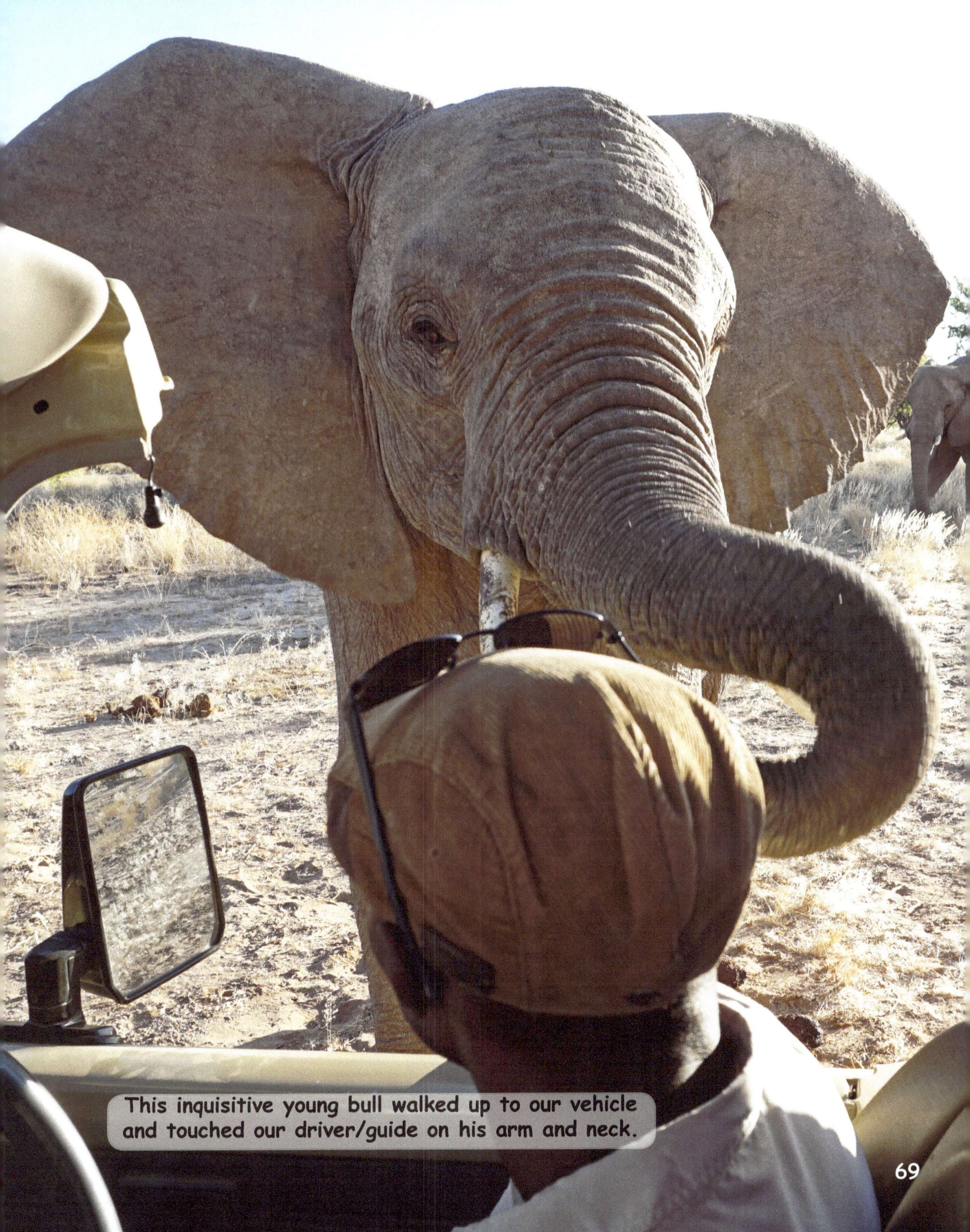

This inquisitive young bull walked up to our vehicle and touched our driver/guide on his arm and neck.

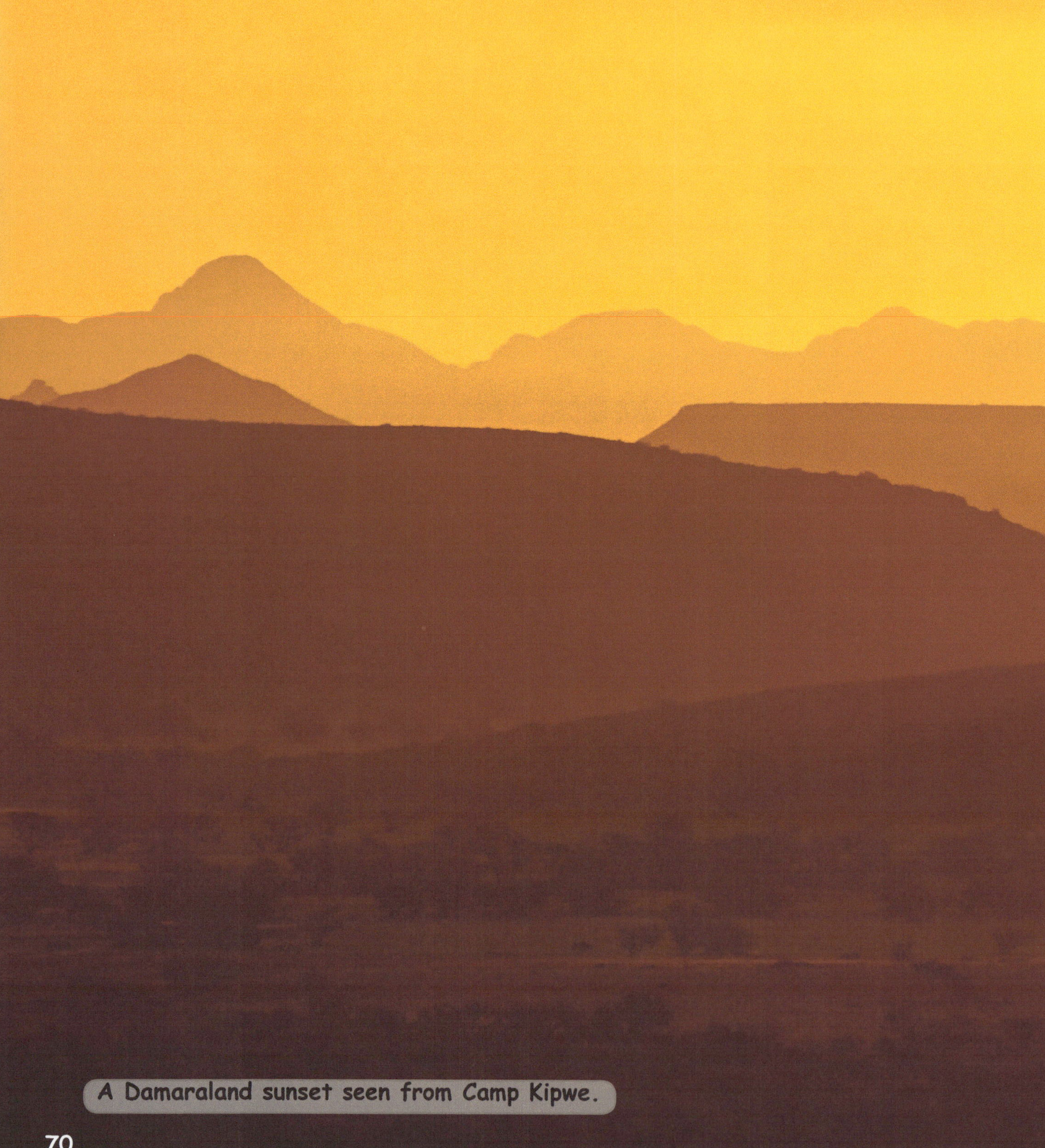

A Damaraland sunset seen from Camp Kipwe.

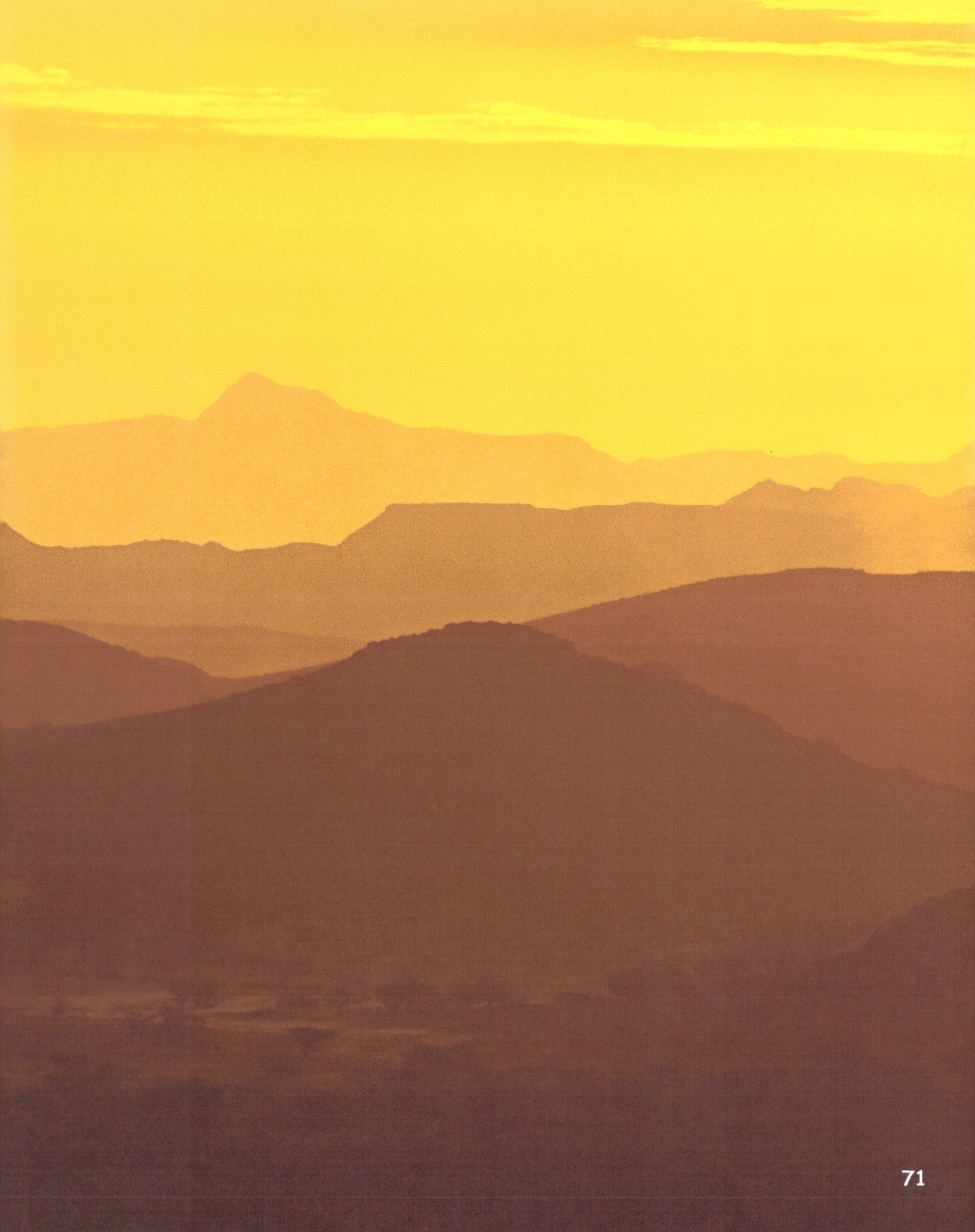

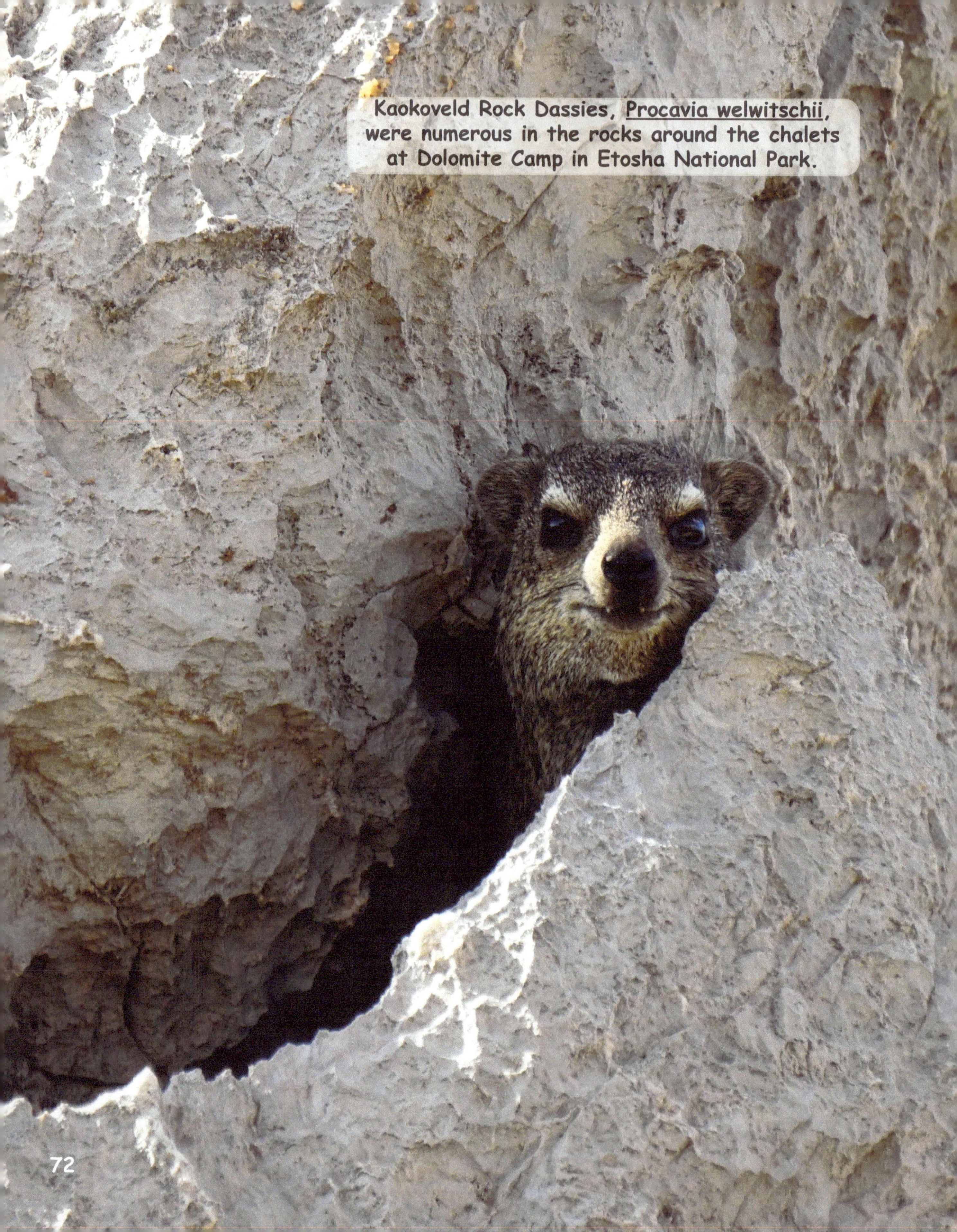

Kaokoveld Rock Dassies, Procavia welwitschii,
were numerous in the rocks around the chalets
at Dolomite Camp in Etosha National Park.

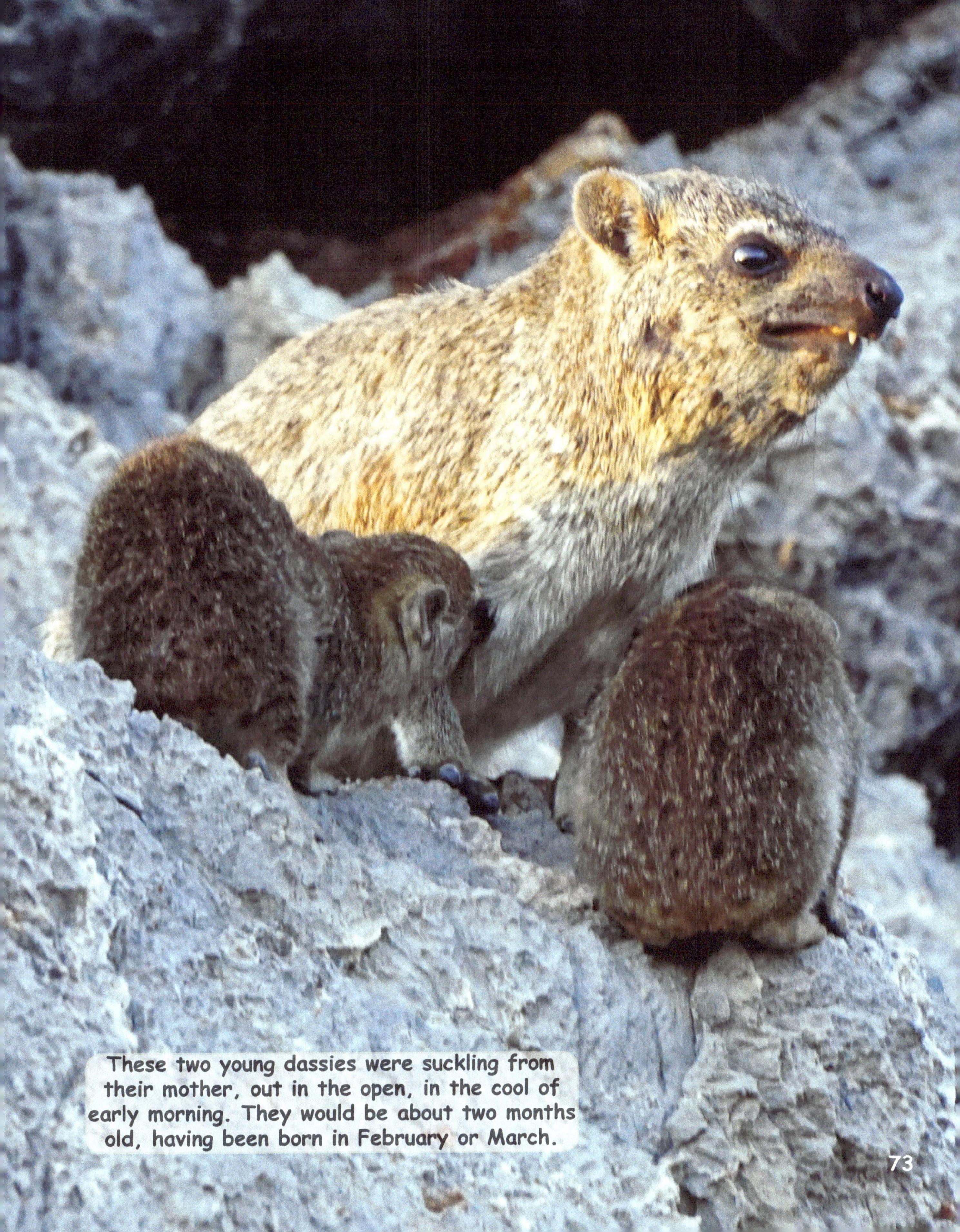

These two young dassies were suckling from their mother, out in the open, in the cool of early morning. They would be about two months old, having been born in February or March.

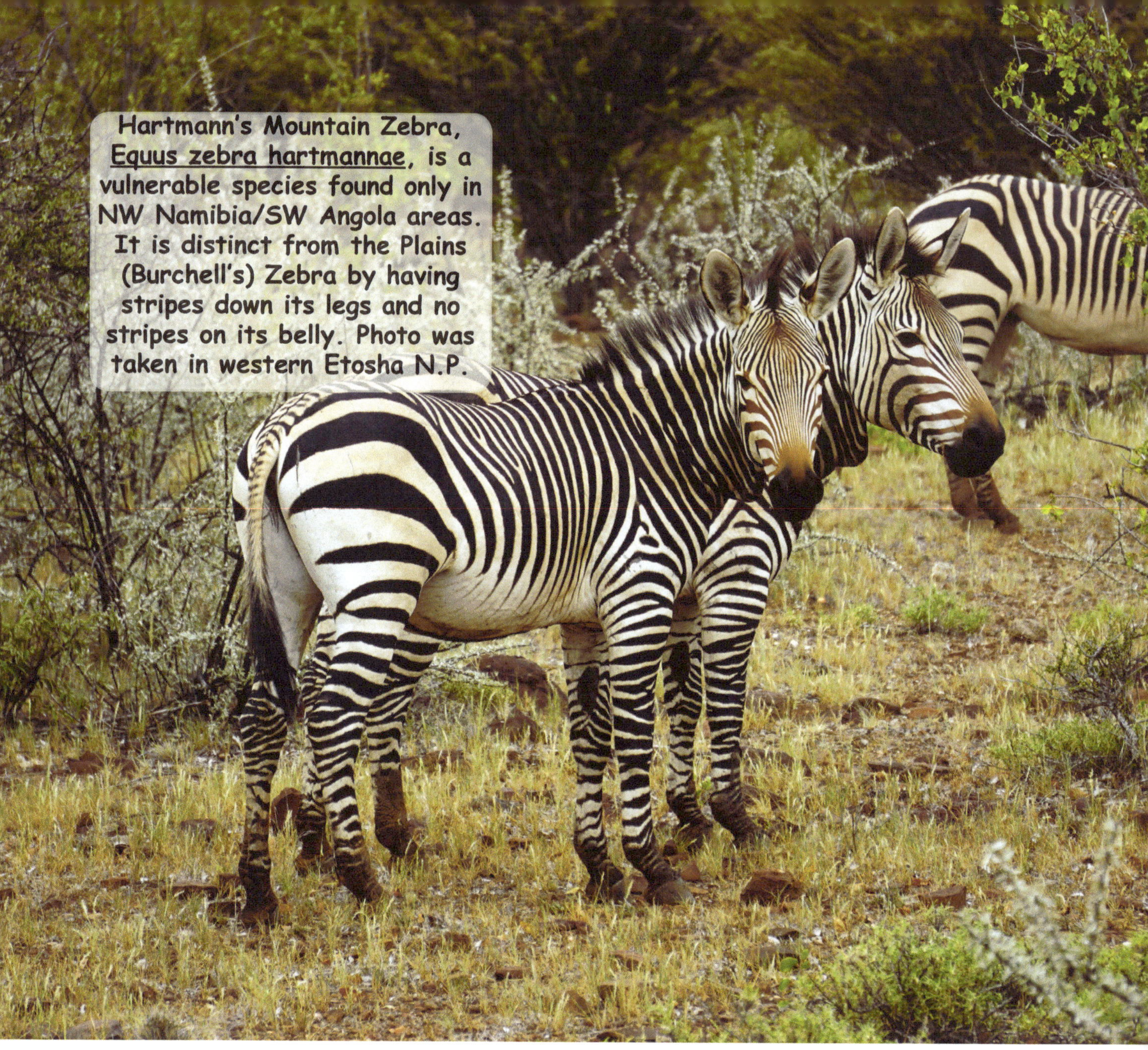
Hartmann's Mountain Zebra, Equus zebra hartmannae, is a vulnerable species found only in NW Namibia/SW Angola areas. It is distinct from the Plains (Burchell's) Zebra by having stripes down its legs and no stripes on its belly. Photo was taken in western Etosha N.P.

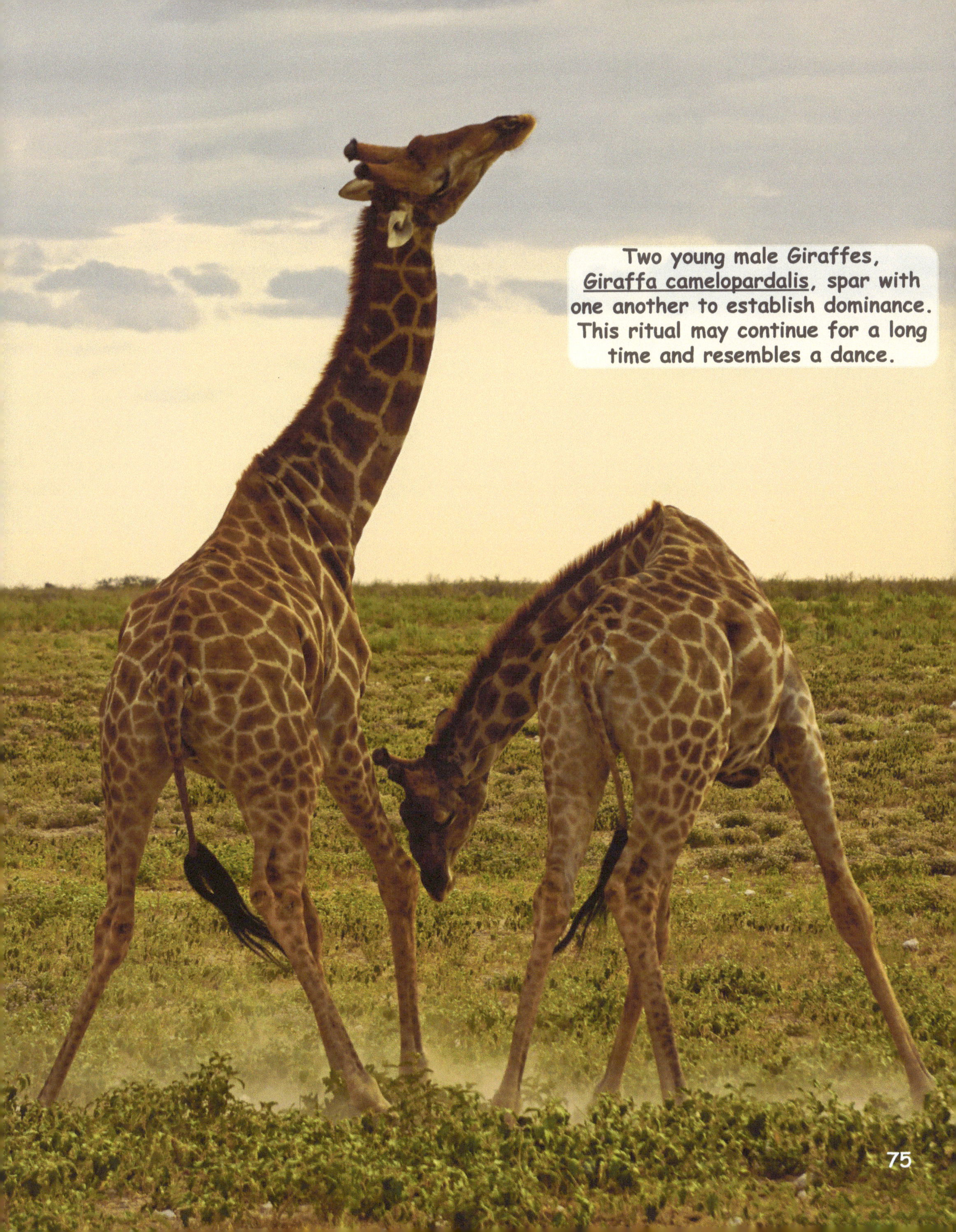

Two young male Giraffes,
Giraffa camelopardalis, spar with
one another to establish dominance.
This ritual may continue for a long
time and resembles a dance.

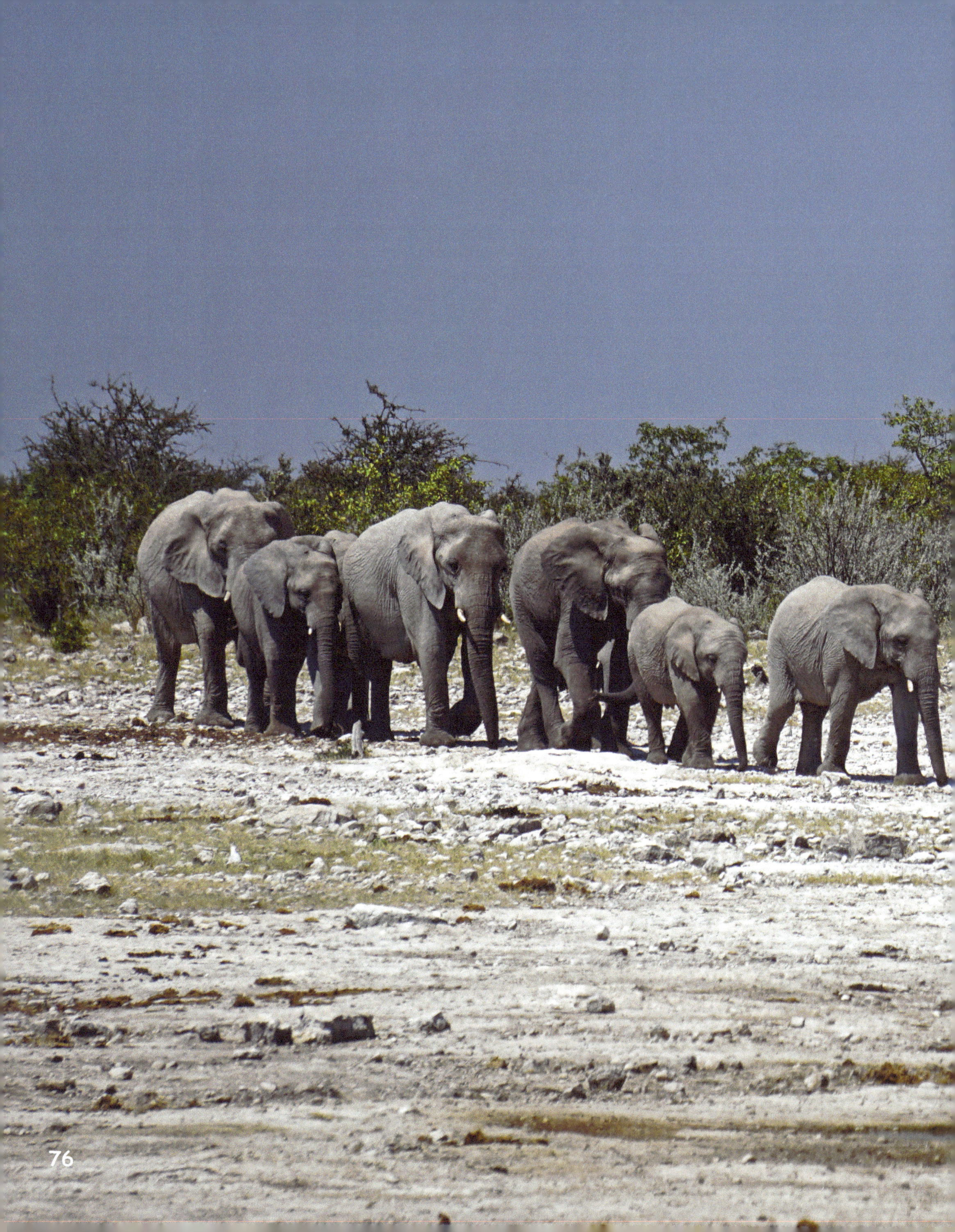

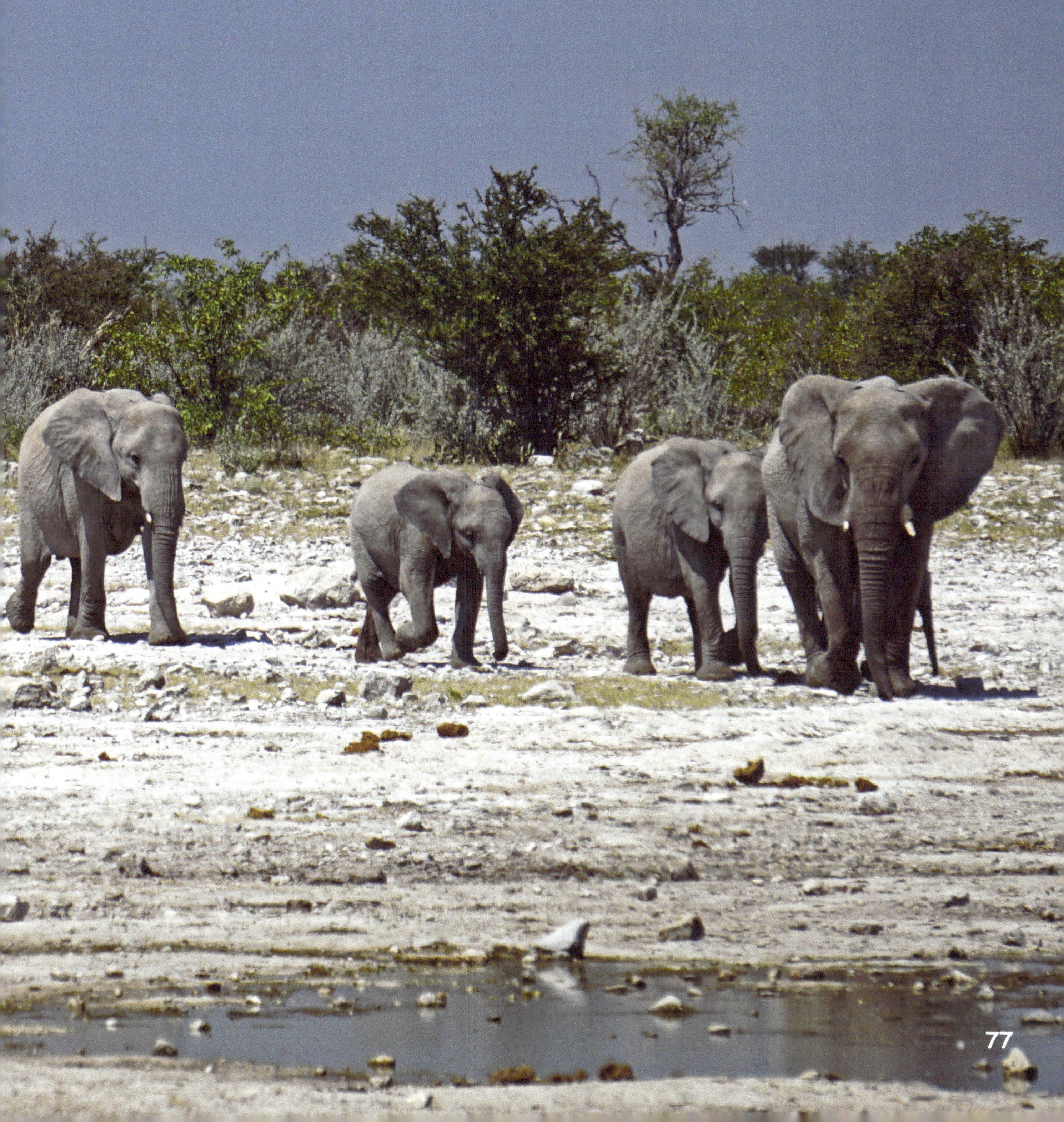

A breeding herd of elephants, Loxodonta africana,
approaches Klippan waterhole in western Etosha N.P.
The herd matriarch brings up the rear.

Two herds meet and there is a lot of interaction.

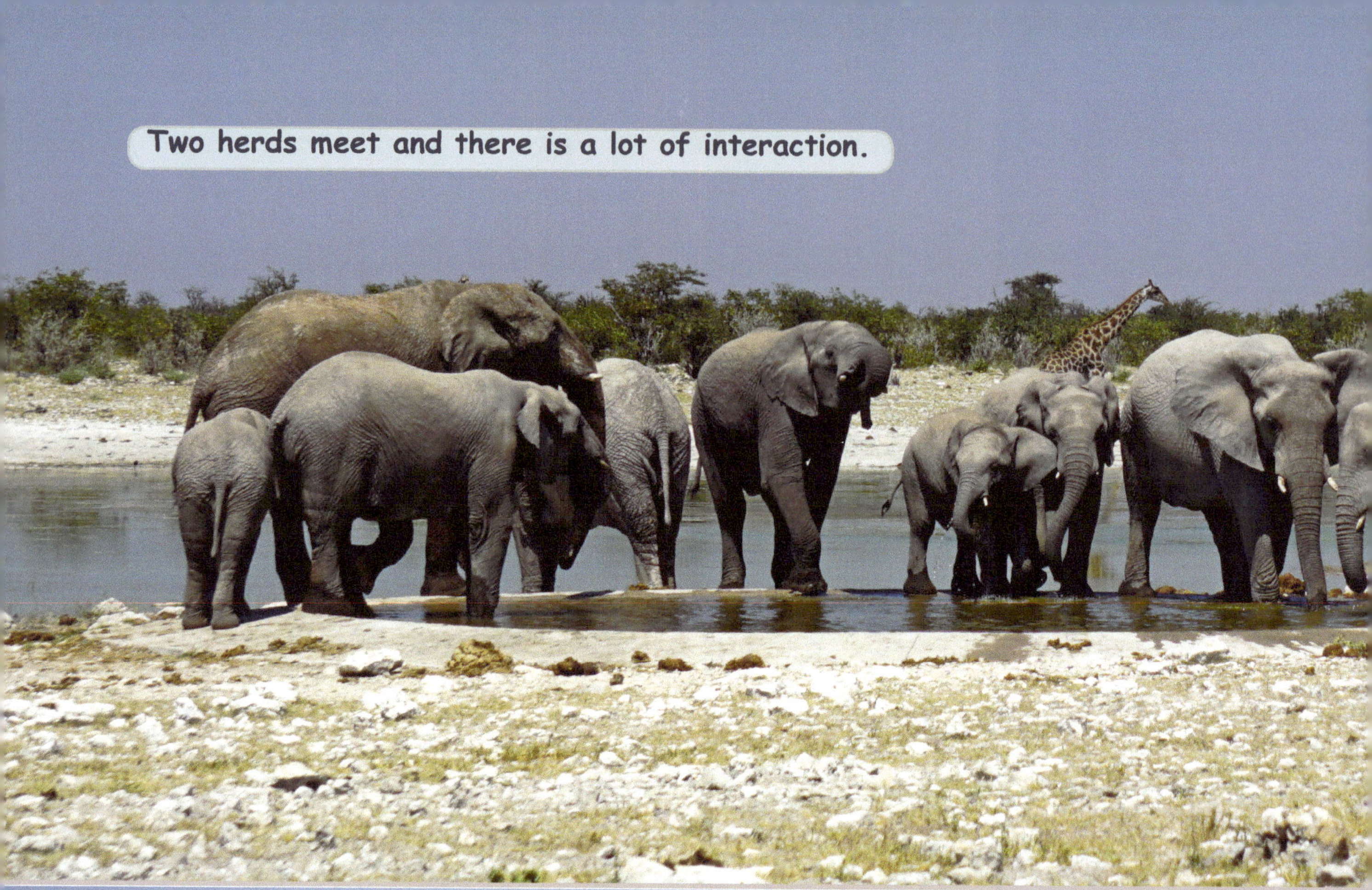

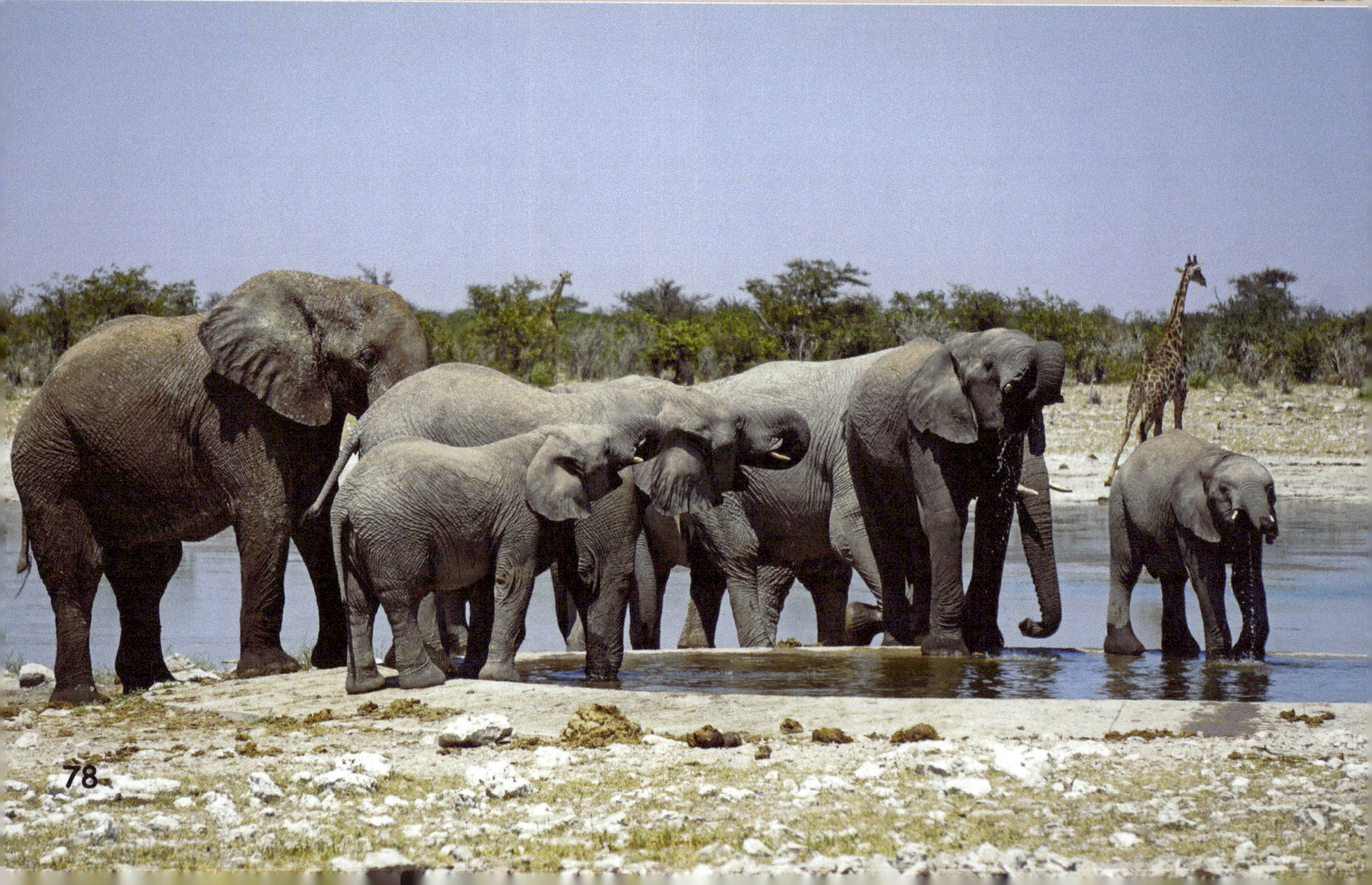

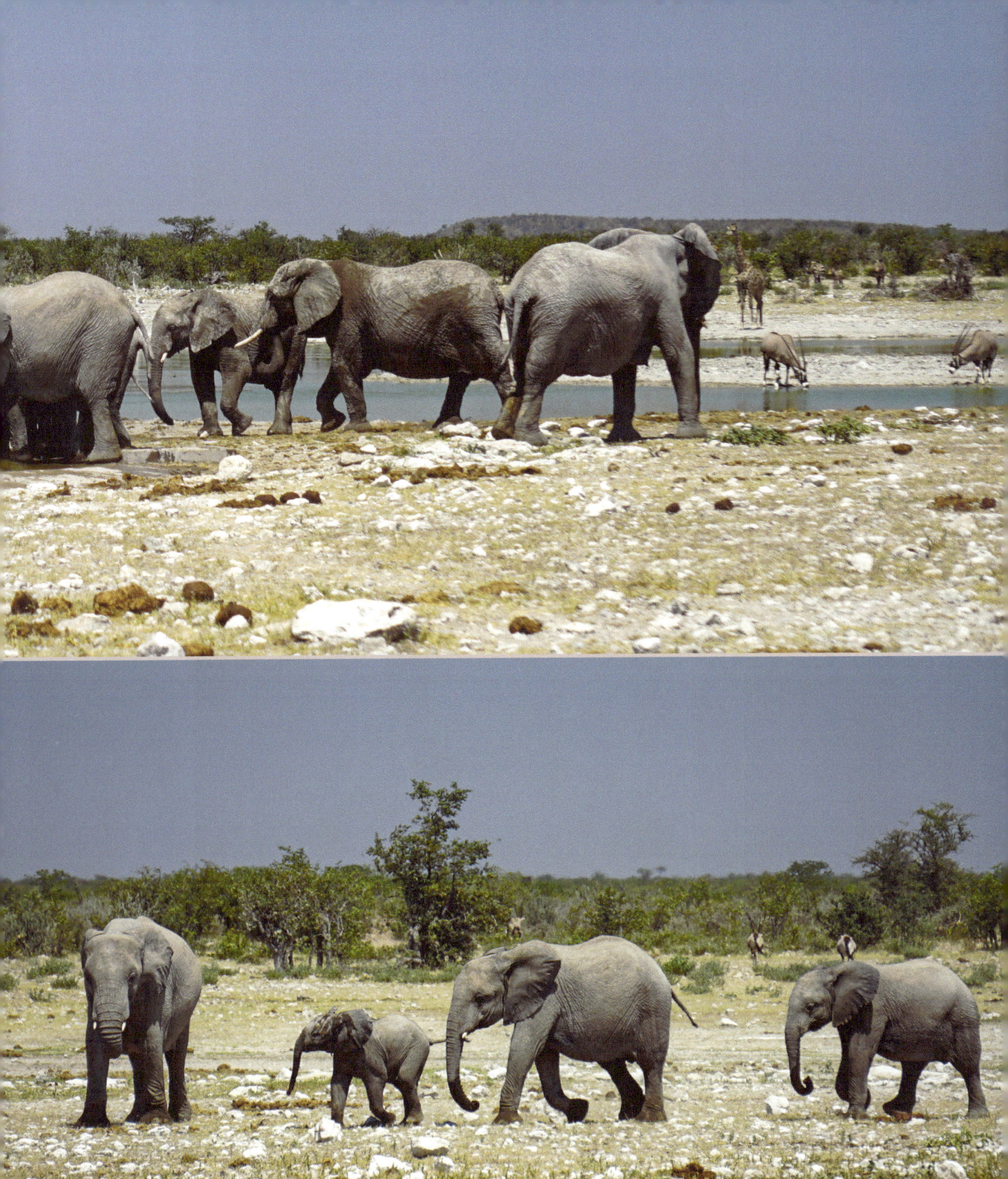

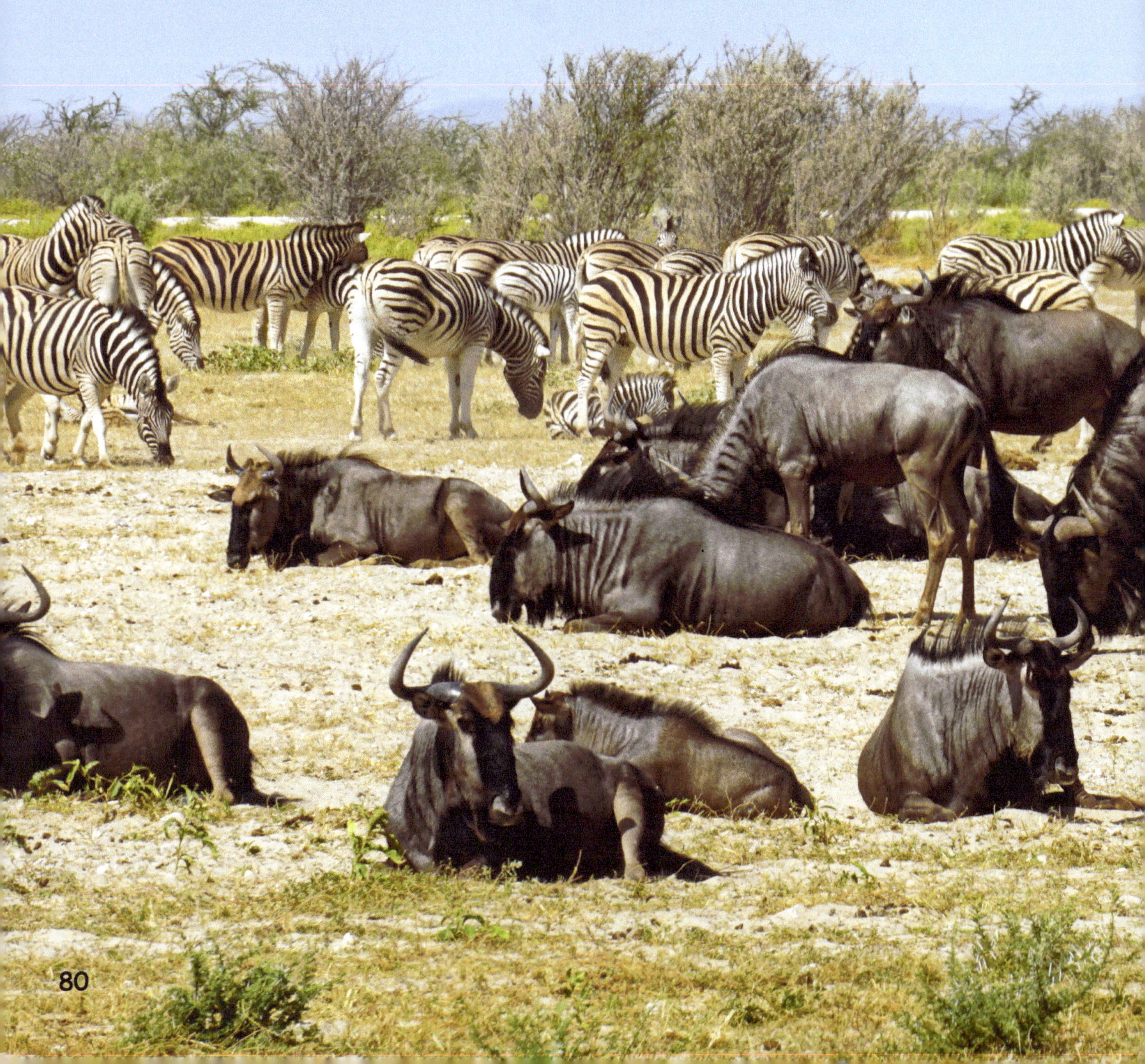
Etosha N.P. has large numbers of Plains
(Burchell's) Zebra, Equus burchellii, and Blue
Wildebeest, Connochaetes taurinus.

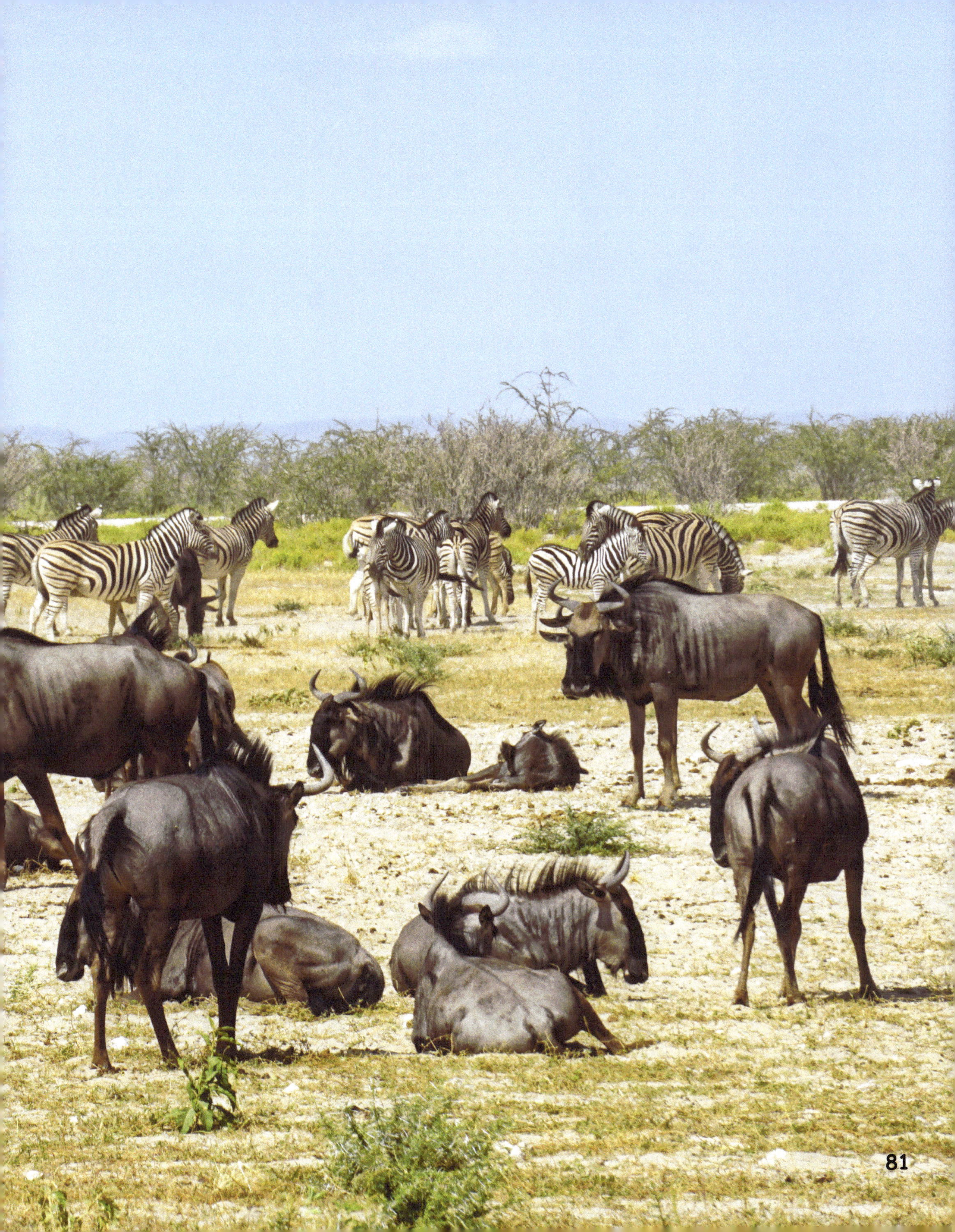

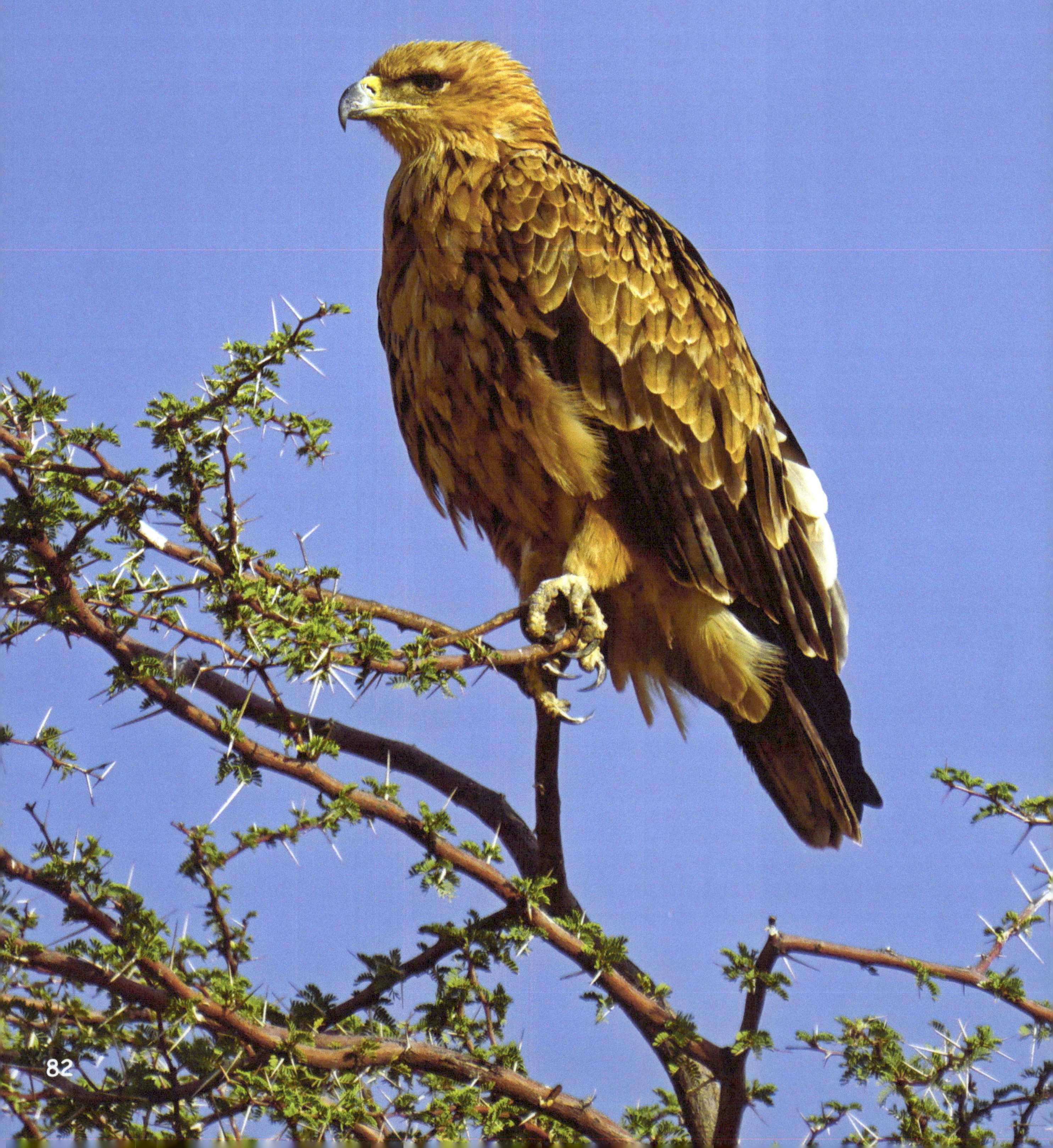

Tawny Eagle, Aquila rapax.
Raptors are plentiful in Etosha
N.P. with 46 species recorded.

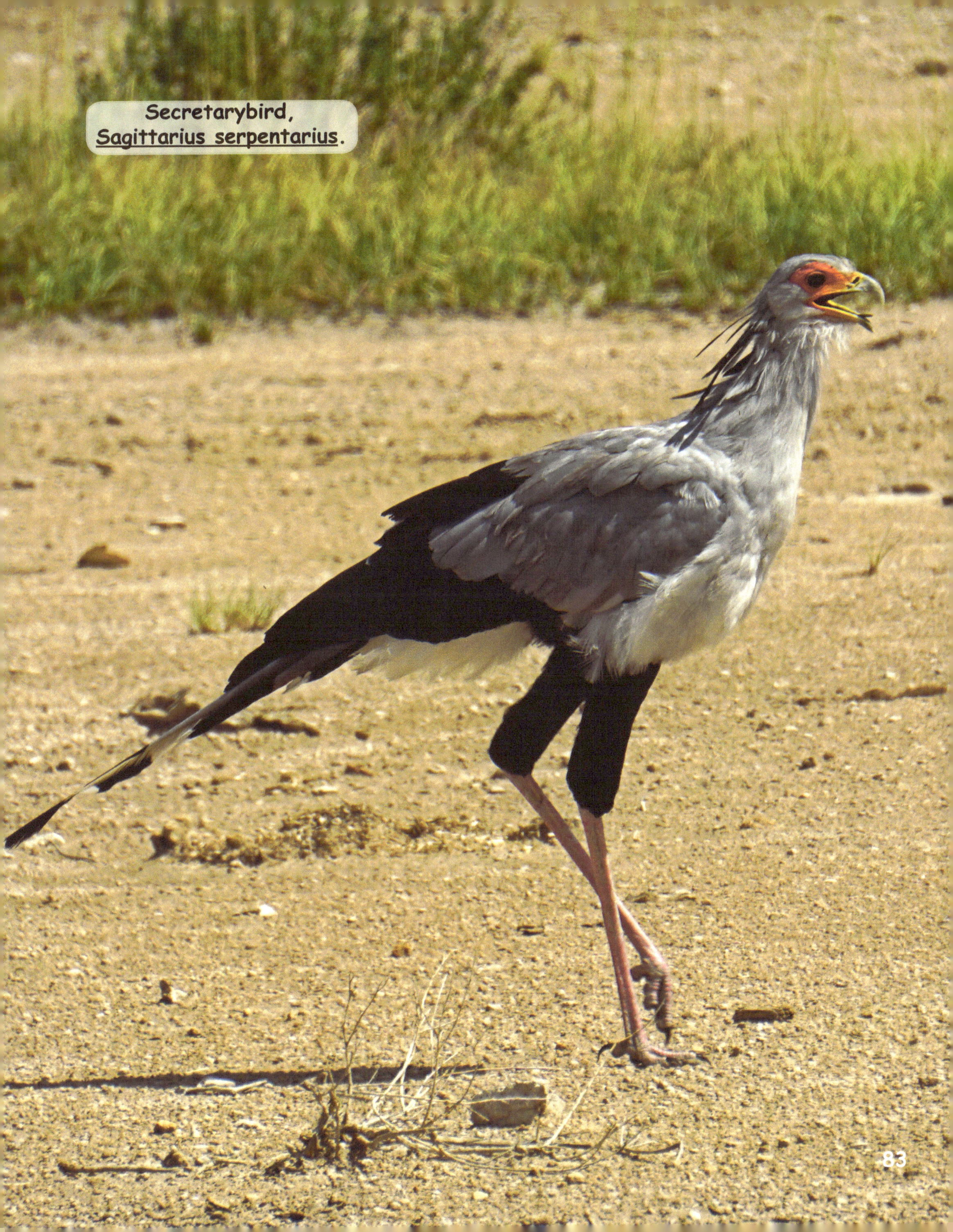

Secretarybird,
Sagittarius serpentarius.

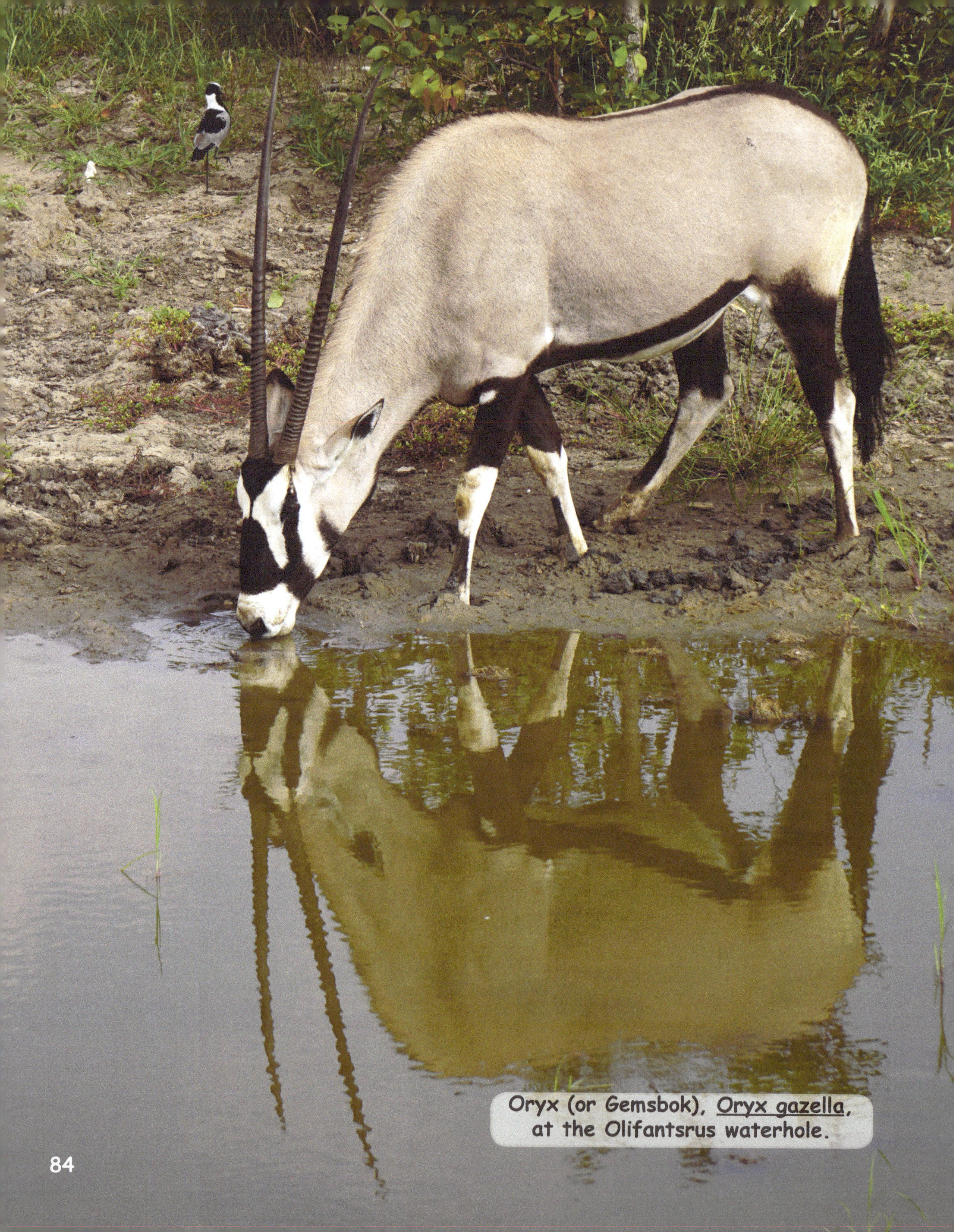

Oryx (or Gemsbok), _Oryx gazella_, at the Olifantsrus waterhole.

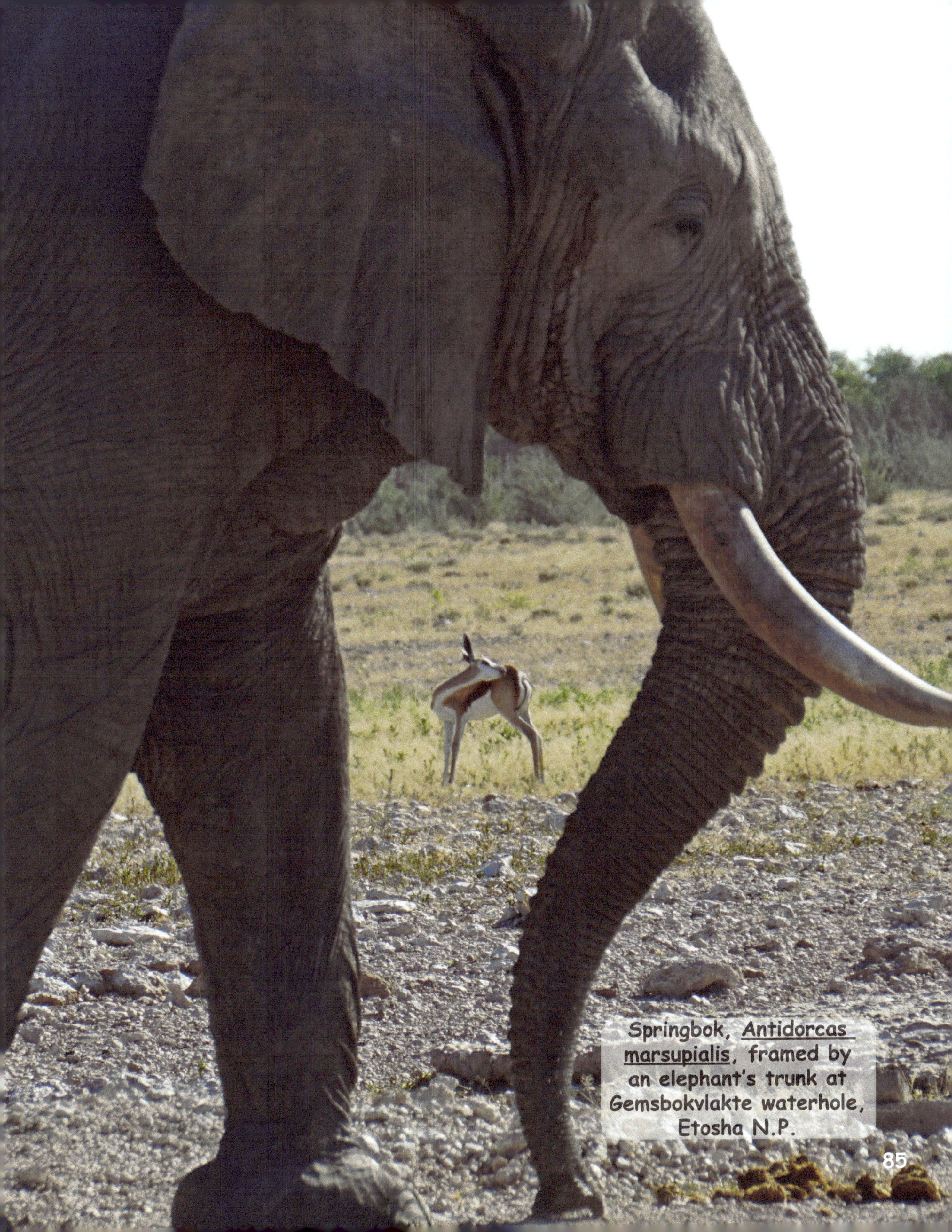

Springbok, _Antidorcas marsupialis_, framed by an elephant's trunk at Gemsbokvlakte waterhole, Etosha N.P.

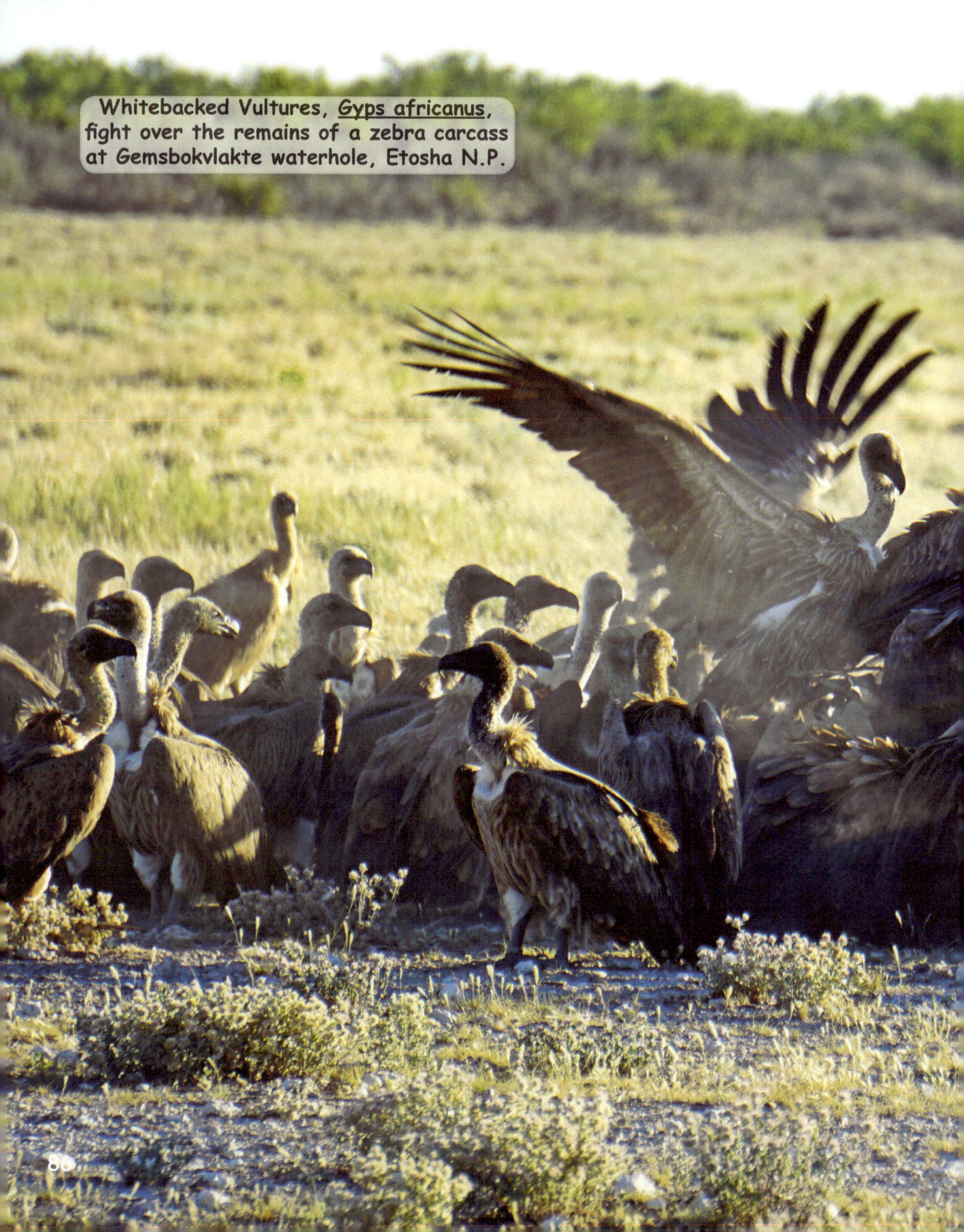

Whitebacked Vultures, Gyps africanus,
fight over the remains of a zebra carcass
at Gemsbokvlakte waterhole, Etosha N.P.

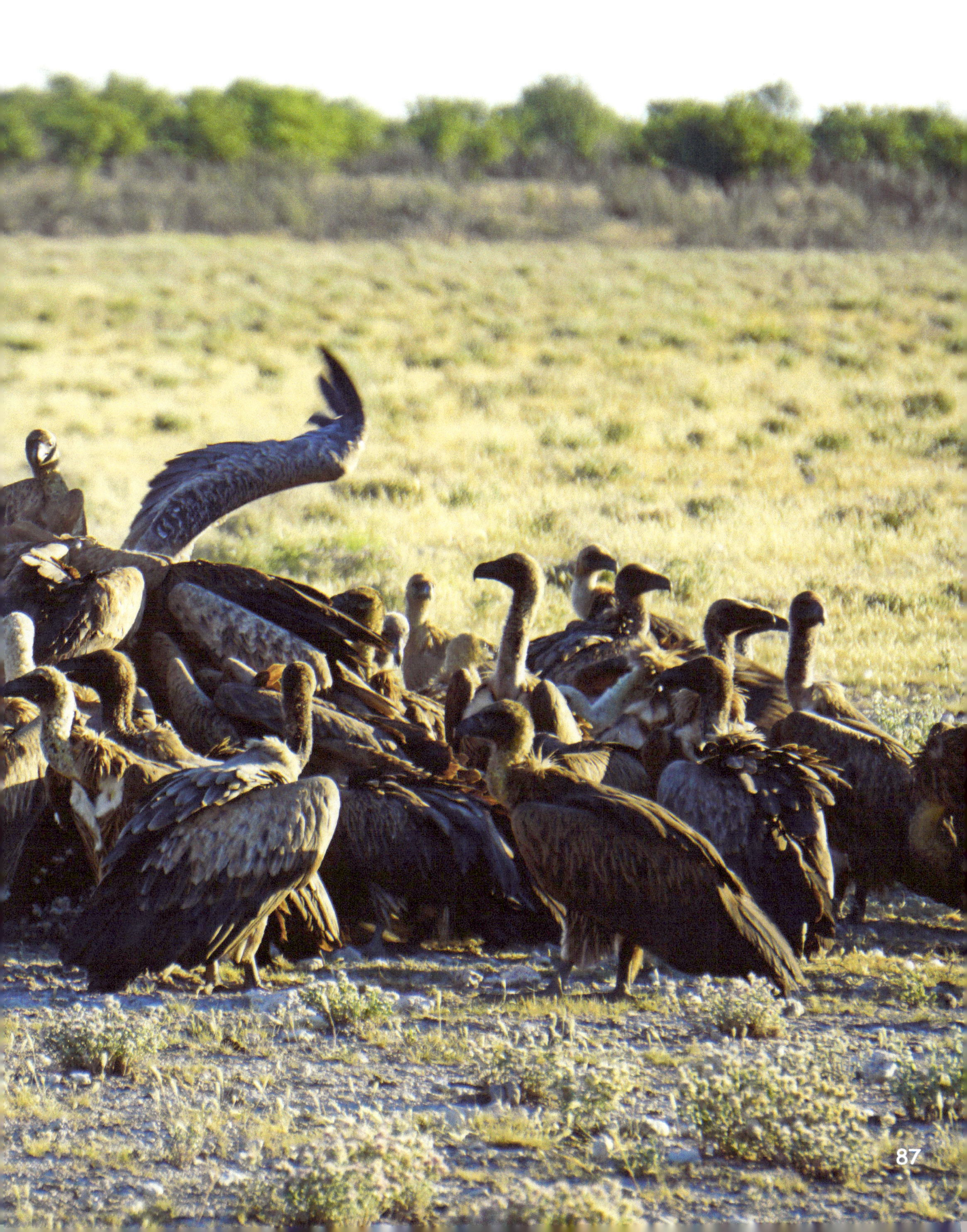

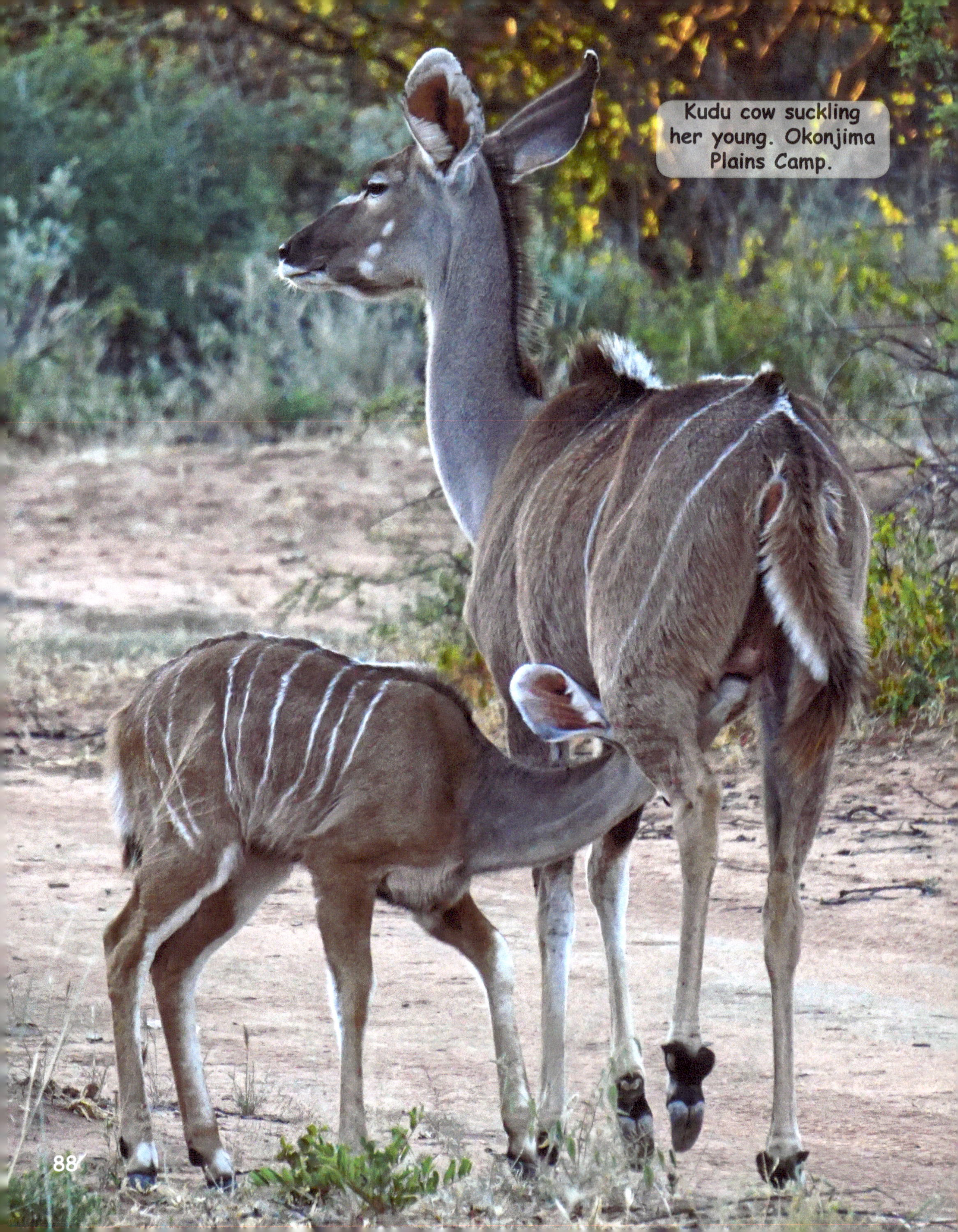

Kudu cow suckling her young. Okonjima Plains Camp.

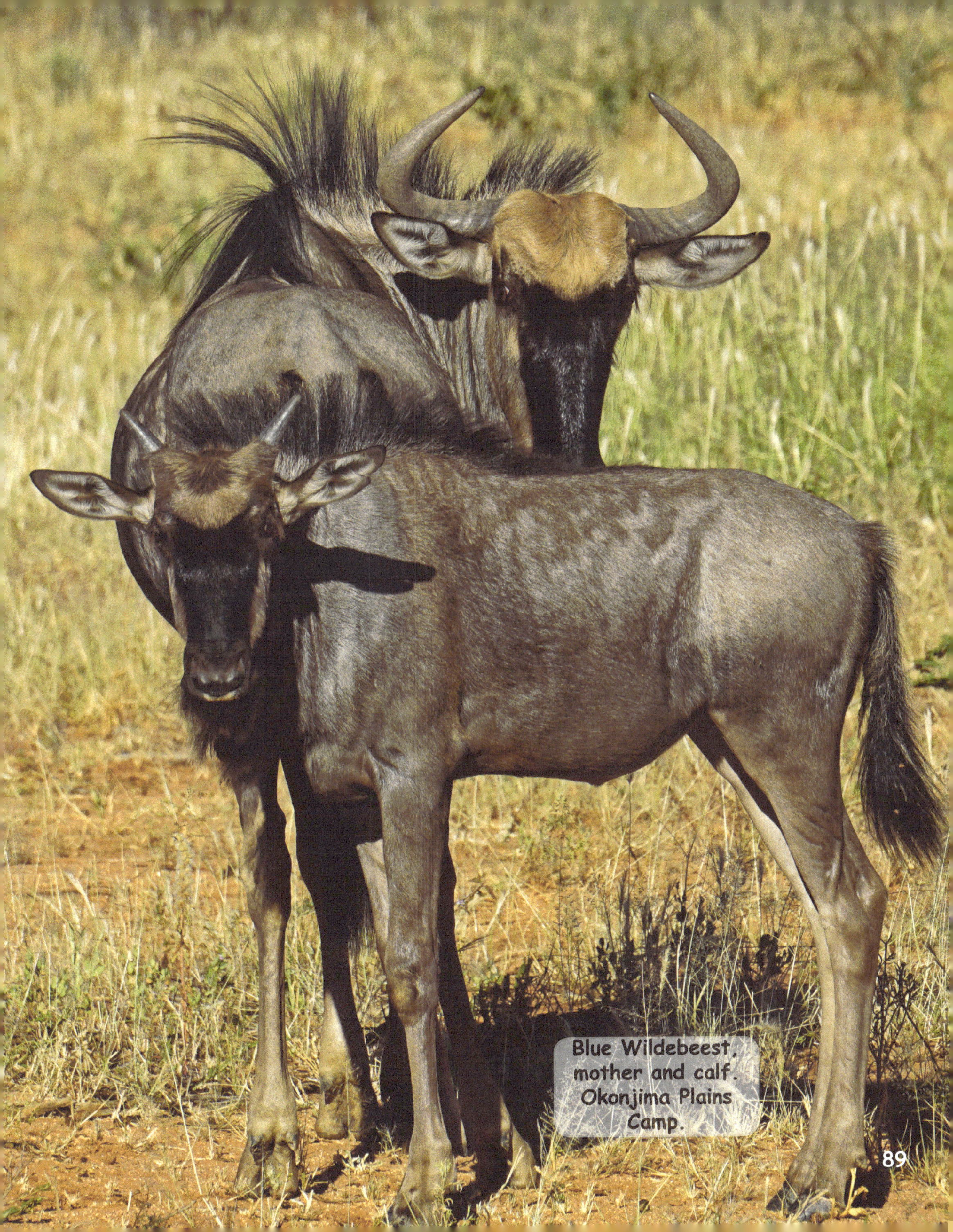

Blue Wildebeest,
mother and calf.
Okonjima Plains
Camp.

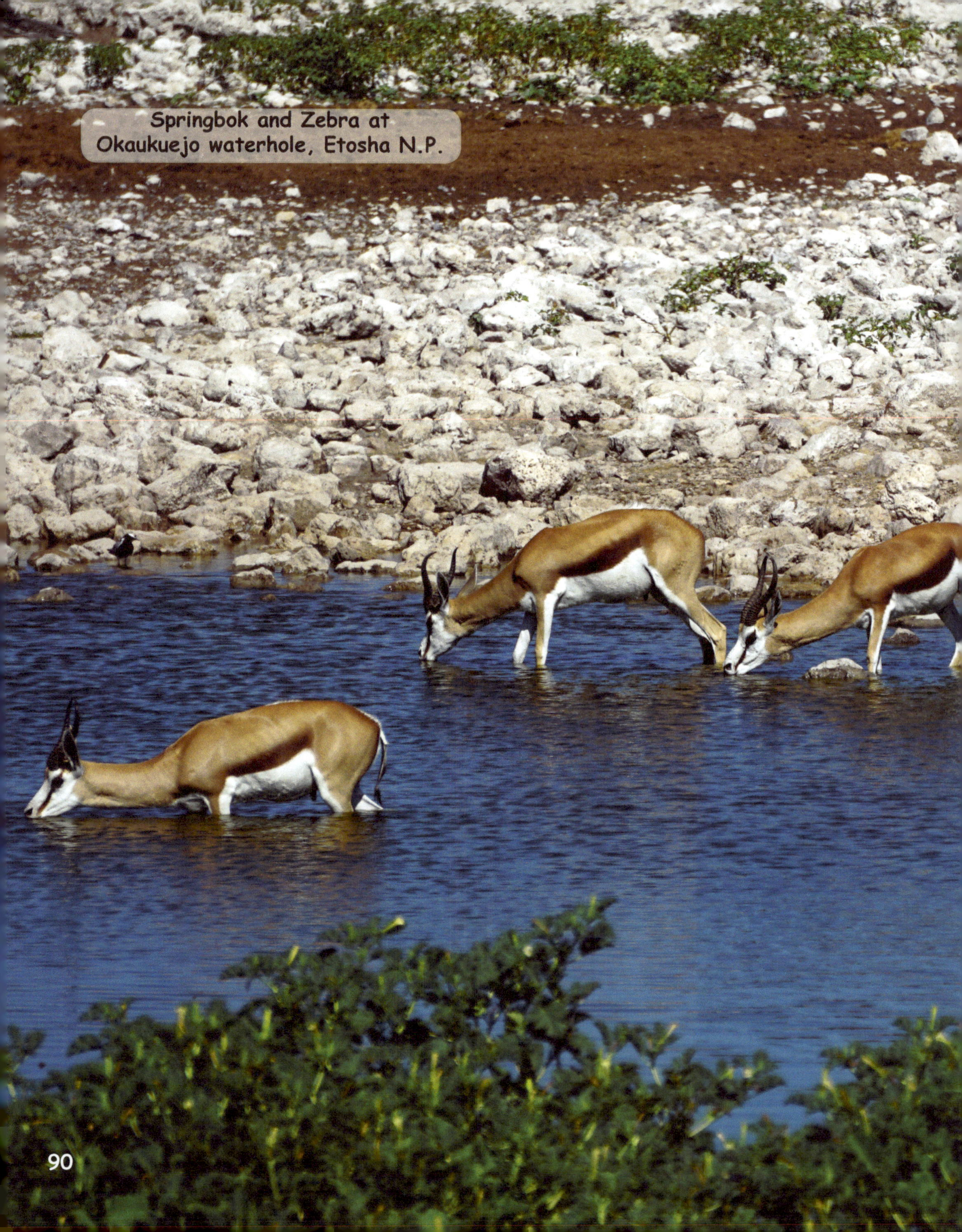

Springbok and Zebra at
Okaukuejo waterhole, Etosha N.P.

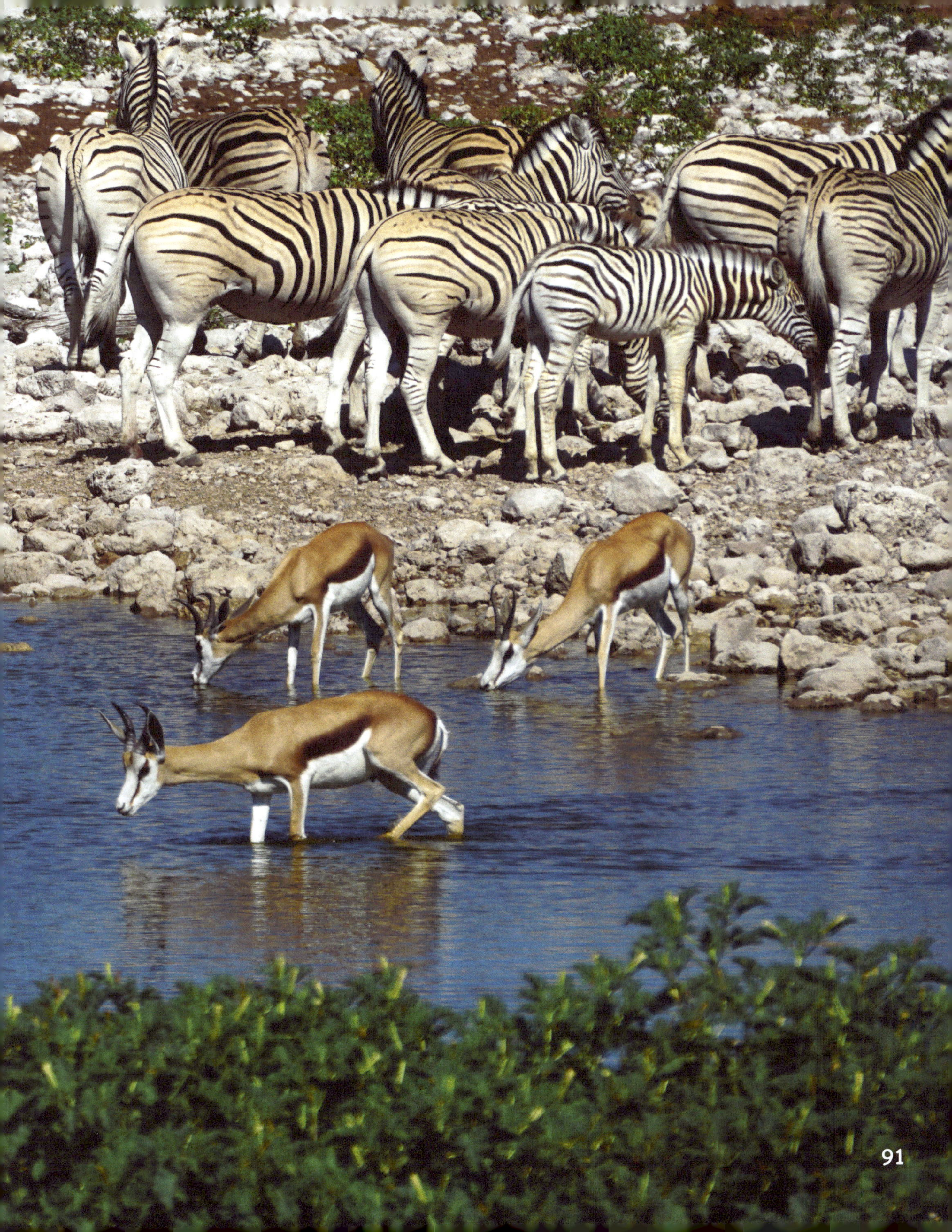

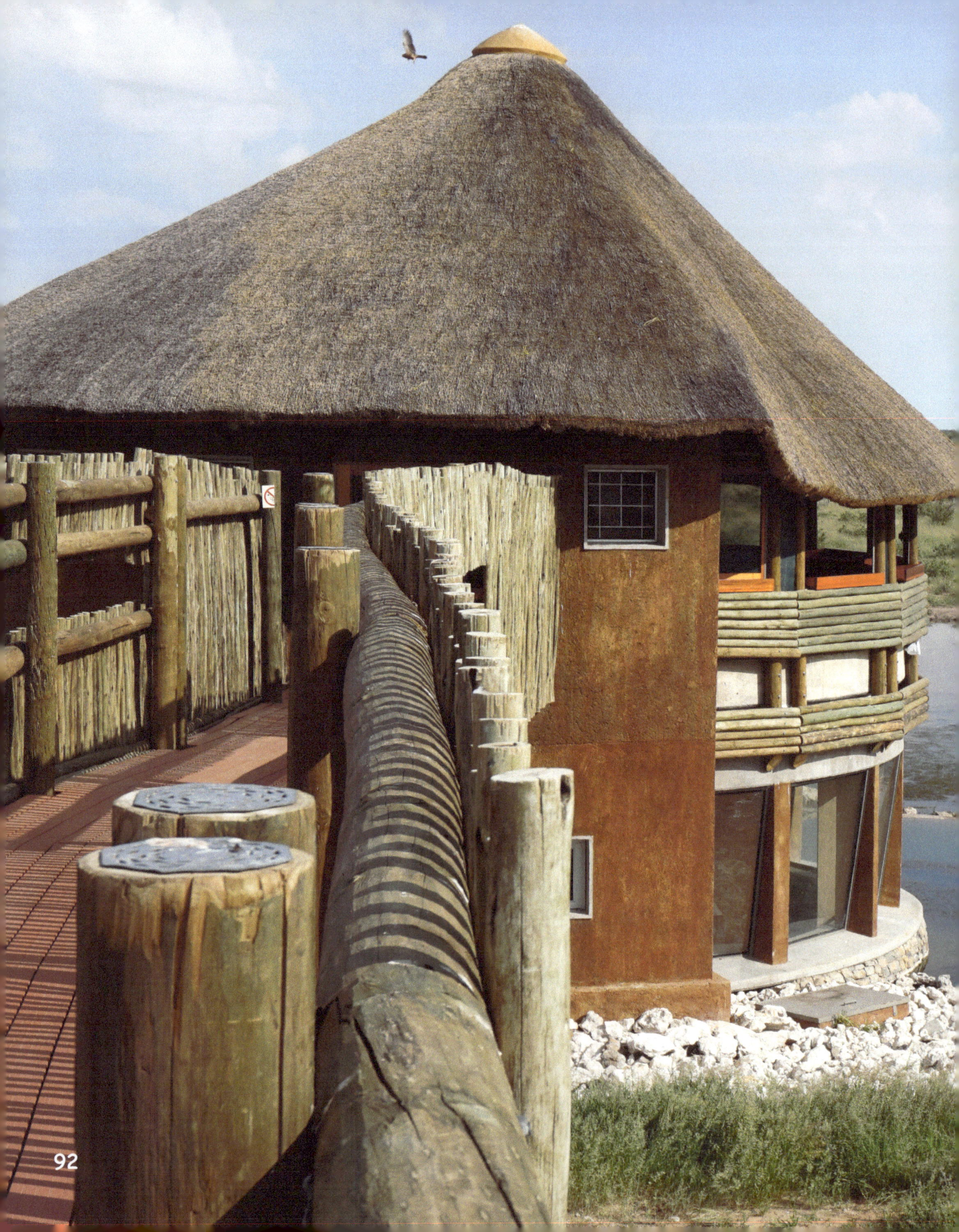

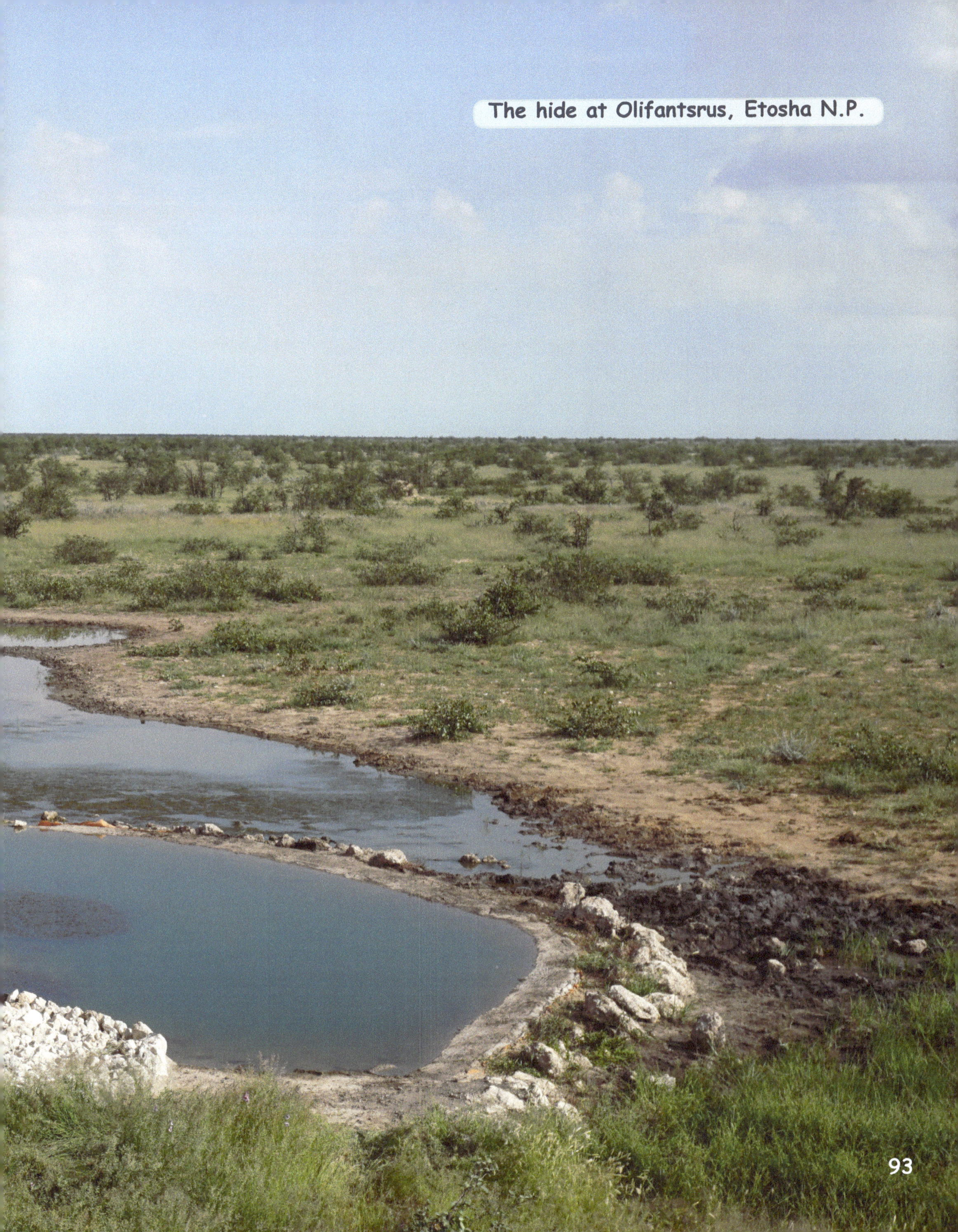

The hide at Olifantsrus, Etosha N.P.

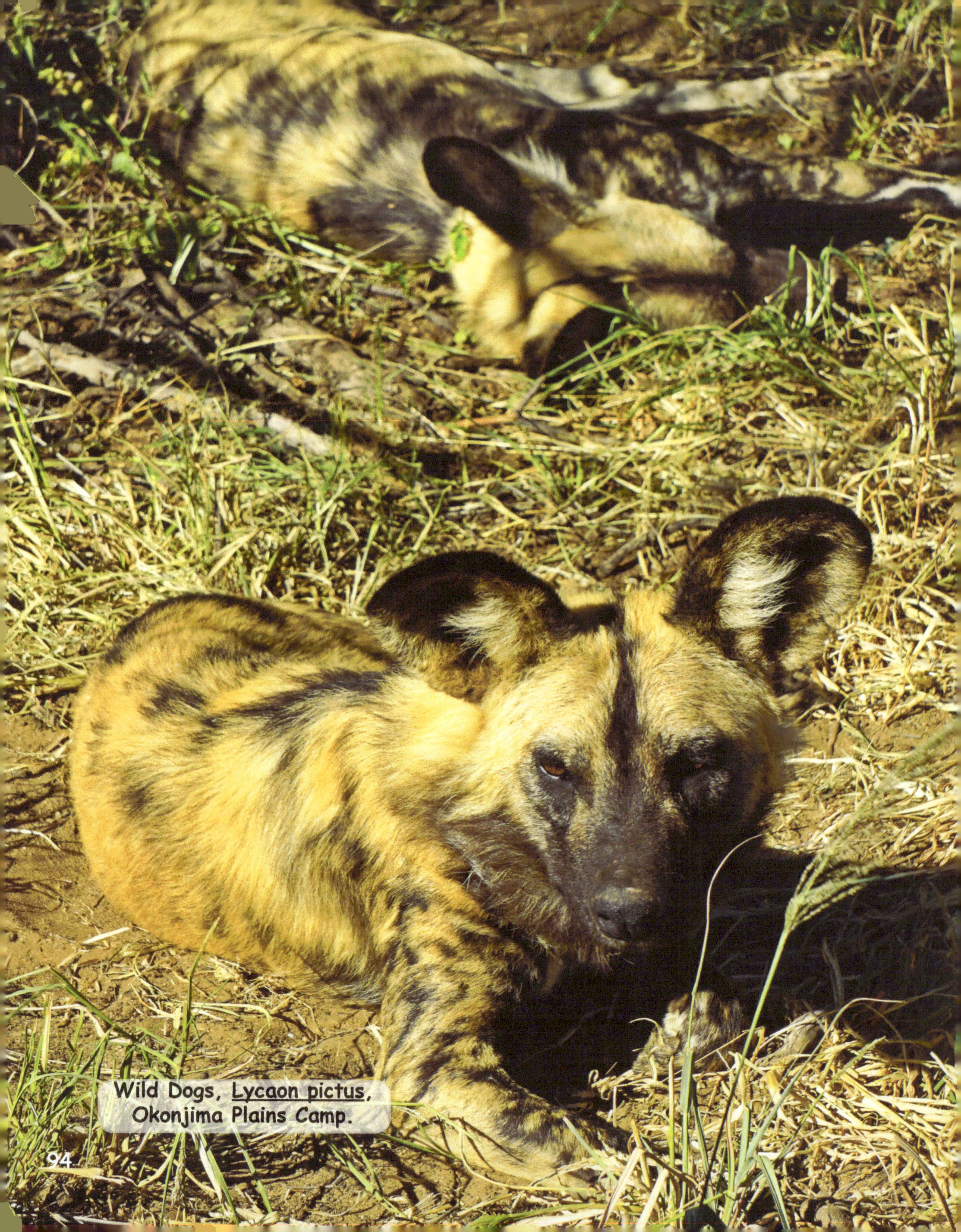

Wild Dogs, *Lycaon pictus*,
Okonjima Plains Camp.

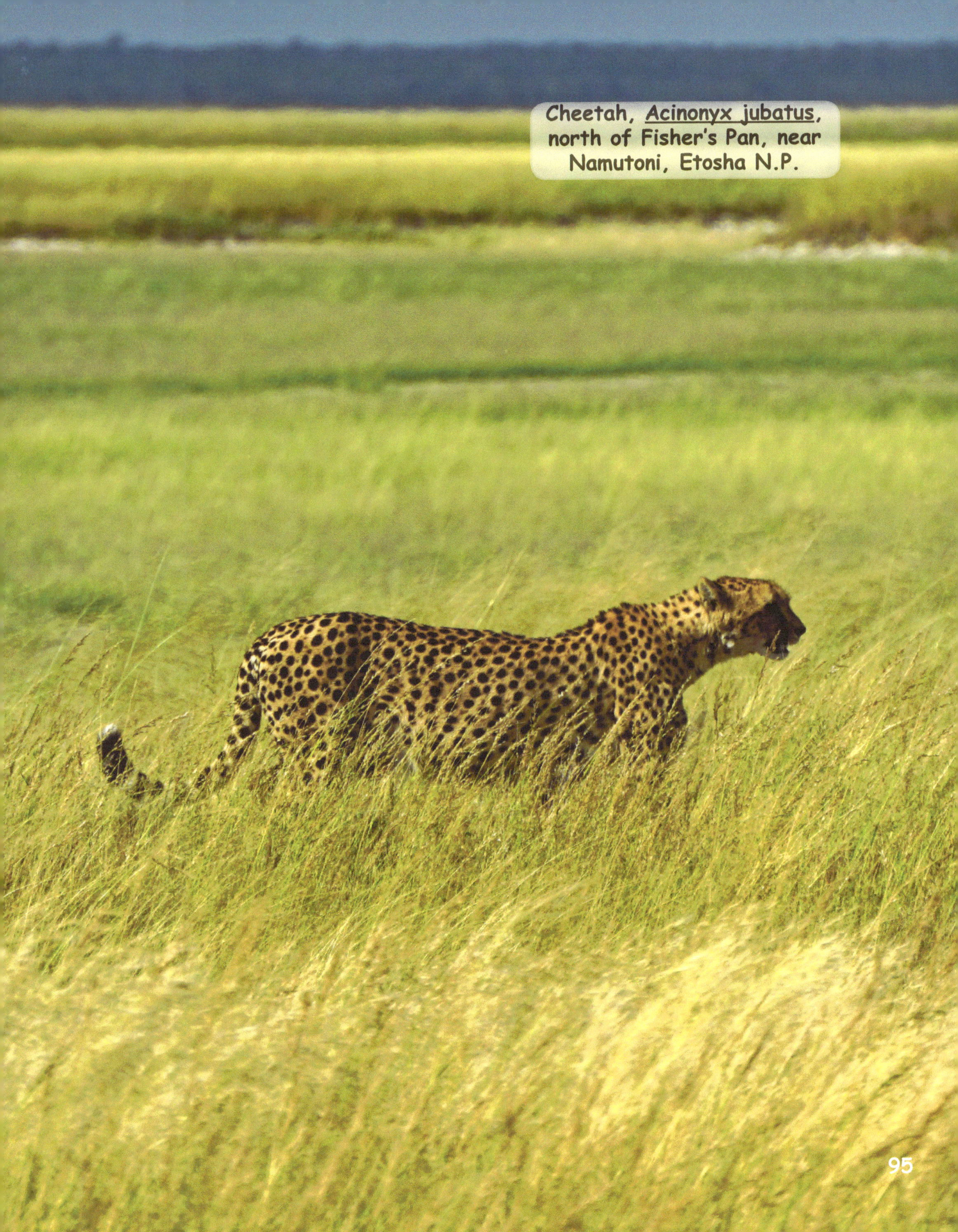

Cheetah, _Acinonyx jubatus_, north of Fisher's Pan, near Namutoni, Etosha N.P.

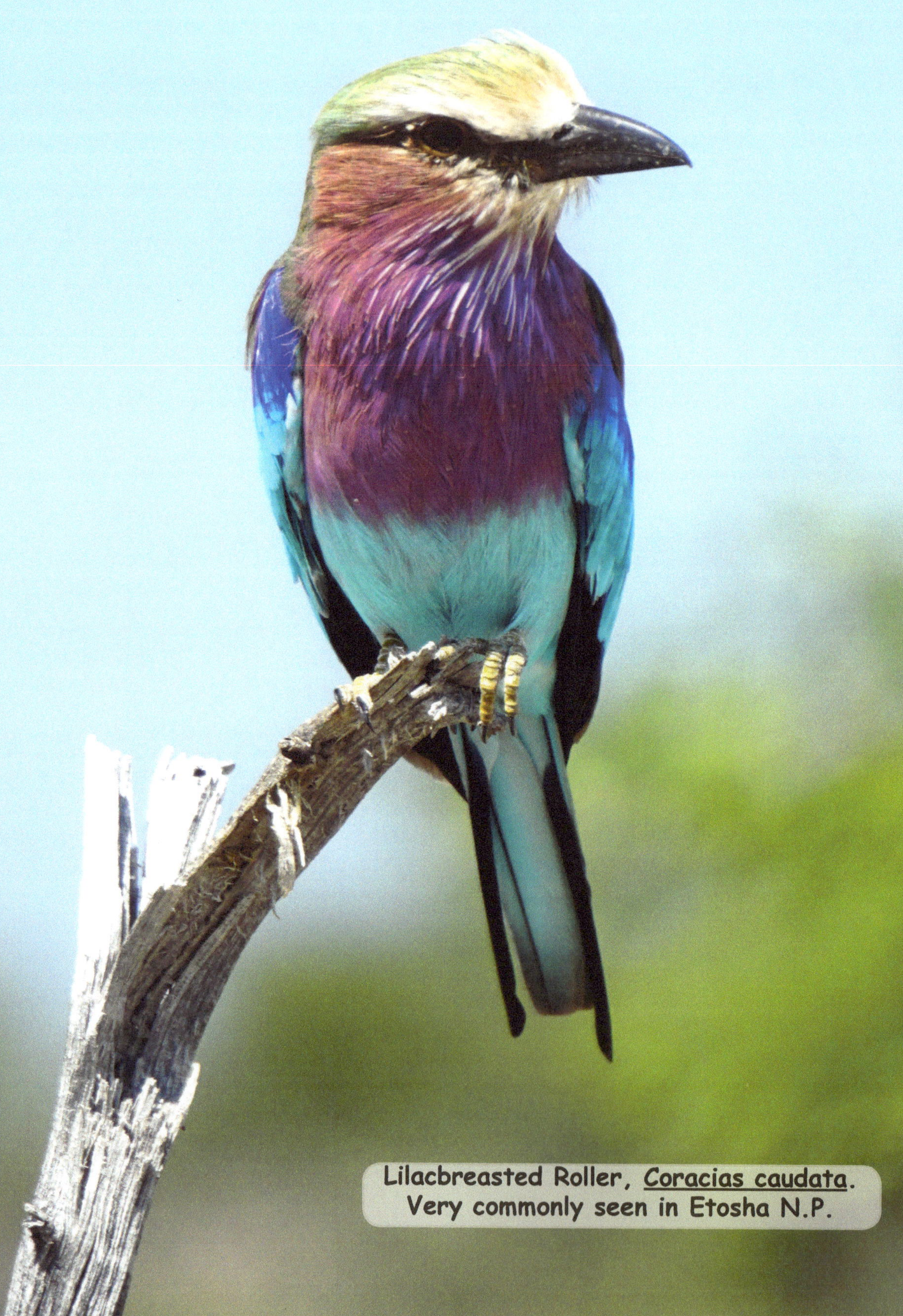

Lilacbreasted Roller, _Coracias caudata_.
Very commonly seen in Etosha N.P.

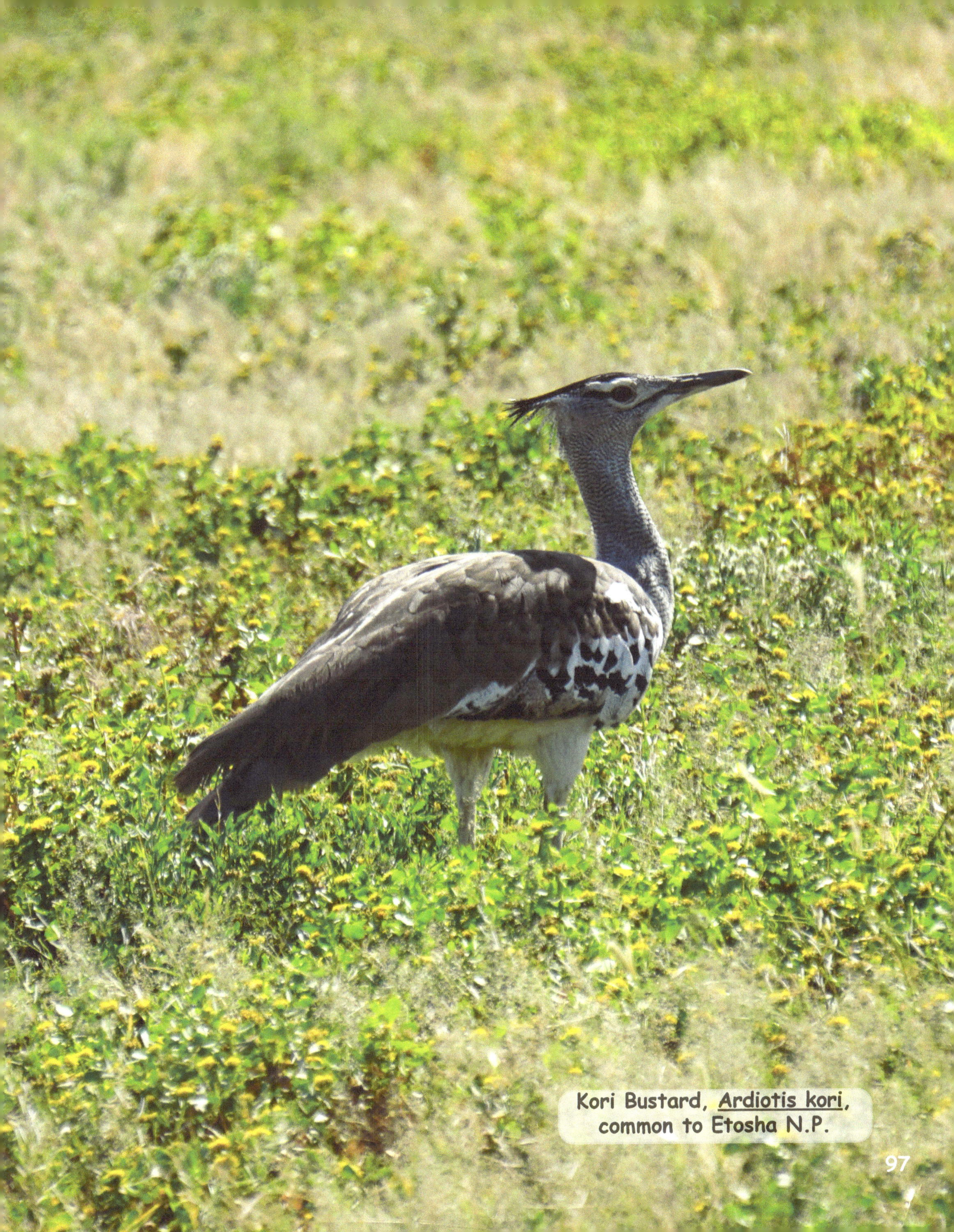

Kori Bustard, _Ardiotis kori_,
common to Etosha N.P.

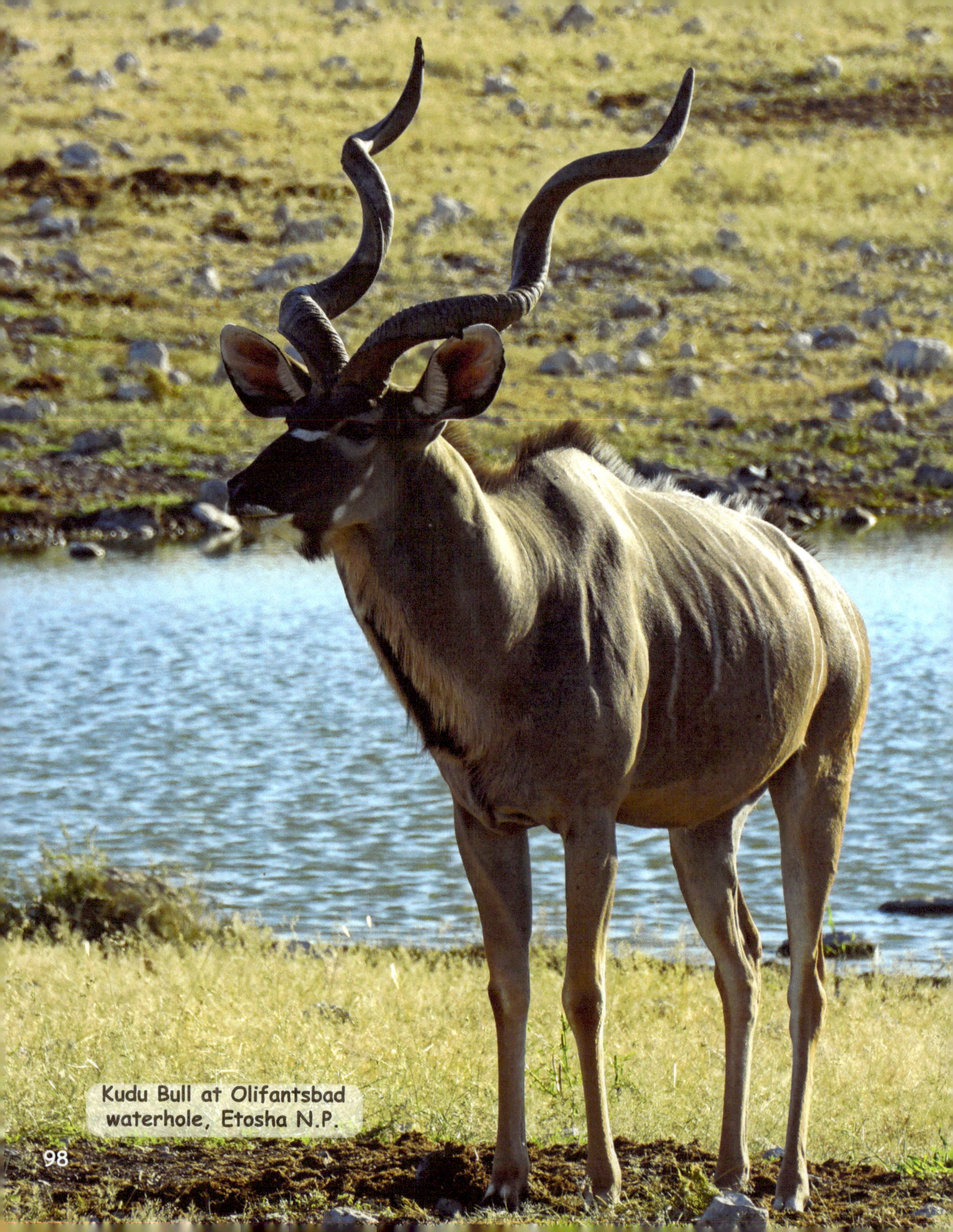
Kudu Bull at Olifantsbad
waterhole, Etosha N.P.

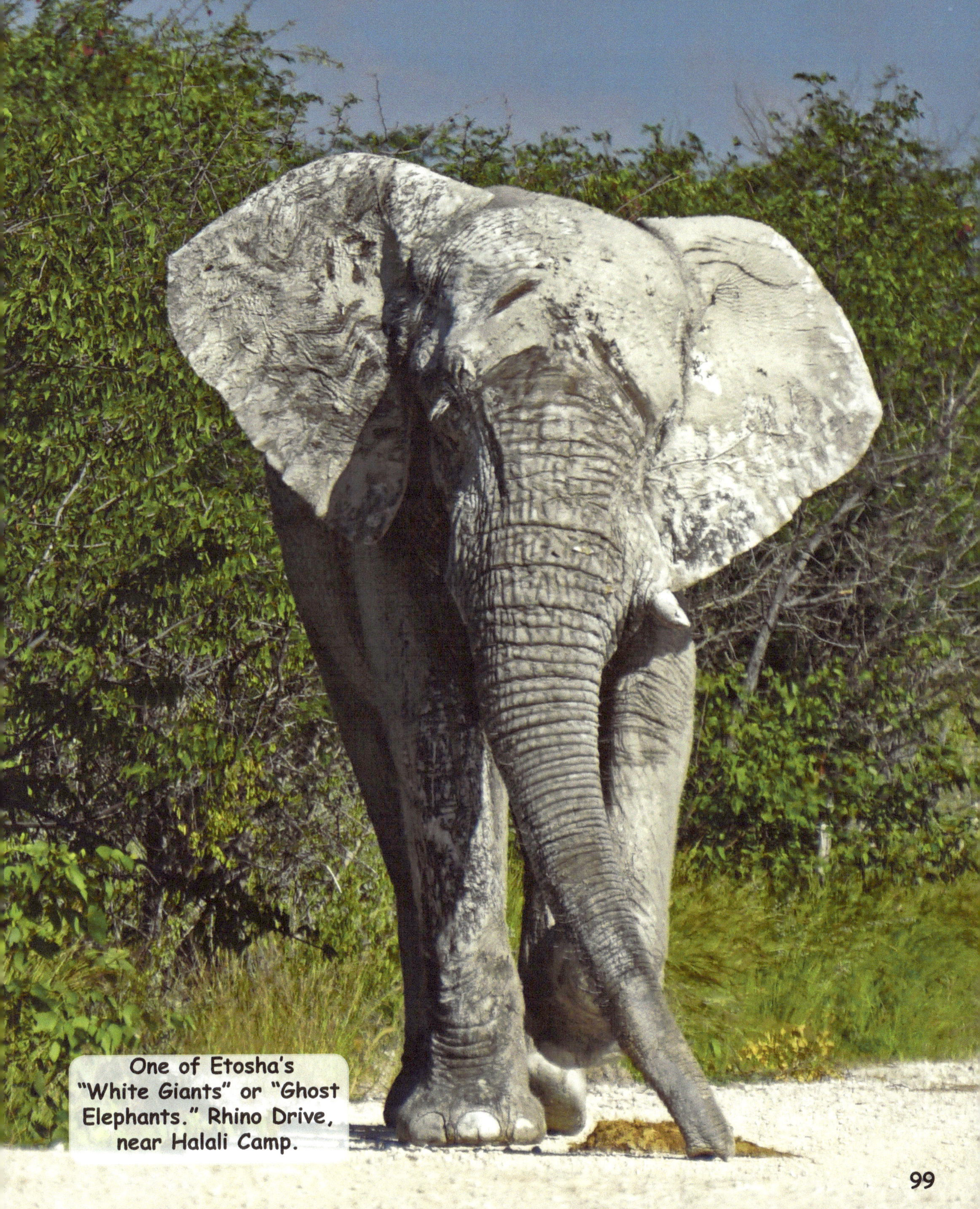

One of Etosha's
"White Giants" or "Ghost
Elephants." Rhino Drive,
near Halali Camp.

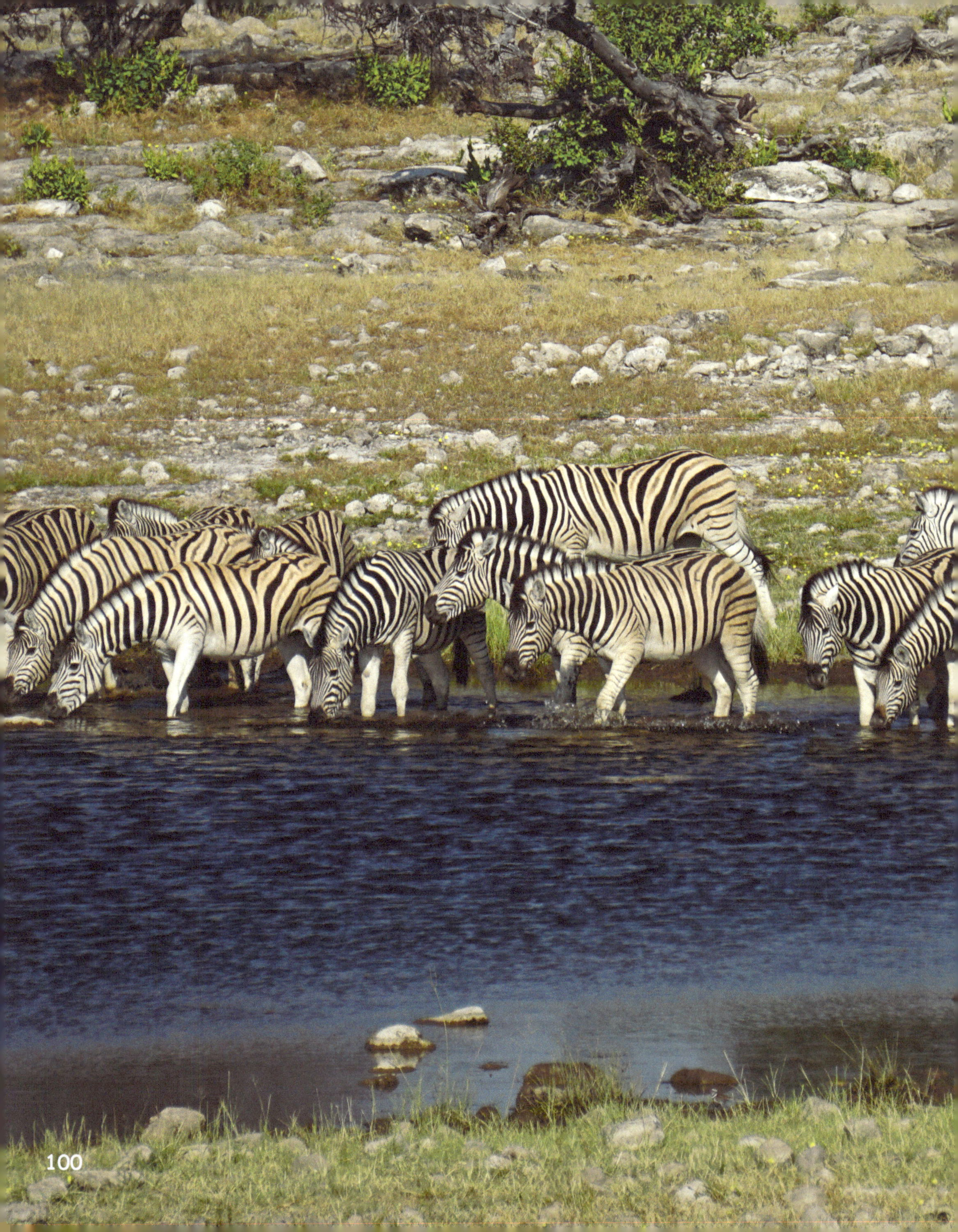

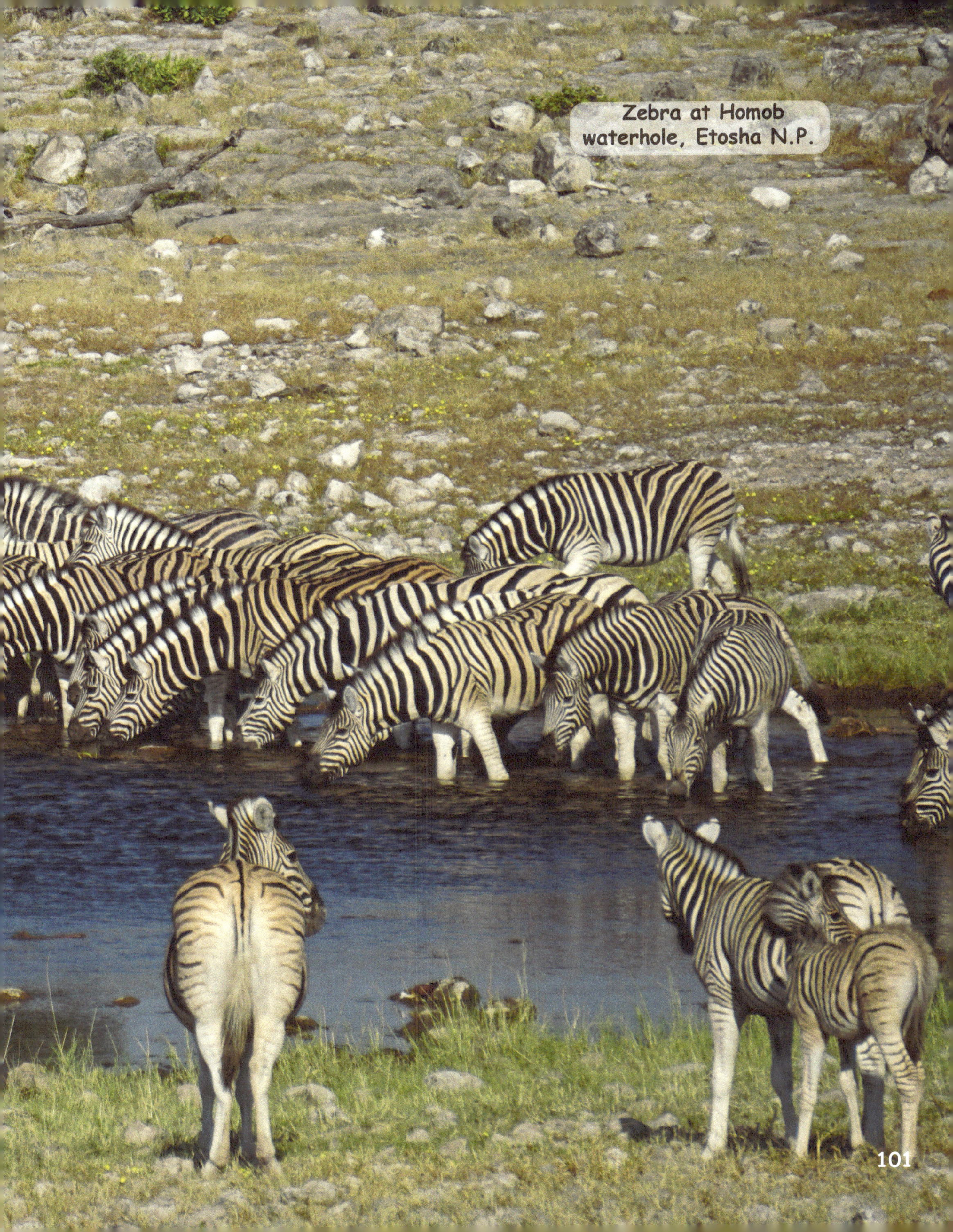
Zebra at Homob
waterhole, Etosha N.P.

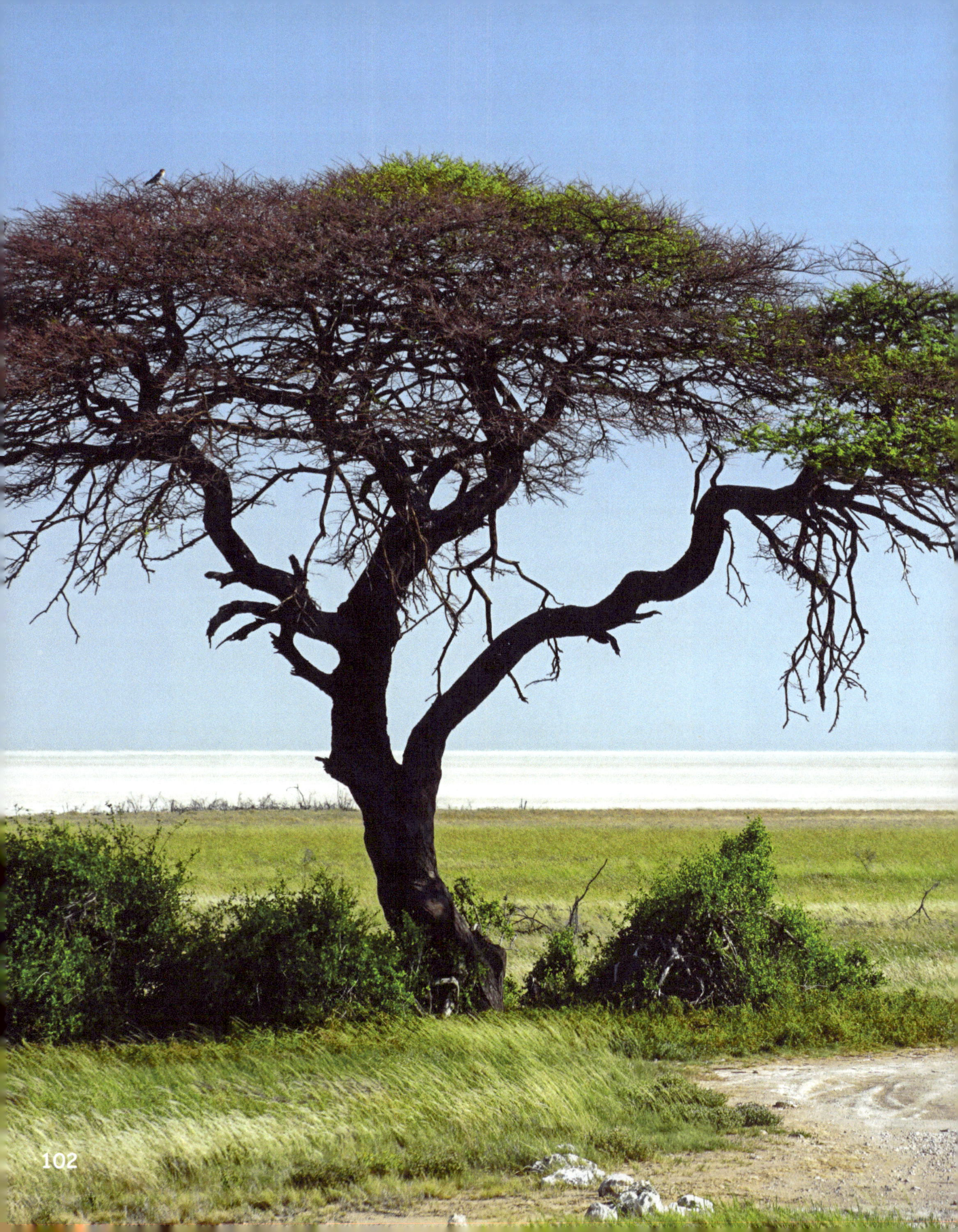

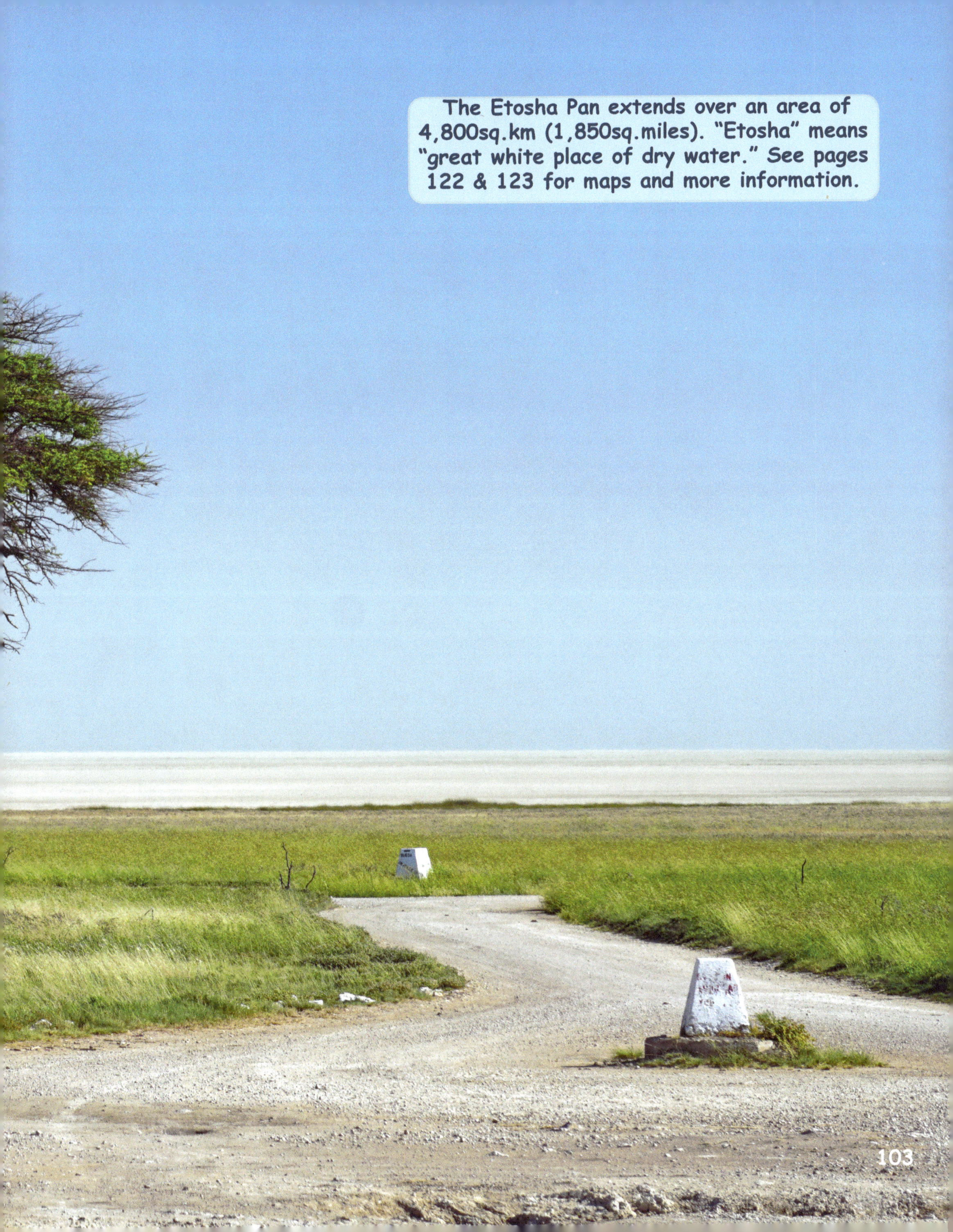

The Etosha Pan extends over an area of 4,800sq.km (1,850sq.miles). "Etosha" means "great white place of dry water." See pages 122 & 123 for maps and more information.

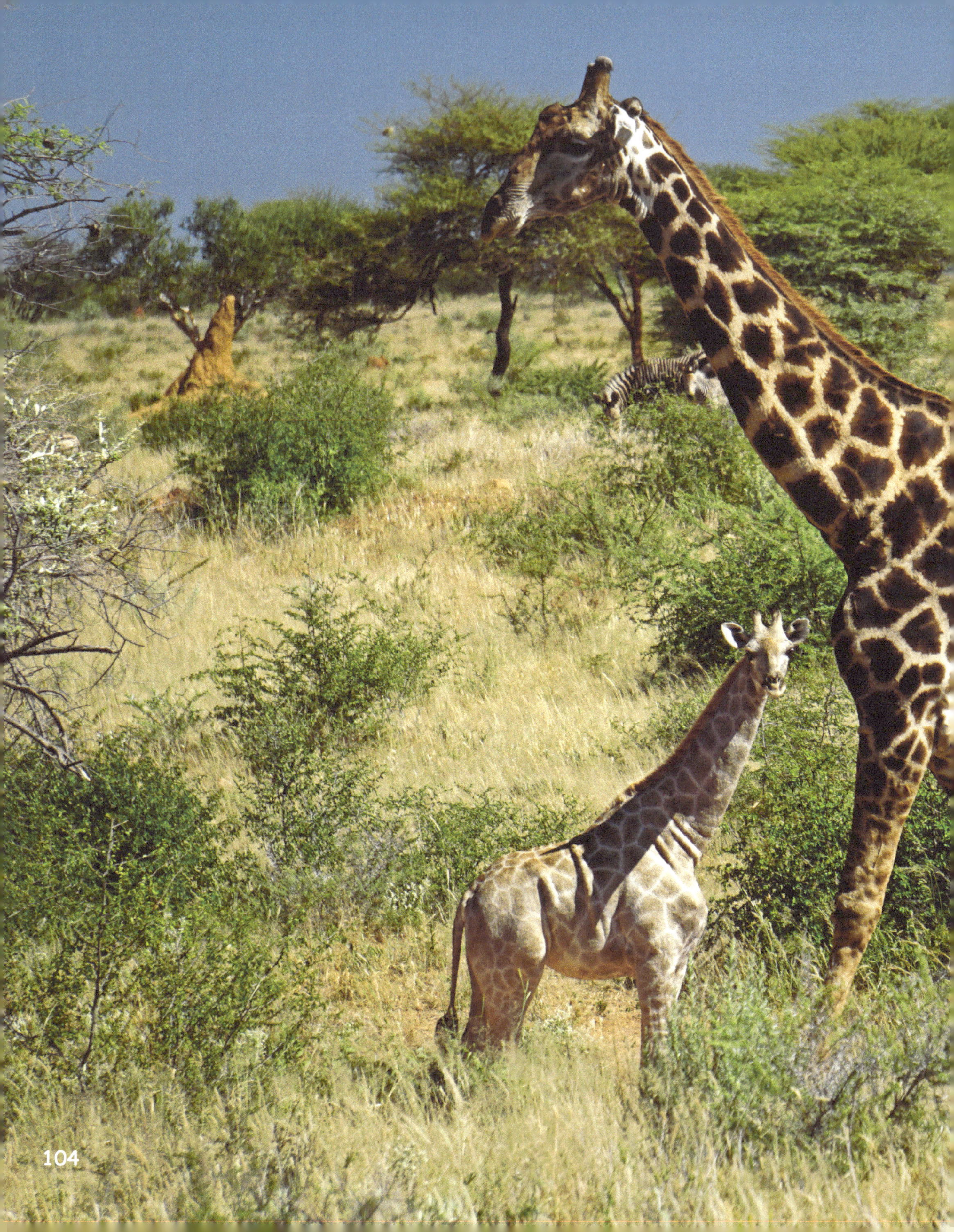

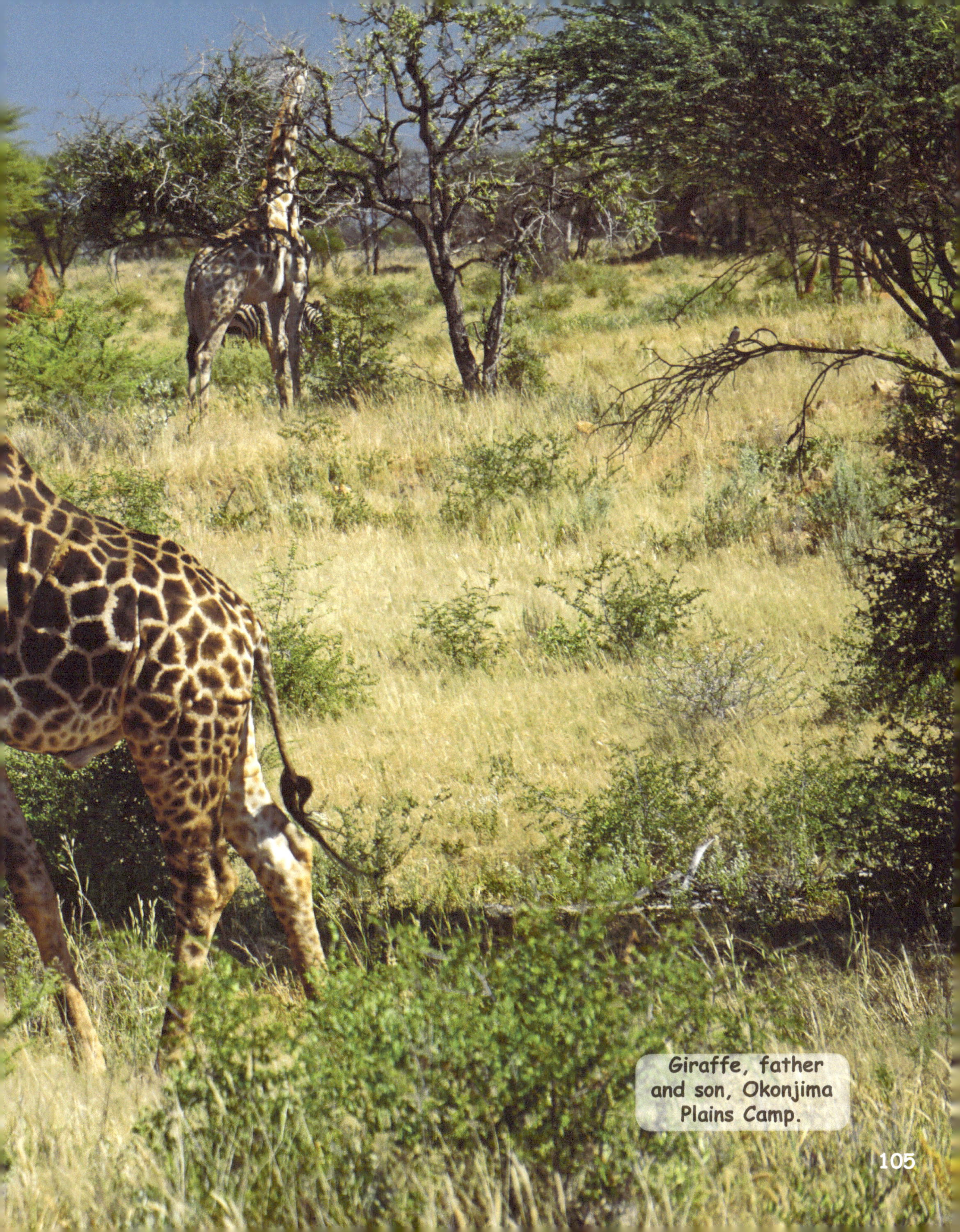

Giraffe, father and son, Okonjima Plains Camp.

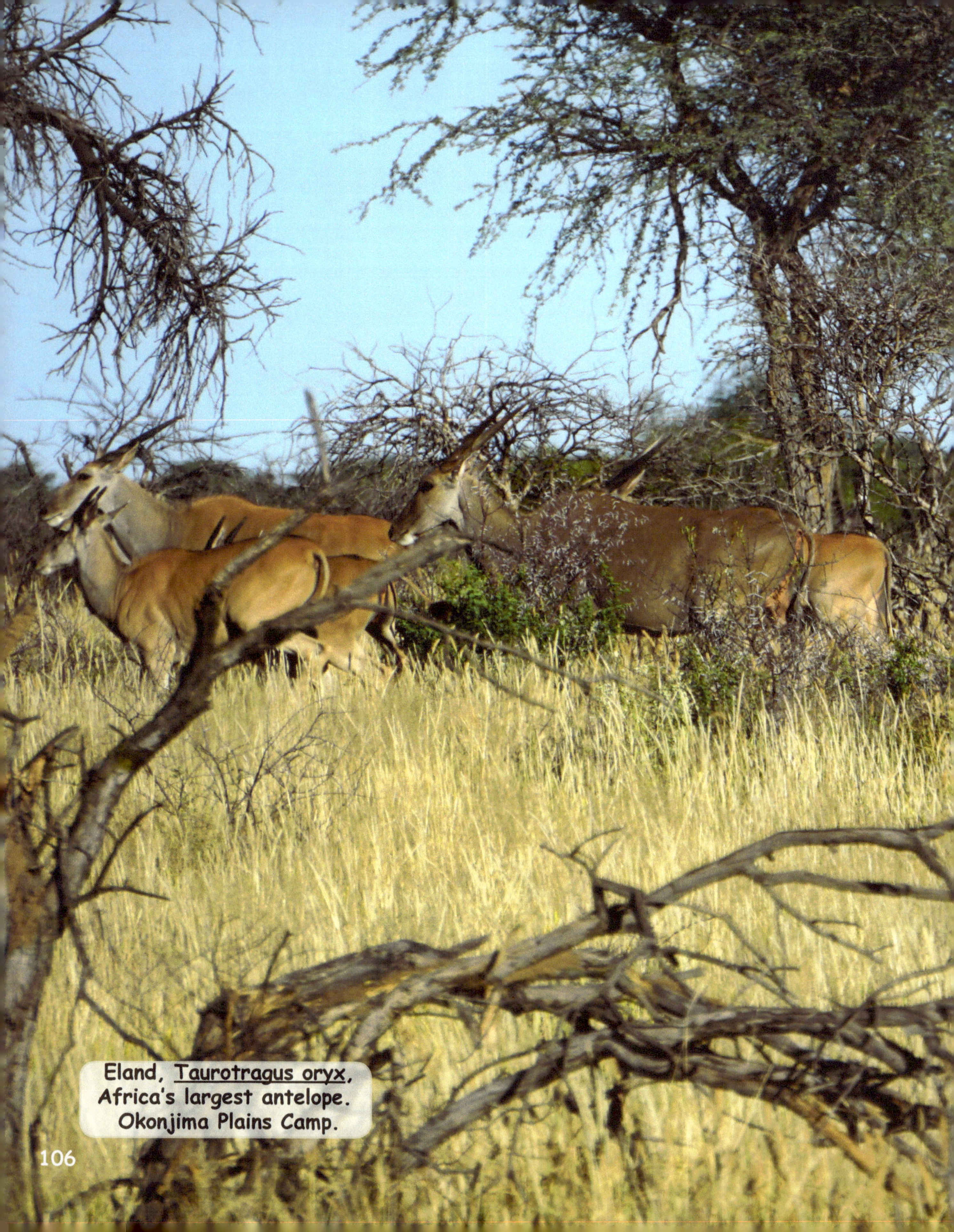

Eland, _Taurotragus oryx_,
Africa's largest antelope.
Okonjima Plains Camp.

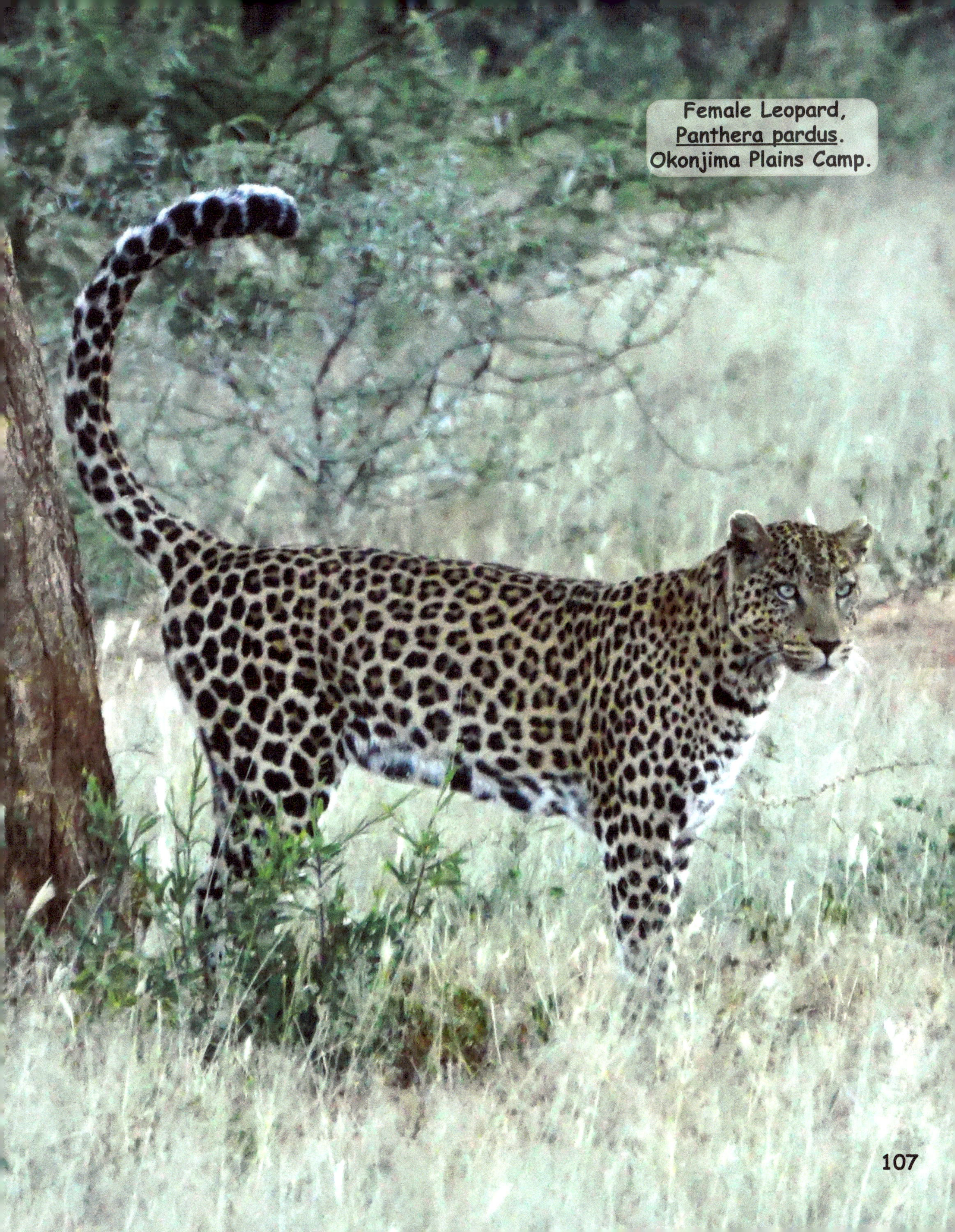

Female Leopard,
Panthera pardus.
Okonjima Plains Camp.

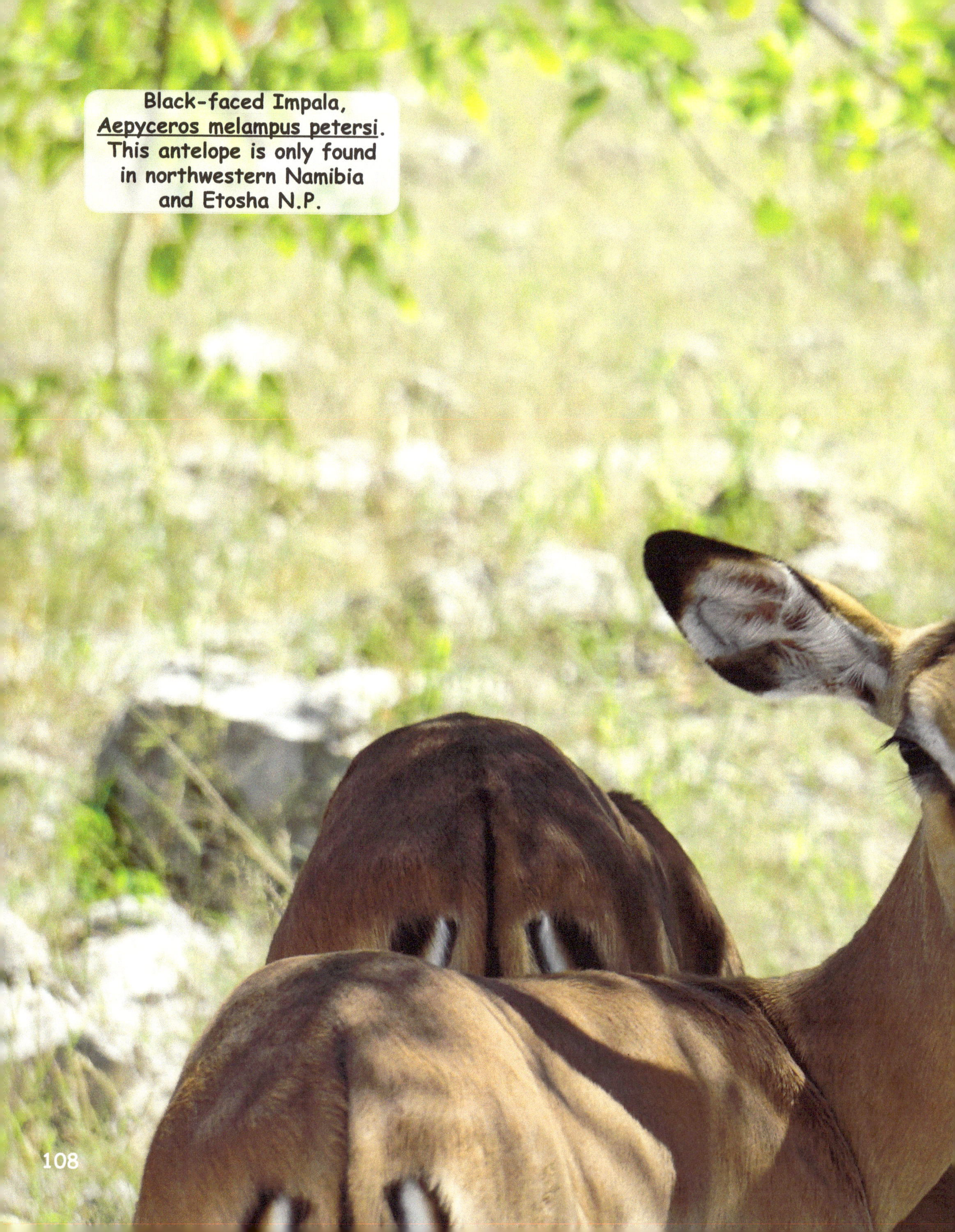

Black-faced Impala,
Aepyceros melampus petersi.
This antelope is only found
in northwestern Namibia
and Etosha N.P.

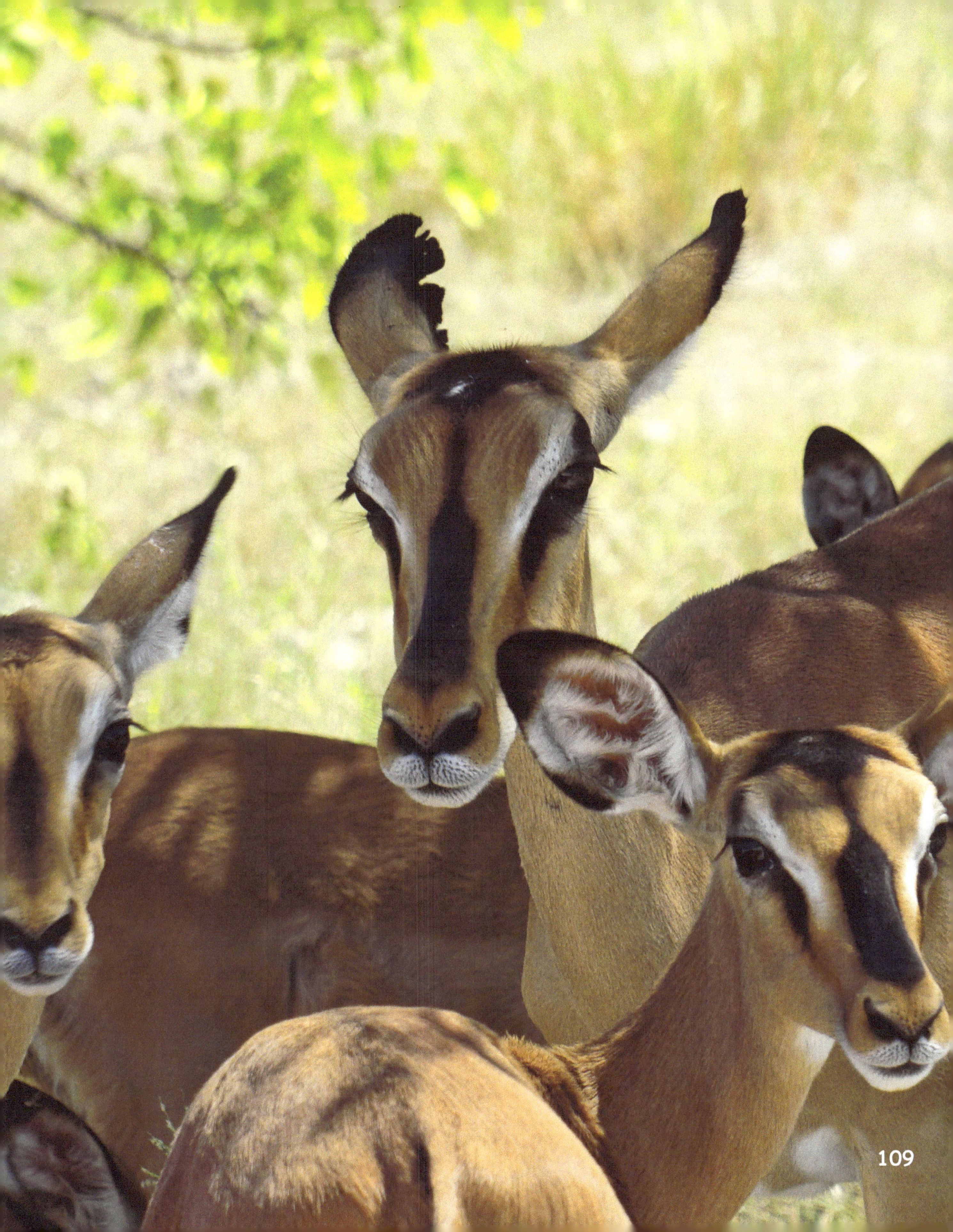

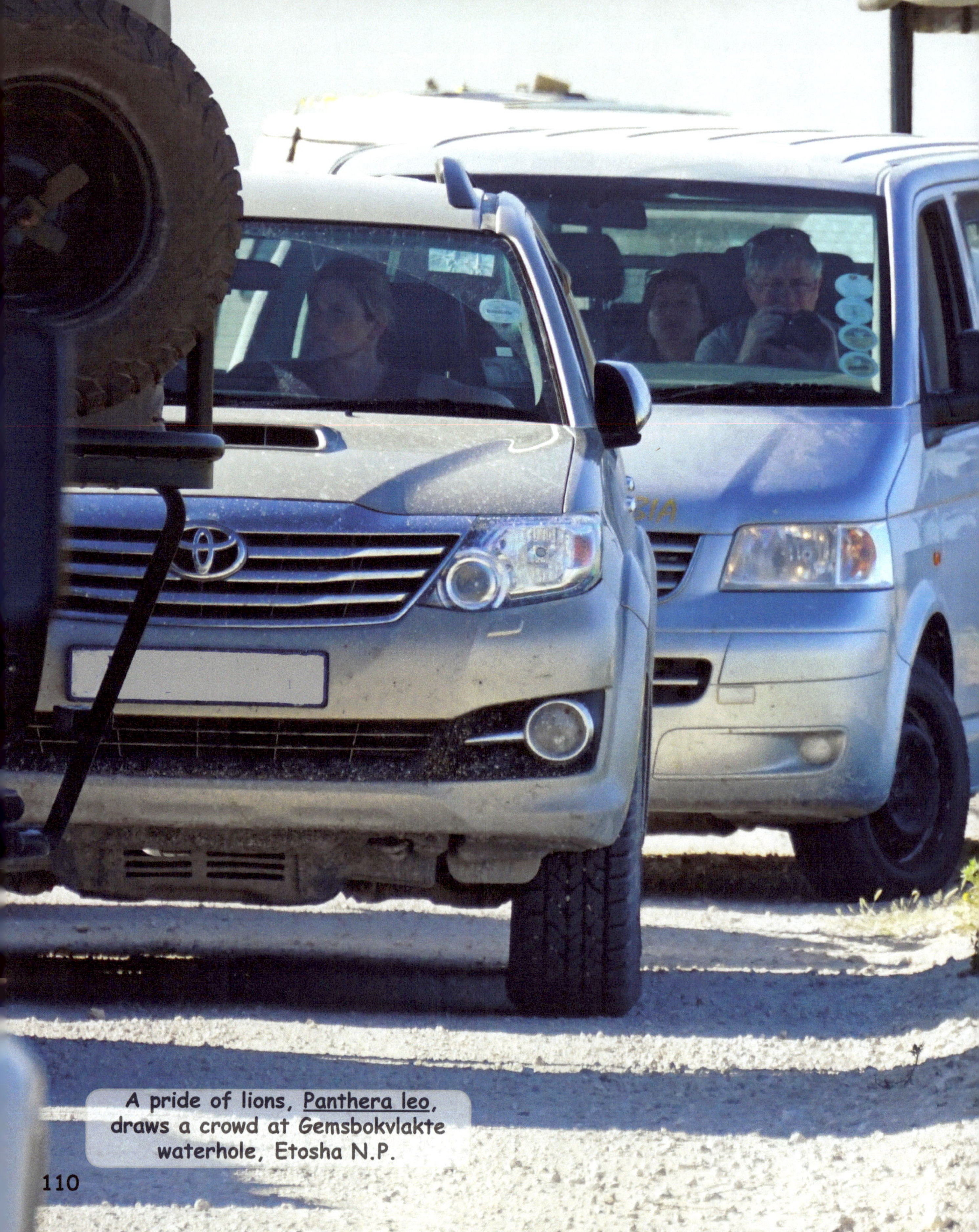

A pride of lions, <u>Panthera leo</u>, draws a crowd at Gemsbokvlakte waterhole, Etosha N.P.

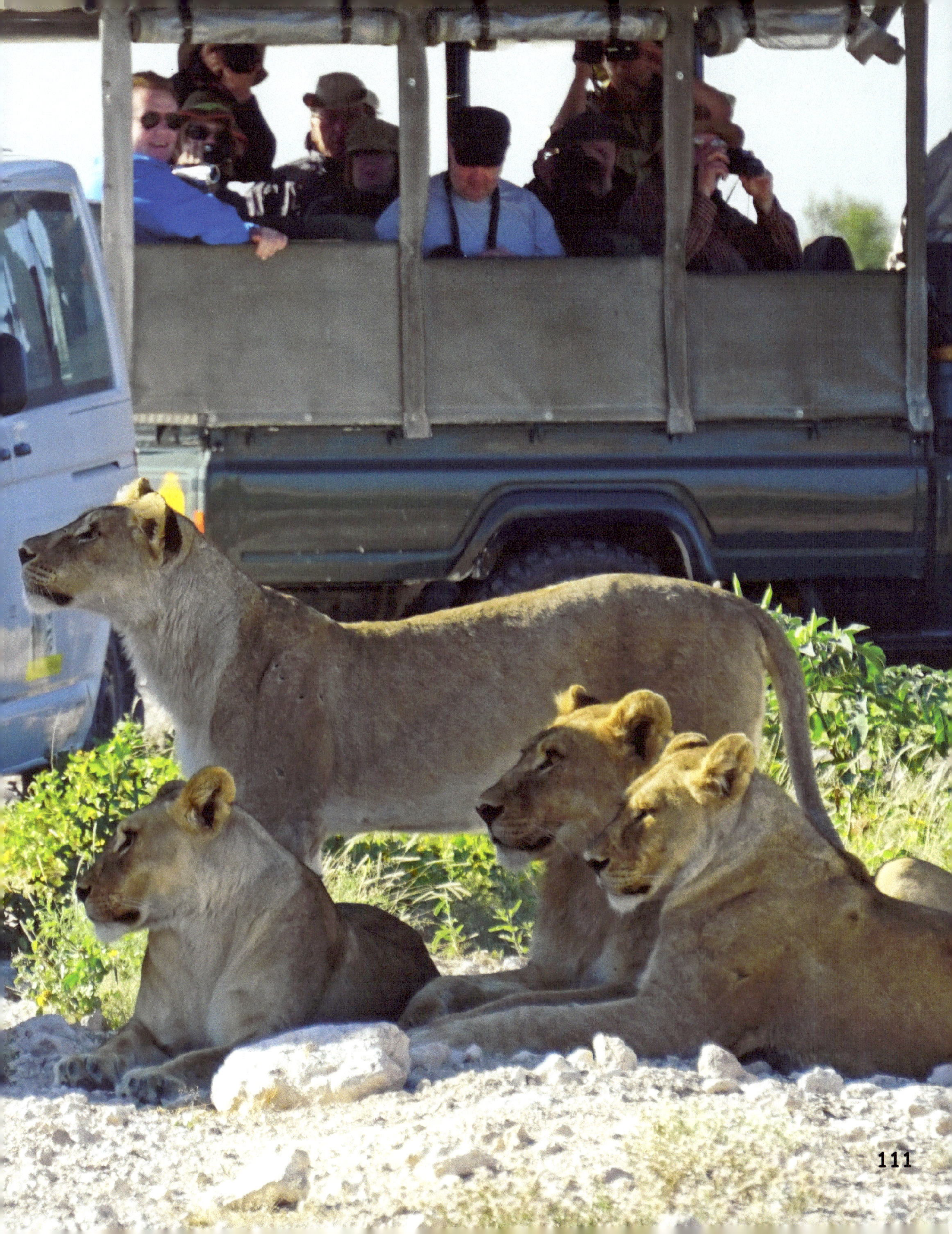

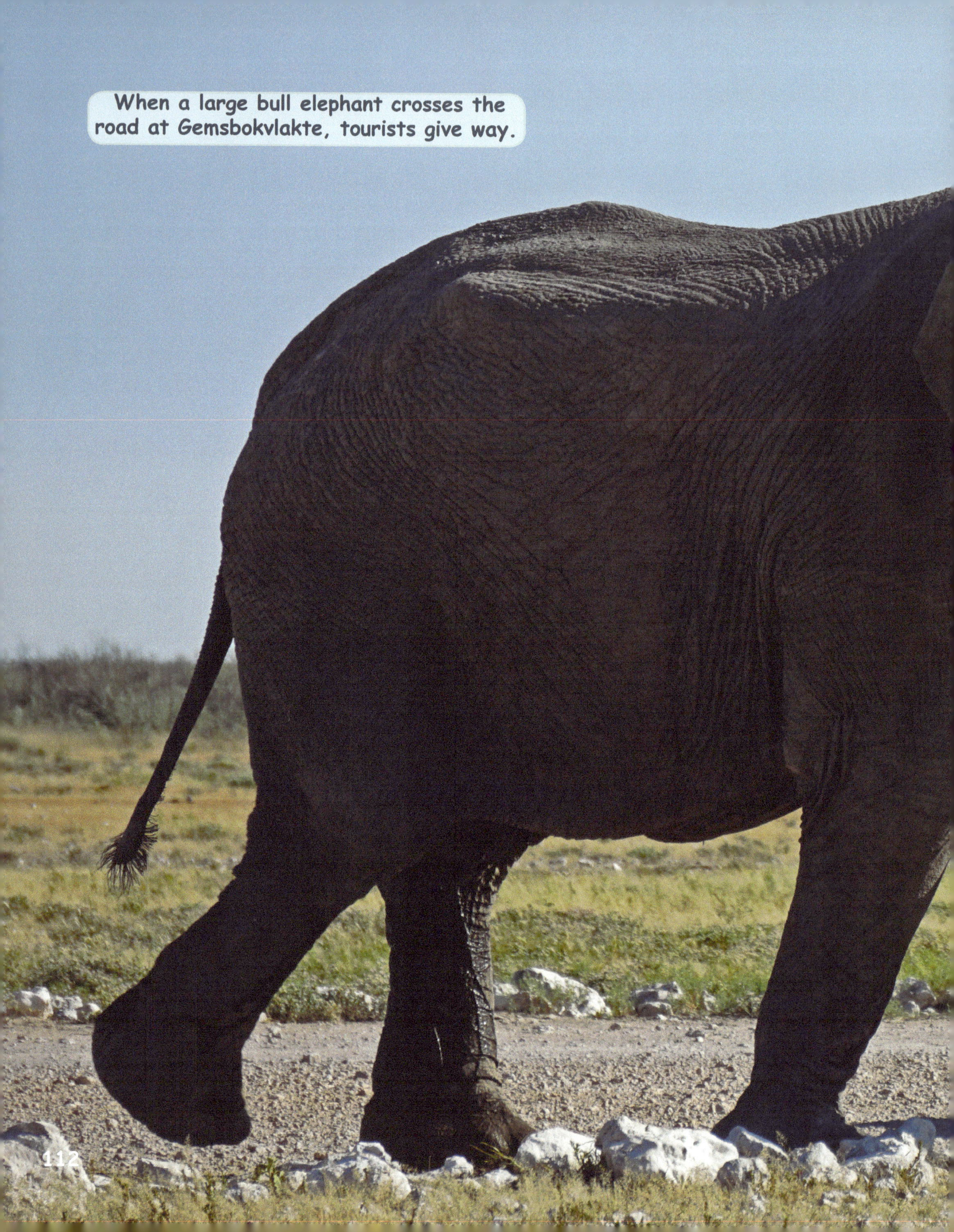

When a large bull elephant crosses the road at Gemsbokvlakte, tourists give way.

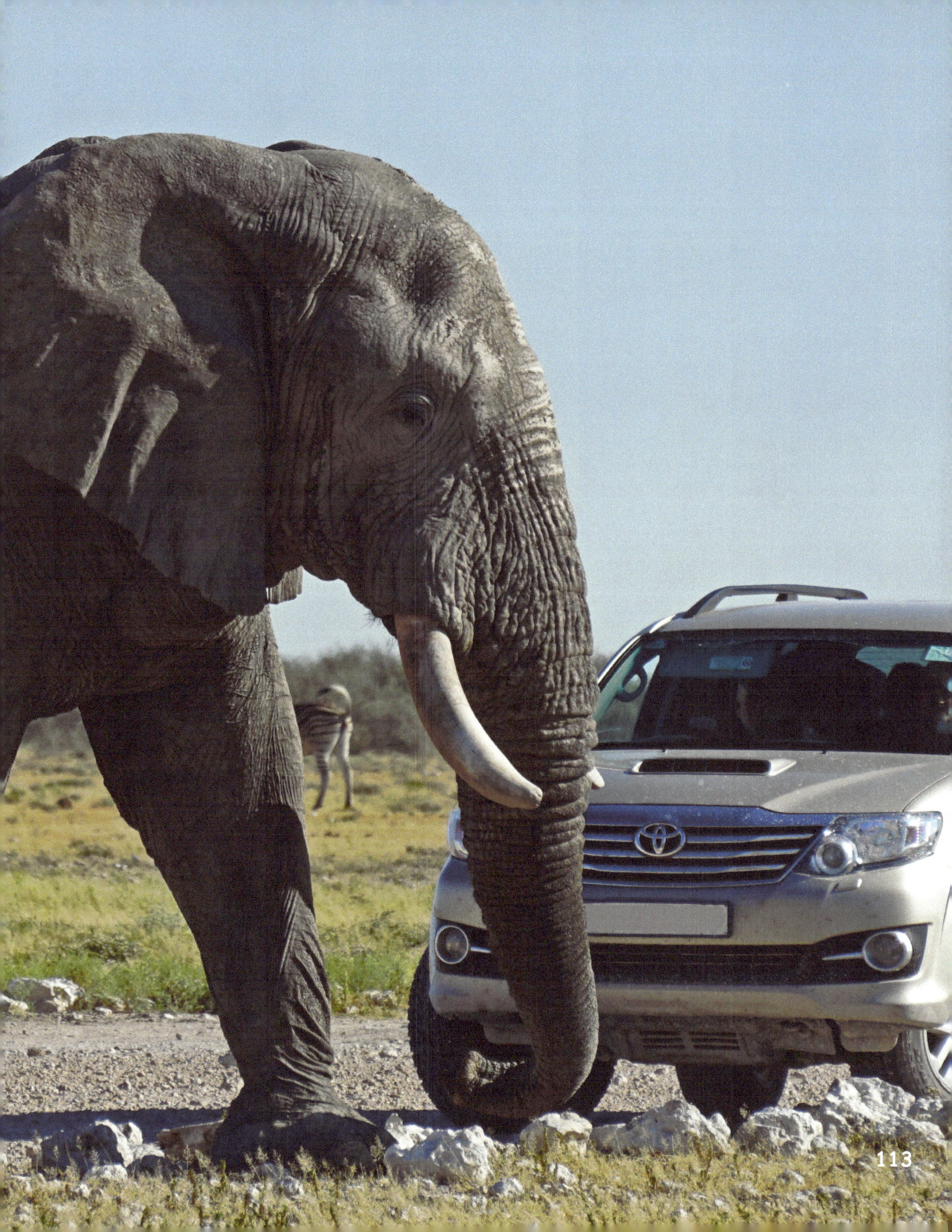

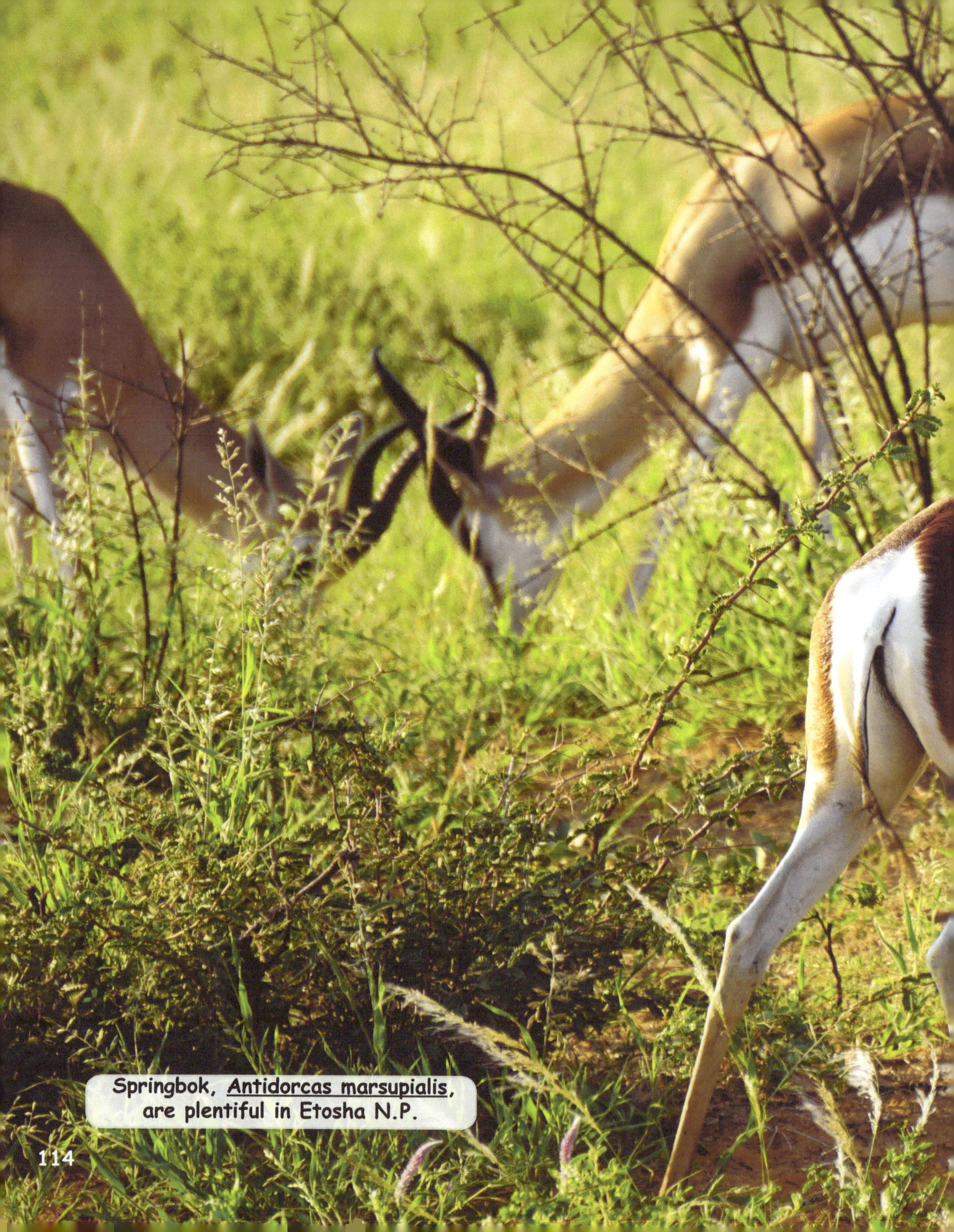

Springbok, Antidorcas marsupialis,
are plentiful in Etosha N.P.

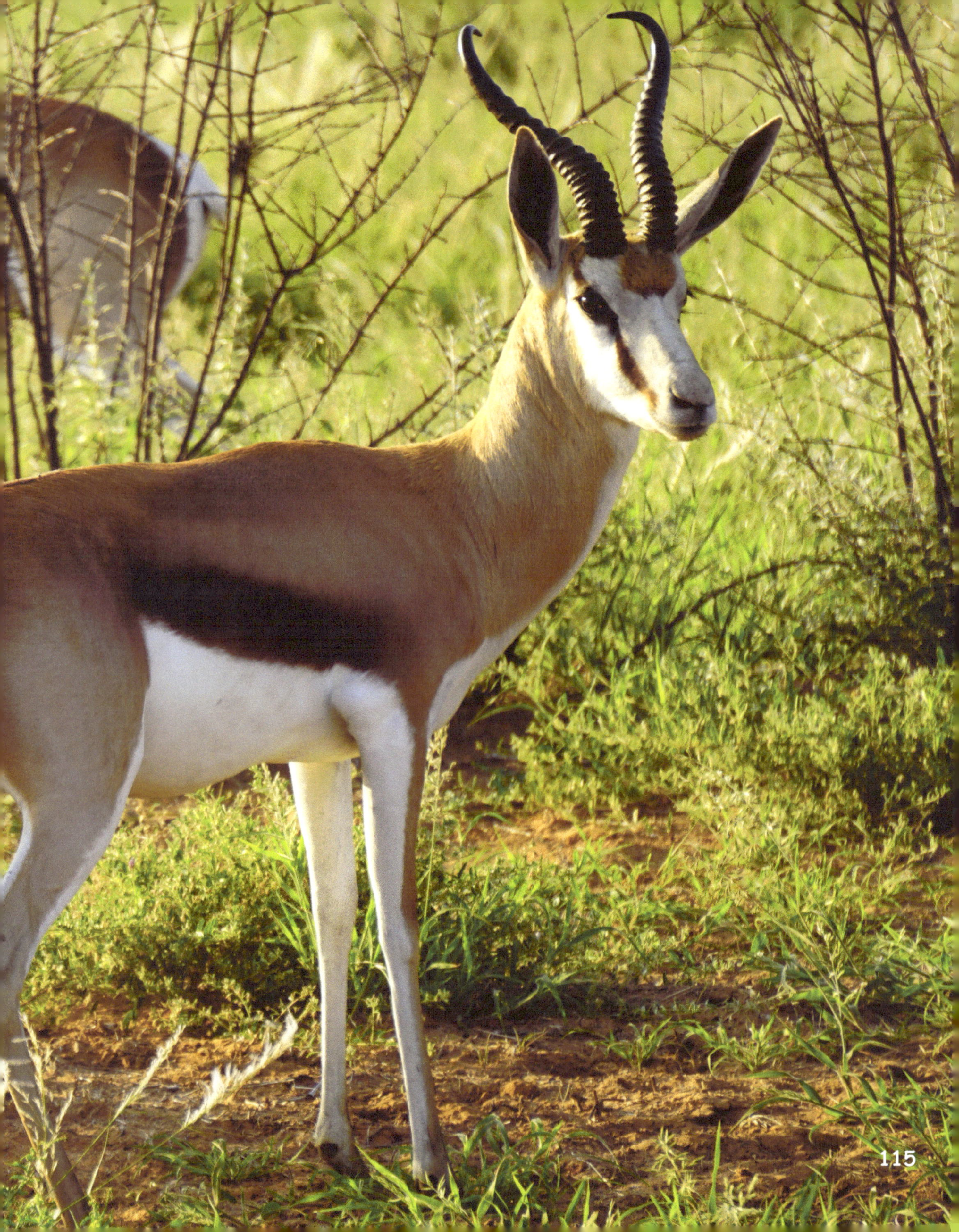

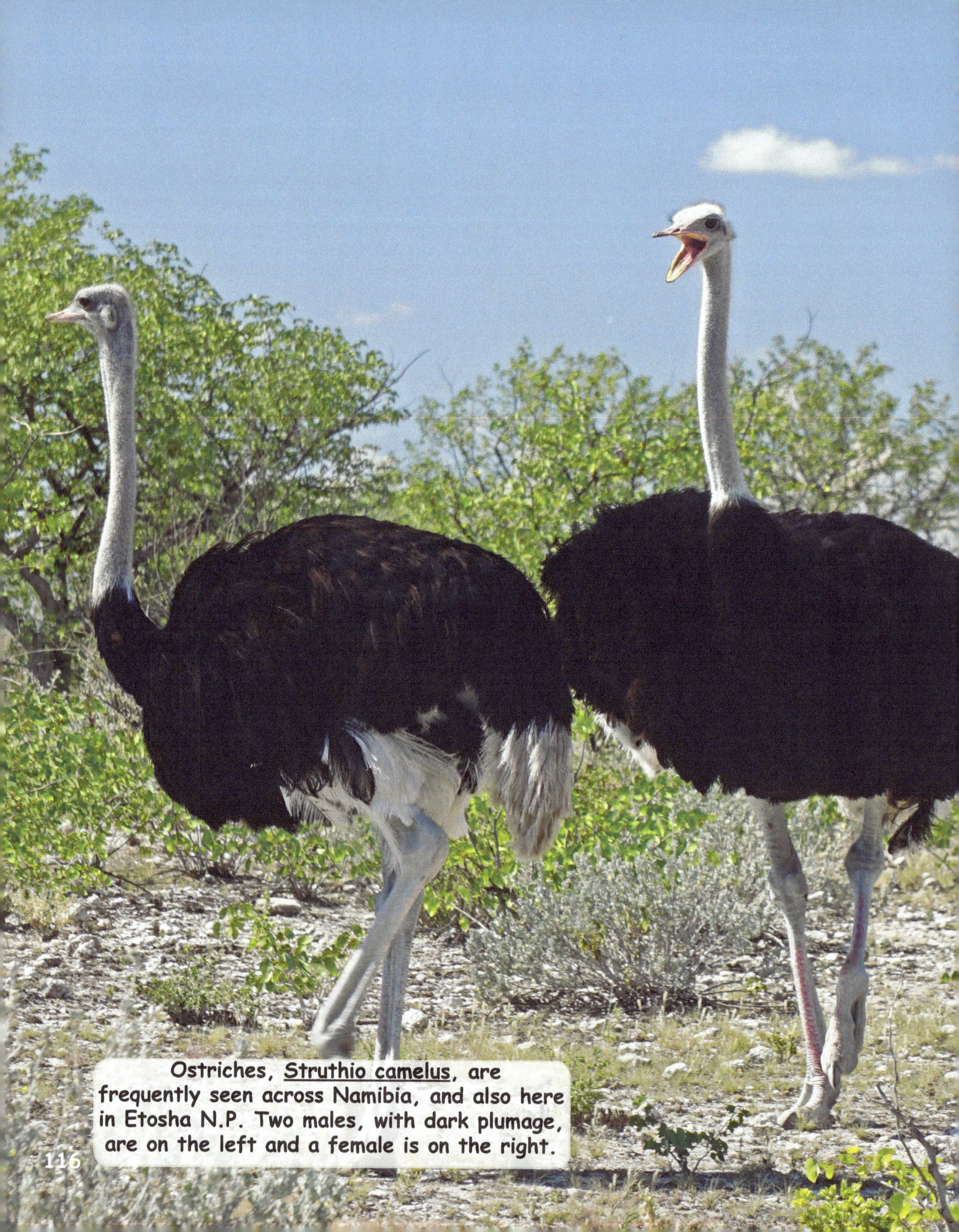

Ostriches, <u>Struthio camelus</u>, are frequently seen across Namibia, and also here in Etosha N.P. Two males, with dark plumage, are on the left and a female is on the right.

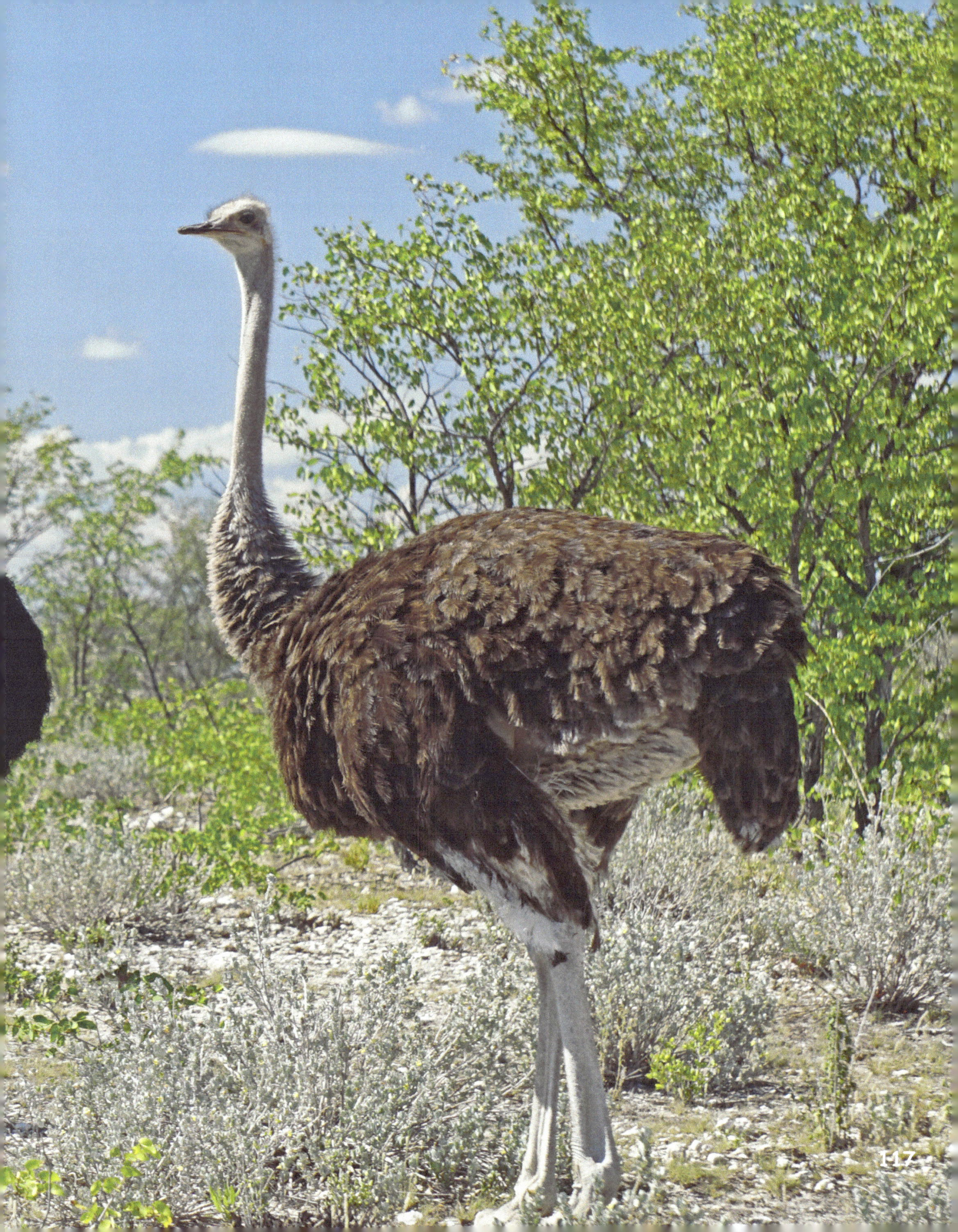

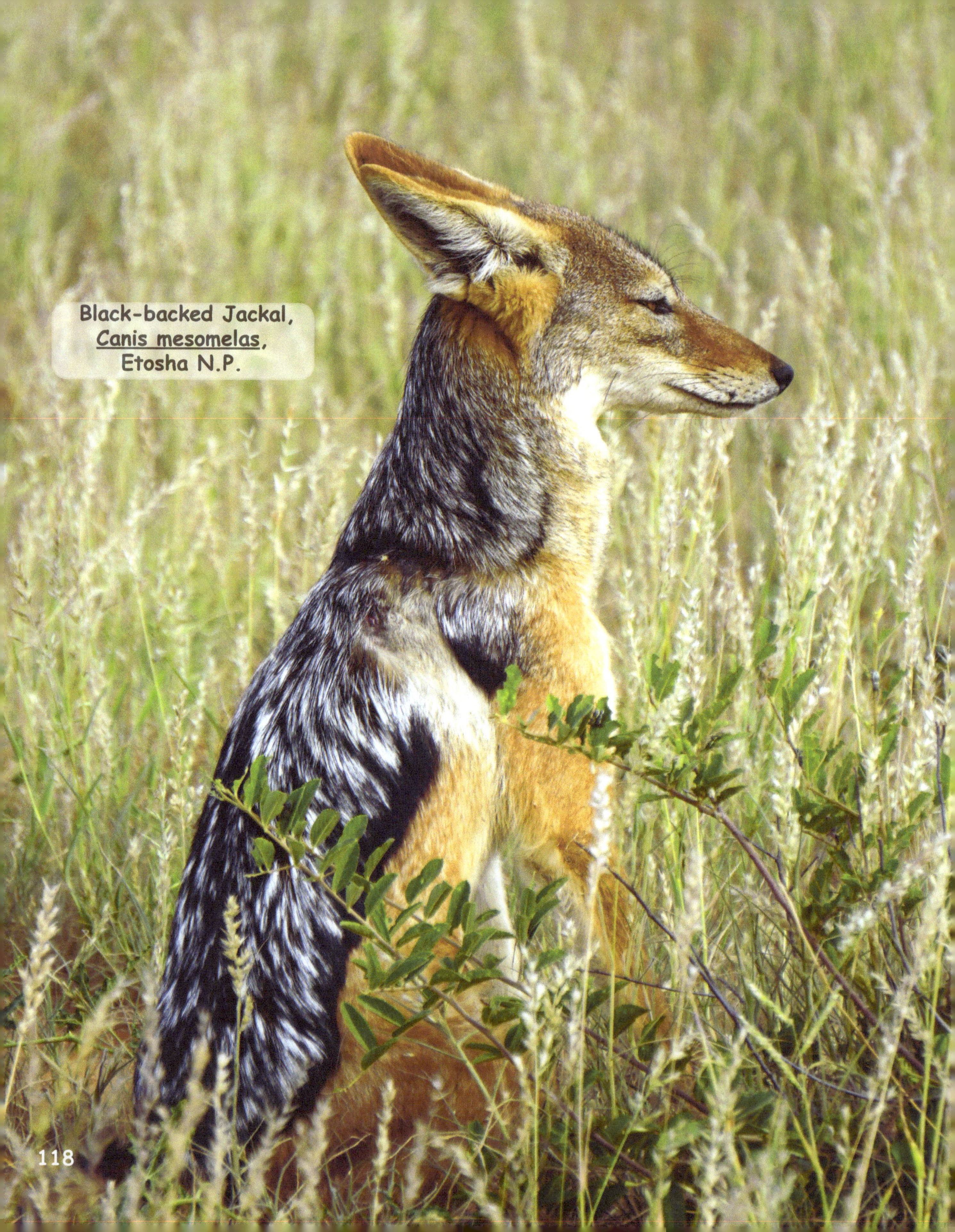

Black-backed Jackal,
Canis mesomelas,
Etosha N.P.

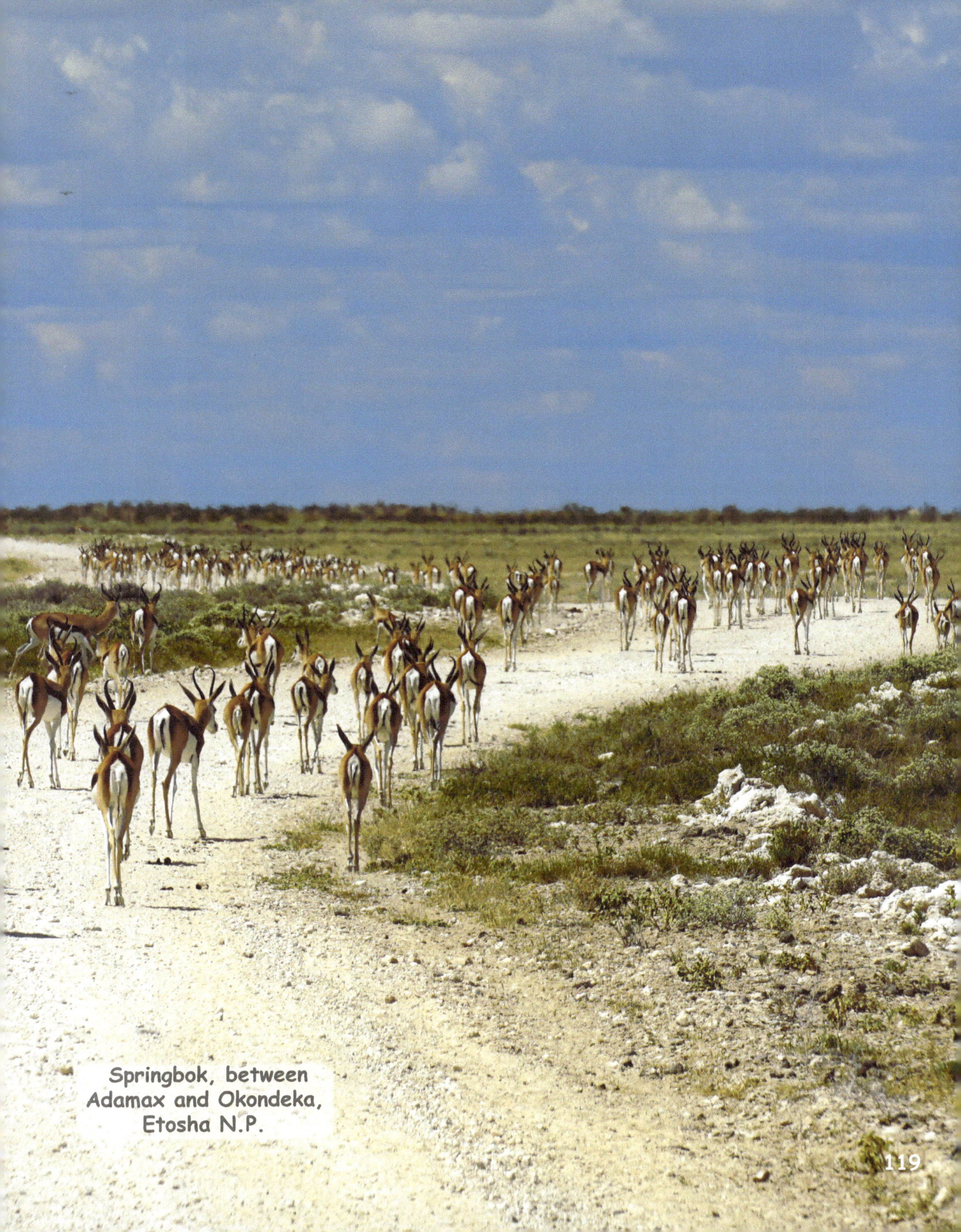

Springbok, between
Adamax and Okondeka,
Etosha N.P.

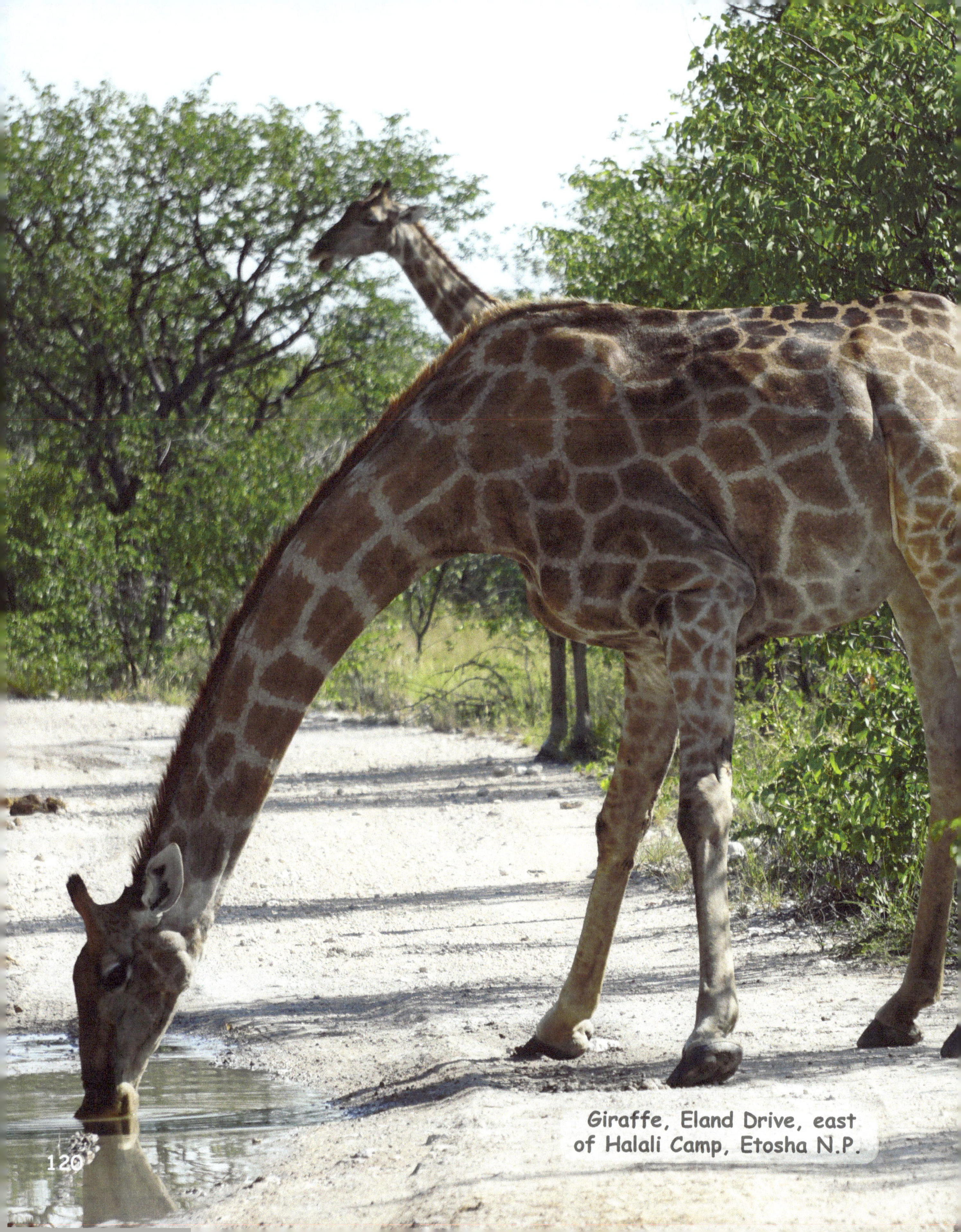

Giraffe, Eland Drive, east of Halali Camp, Etosha N.P.

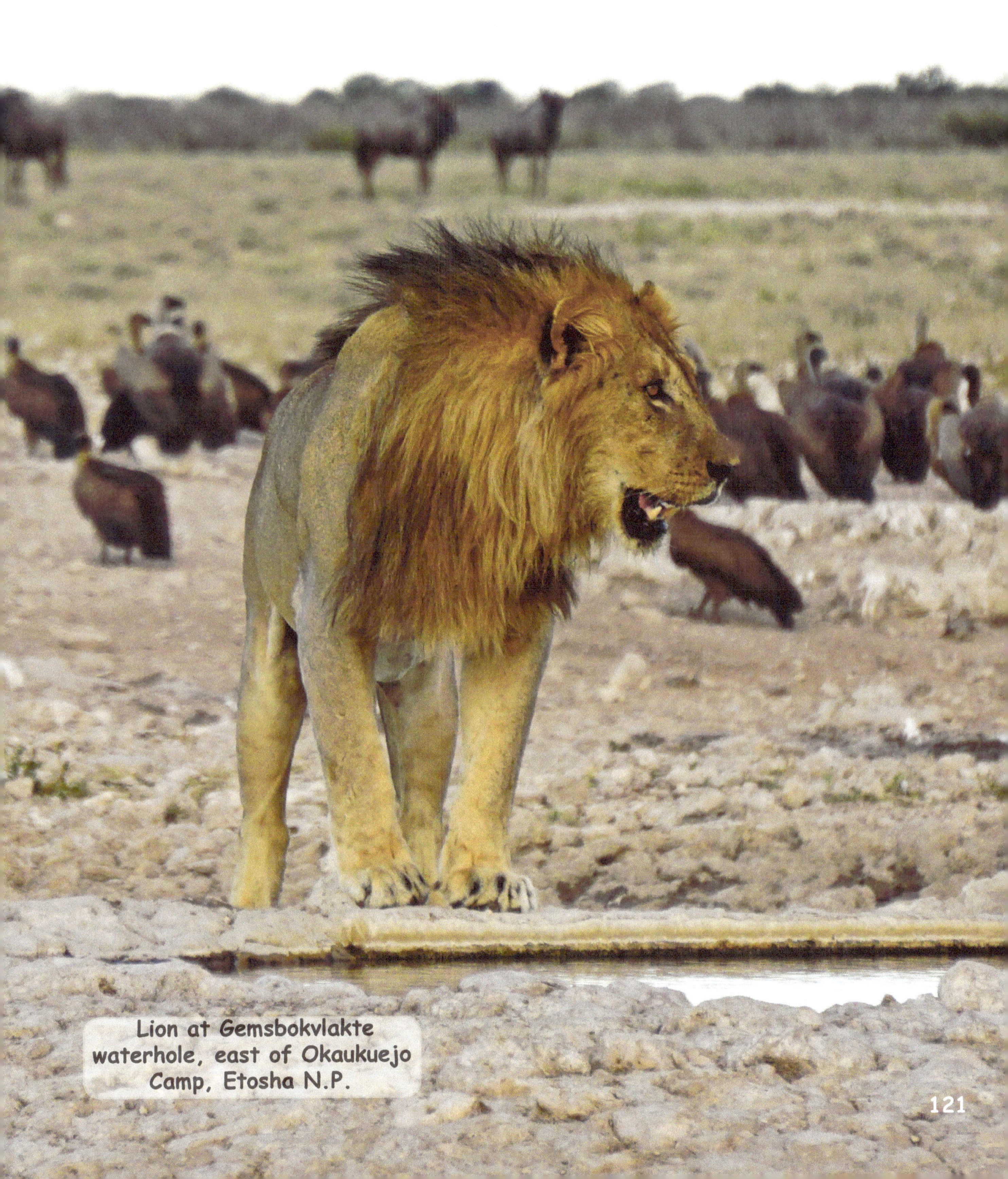

Lion at Gemsbokvlakte
waterhole, east of Okaukuejo
Camp, Etosha N.P.

The western half of Etosha N.P. has only been open
to the public since 2011, with the establishment of
Dolomite Camp and the opening of Galton Gate.

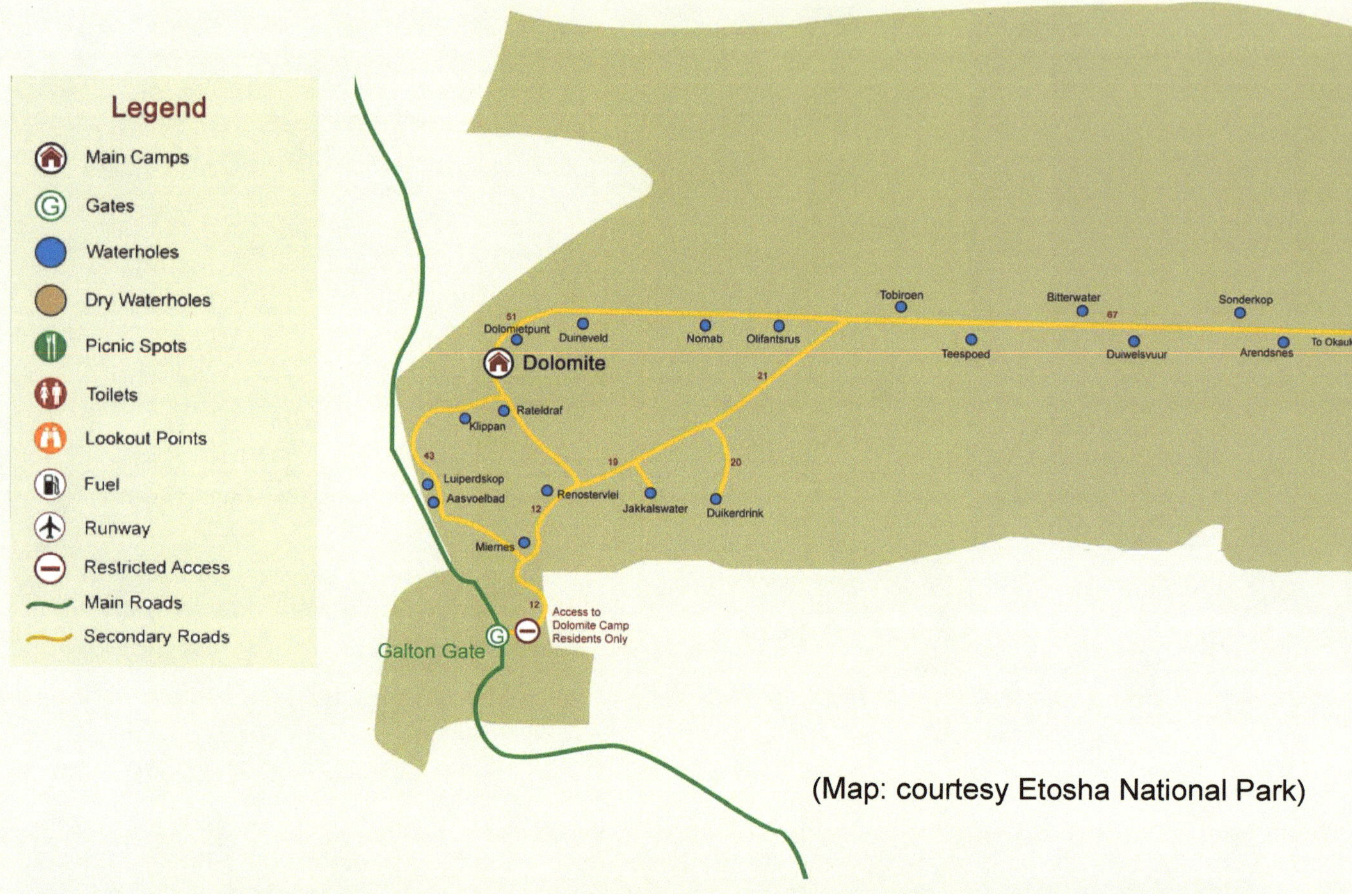

(Map: courtesy Etosha National Park)

Etosha National Park is one of the world's great wildlife viewing venues. It covers an area of 22,270sq.km (8,600sq.miles). The park's name, which means "great white place of dry water," is taken from the vast white and greenish colored Etosha Pan. (See map and satellite image on the next page.) The surrounding woodlands and grasslands provide habitats for a huge variety of mammals, birds and vegetation.

The Etosha Pan spreads over an area of 4,800sq.km (1,850sq.miles) It developed through tectonic plate activity over about ten million years. Around 16,000 years ago, when ice sheets were melting across the northern hemisphere, a wet climate phase in southern Africa filled Etosha Lake. Today, it is mostly dry clay mud split into hexagonal shapes as it dries and cracks, and is seldom seen with even a thin sheet of water covering it. It is approximately 80 miles long by 30 miles wide.

Etosha N.P. was first proclaimed a reserve in March, 1907, by the governor of German South West Africa.

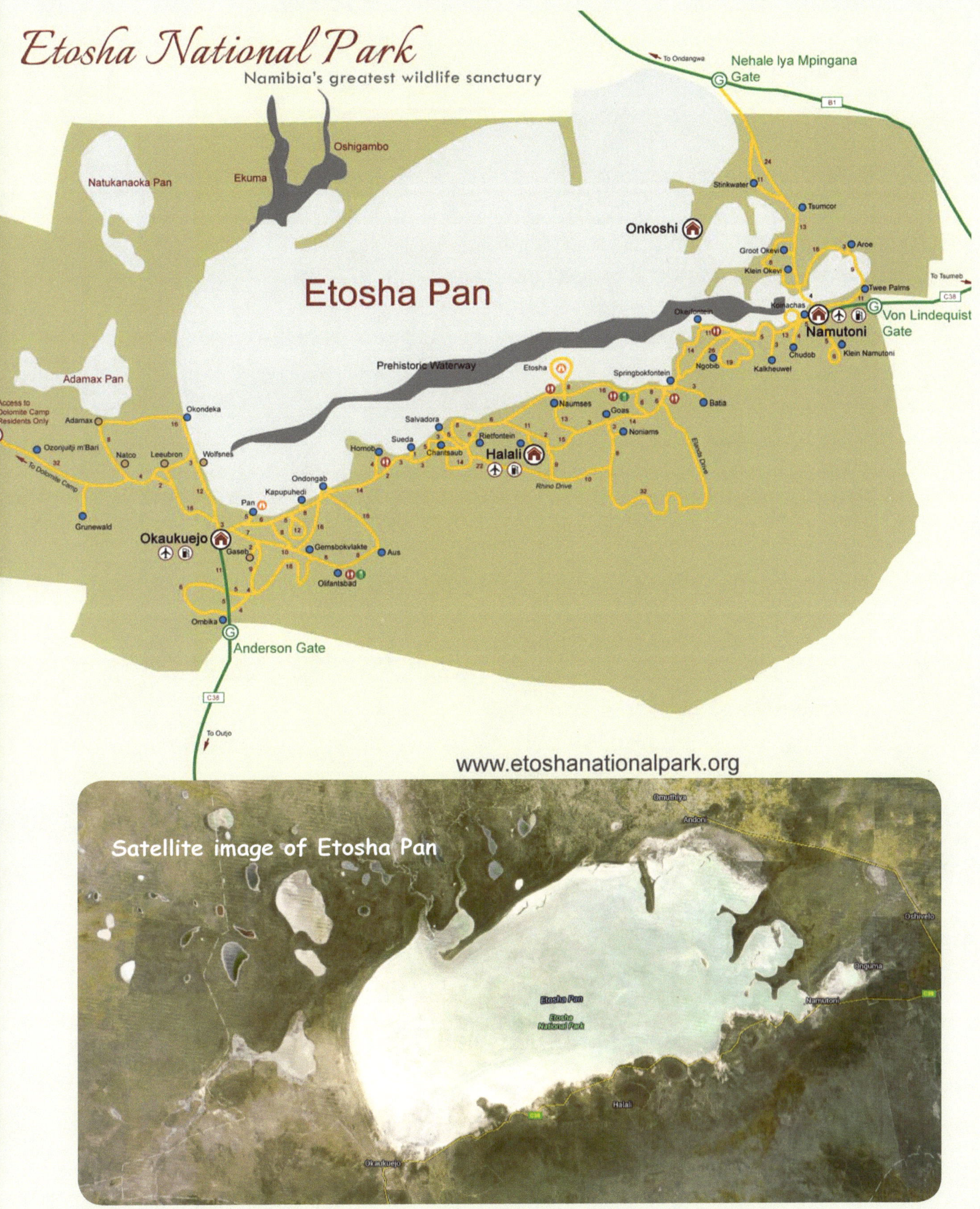

Etosha National Park
Namibia's greatest wildlife sanctuary
Natukanaoka Pan
Oshigambo
Ekuma
Onkoshi
Etosha Pan
To Ondangwa
Nehale Iya Mpingana Gate
Stinkwater
Tsumcor
Groot Okevi
Aroe
Klein Okevi
Twee Palms
To Tsumeb
Komachas
Okerfontein
Von Lindequist Gate
Namutoni
Chudob
Klein Namutoni
Prehistoric Waterway
Etosha
Springbokfontein
Ngobib
Kalkheuwel
Adamax Pan
Access to Dolomite Camp Residents Only
Okondeka
Naumses
Goas
Batia
Adamax
Salvadora
Noniams
Ozonjuitji m'Bari
Natco
Leeubron
Sueda
Rietfontein
To Dolomite Camp
Wolfsnes
Homob
Chantsaub
Halali
Etosha Drive
Grunewald
Ondongab
Kapupuhedi
Rhino Drive
Okaukuejo
Pan
Gaseb
Gemsbokvlakte
Aus
Olifantsbad
Ombika
Anderson Gate
To Outjo
www.etoshanationalpark.org
Satellite image of Etosha Pan
Omuthiya
Andoni
Etosha Pan
Etosha National Park
Oshivelo
Namutoni
Onguma
Halali
Okaukuejo

Namibia Facts

- Namibia (formerly South West Africa) is named for the coastal Namib Desert; the name "namib" means "vast place" in the Nama/Damara language.
- The country gained its independence from South African Mandated rule in March, 1990.
- With an area of 824,292sq.km (318,260sq.miles), it is the 34th largest country in the world and the 15th largest in Africa.
- Mean elevation is 1141M (3,704ft).
- Namibia is the first country in the world to incorporate the protection of the environment into its constitution. Some 14% of the land is protected, including the entire Namib Desert coastal strip.
- The population is 2,212,000, comprised of black 87.5%, white 6%, mixed 6.5% ethnic groups.
- English is the official language, although there are 13 recognized national languages.
- Religions are Christian 80% to 90% (at least 50% Lutheran), and indigenous beliefs 10% to 20%.
- Literacy rate of total population is 81.9%.
- The country exports diamonds, uranium, zinc, copper, lead, fish, and livestock.

Namibia's National Flag

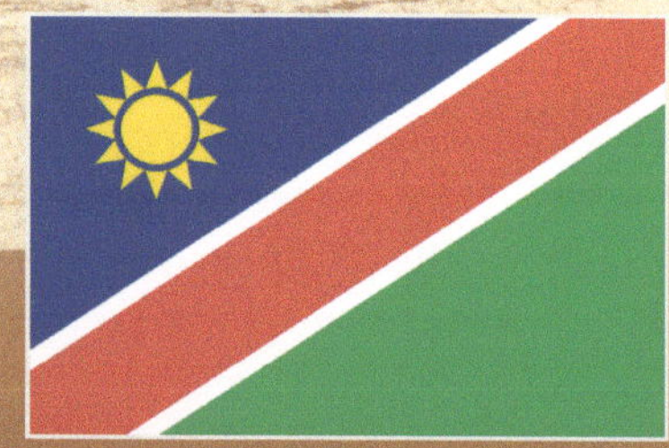

Africa smiled a
little, when you left. "We know
you," Africa said. "We have seen and
watched you. We can learn to live without
you, but we know we needn't yet."
And Africa smiled a little, when you left...
"You cannot leave Africa," Africa said. "We are
always with you, there inside your head. Our rivers
run in currents in the swirl of
your thumbprints; our
drumbeats counting out
your pulse; our
coastline the
silhouette of your
soul." So Africa smiled
a little, when you
left. "We are in
you," Africa said.
"You have
not left us
yet."

ANONYMOUS

125